COSMOS IN THE CHAOS

COSMOS *in* *the* CHAOS

Philip Schaff's Interpretation of Nineteenth-Century American Religion

STEPHEN R. GRAHAM

WILLIAM B. EERDMANS PUBLISHING COMPANY
GRAND RAPIDS, MICHIGAN / CAMBRIDGE, U.K.

255 Jefferson Ave. S.E., Grand Rapids, Michigan 49503 /
P. O. Box 163, Cambridge CB3 9PU U.K.

Printed in the United States of America

00 99 98 97 96 95 7 6 5 4 3 2 1

Library of Congress Cataloging-in-Publication Data

Graham, Stephen R. (Stephen Ray), 1957-
Cosmos in the chaos: Philip Schaff's interpretation of nineteenth-century American religion / Stephen R. Graham.
p. cm.
Originally presented as the author's thesis (Ph.D.) — University of Chicago, 1989.
Includes bibliographical references.
ISBN 0-8028-0841-7 (pbk.)
1. United States — Church history — 19th century — Study and teaching — History.
2. Schaff, Philip, 1819-1893 — Views on 19th century American Christianity. I. Title.
BR525.G65 1995
277.3'081'092 — dc20 95-37727
CIP

To Sharon
with love

Contents

Acknowledgments

One of my greatest joys in bringing this project to completion is the opportunity to express publicly and in print my gratitude to a number of people whose assistance has made it possible. My most profound debt is to Martin E. Marty, who directed the dissertation on which this book is based. His cheerful encouragement, fertile imagination, genuine friendship, and modeling of graciousness and scholarship have shaped me as a scholar, and as a person. The other members of my dissertation committee, Jerald C. Brauer and W. Clark Gilpin, offered insightful critique and encouragement. Mark A. Noll, whose example as a teacher and scholar first inspired me to pursue this vocation, offered words of encouragement at just the right times.

I cannot imagine a finer group of colleagues than those with whom I have been privileged to work at North Park Theological Seminary. Special thanks goes to Phil Anderson, colleague in church history, who read and critiqued this manuscript, and to archivist Tim Johnson of the Covenant Archives and Historical Library, who prepared the index. Both are valued friends and co-workers in the heritage we all cherish. I thank former Dean Rob Johnston and former Dean of Faculty Klyne Snodgrass for their encouragement of scholarship, and the faculty development committee of North Park Theological Seminary for generous grants that allowed me to revisit the archives at the Burke Library of Union Theological Seminary and the Evangelical and Reformed Historical Society at Lancaster Theological Seminary. The staffs of those archives made working in each of them a pleasure. I also thank the staffs of the Joseph Regenstein Library at the University of Chicago, the Buswell Memorial Library of Wheaton College, and the Mellander Library of North Park Theological Seminary.

I dedicate this book to my wife Sharon, whose contributions to my life cannot be captured in mere words.

STEPHEN R. GRAHAM

Foreword

Let's make too little, for starters, of Philip Schaff, the subject of this welcome book. It is good to start modestly, lest the temptation to make claims of the sort motion picture advertisers favor — S*P*E*C*T*A*C*U*L*A*R and all that — becomes too strong.

No, viewed from some angles, Schaff is overlookable. He straddled the decades of the previous century, while present-minded Americans have enough trouble getting curious about the recent past of their own. He fought no wars; his sex life was not interesting; the little hint of moral flaw that seemed to tear adolescent Philip apart would go unnoticed today. He never ran for office and never tried to buy off those who did. His was the world of religion and ours is both religious and secular. He inhabited the Protestant ethos, about which few get stirred today.

Within that religious, Christian, and Protestant world, Schaff spent his years in the then very small seminary sphere. Even today, with the theological school much larger, one does not expect to make bestsellers, even in church circles, out of studies dealing with seminary professors. And we who teach religious, or Christian, or church history know our place. The subject of this book, its author, and the writer of this Foreword alike know that dealing with the story of Christianity is not the way to make news, nor the way to poise one's self to be in the front lines of theological battles. For Graham to rouse us from apathy or boredom by telling the story of a seminary professor church historian who came from uninteresting cuckoo clock–land Switzerland (of Swiss descent, I speak as a fool; but have you seen any Swiss Power bumper stickers, or Swiss Day parades?) to the backwoods of Pennsylvania for much of his career is expecting much.

Of course, I am playing games in this effort to provide perspective. From other angles, and I hope we do play the angles in life, Schaff is a Rather Big Deal. So, now, consider reasons to take him and this book seriously. The externals of his career achievements are not the most important elements. While church history may not be a "page one" discipline, Schaff was not only the first and principal exemplar of the crafts that go with being a church historian, the biggest fish in its pondlet. He also was the main founder of the American Society of Church History. While he died in the year of the World's Parliament of Religions, 1893, the interfaith forum that provided the stage for his swan song, Schaff was a pioneer who ventured into the places where high risk religious encounters were not yet taken for granted. If one had to name the precursor, even the inventor of what became the ecumenical movement in its American version, it would be hard to come up with any to compete with Philip Schaff. His bibliography, while not representative of what scholars today read to get accurate knowledge of Christian history, remains an impressive monument and is worth reading at least for those who would see how the best of the historians a century ago told the Christian story for Americans.

Still, all that has to do with what I have called the externals of Schaff's achievements. While Stephen Graham knows that readers need the detailed fleshing out of the plot of Schaff's life, he has a different interest, one that compels careful attention to the subject of this book. By focusing on the mirror Schaff held up to America and on what that mirror tells about both the holder and the scene, Graham contributes to our understanding of an America that needed mirroring help in the second half of the nineteenth century as it does at the end of the twentieth.

The United States, diverse ethnically, pluralist religiously, and confused morally, has often and well been served by the visits of Europeans, who left diaries, letters, or treatises on the meaning of America to help citizens find their identity and purpose. By far the best known of these hundreds of chroniclers was Alexis de Tocqueville, a democrat of aristocratic French background whose *Democracy in America* is a classic to which the native-born looked and look when they want to find out something of who they were and are. Tocqueville made much of "associations," including the churches, so one can learn from his observations. But his viewing of religion was not sustained.

Philip Schaff, on the other hand, a kind of product of an early "Ph.D." glut in Germany, came to stay. One of his most important reflections came when he visited the Old Country to tell it about the new world. But they would slight Schaff and be slighted in turn who concentrated only on his concentrated work *America.* All through his career the church historian and ecumenist, first at Mercersburg Seminary and then at Union Theological Seminary in New York, kept interpreting America in the light of what was for its day a generous, cosmopolitan vantage.

What makes the reading of Schaff and Graham on Schaff so rewarding is this: Schaff was not only a mirror or a mirror holder. He was an agent on the scene about which he wrote. He knew enough about theological change in Germany to ponder what the "crisis of historical consciousness," as it has been called, meant for the faith itself. He knew enough about the sectarian influences that flowed from the British Isles to provide counsel on efforts toward church unity in America. He was sufficiently realistic to spell out the problems of divided, contentious Christianity and hopeful enough to suggest that the various elements of the church could find better ways to relate to each other.

Schaff was, in a way, a philosopher of history, who set the raw data of American religious life to the music of theology. That effort would no doubt have kept him from getting tenure in liberal arts colleges or universities today, and not all theological school historians would favor his approach. In some ways he anticipates not the narrating historians, from Leonard Bacon, who was coming on to the scene Schaff would leave in 1893, through William Warren Sweet in the middle of our century, to almost everyone in the business today; instead, he foreshadows the later theologians who make use of the empirical life of the church in the interest of providing direction in their own time. Not as theologically profound as H. Richard Niebuhr, Schaff did write his own version of *The Kingdom of God in America* and anticipated Niebuhr's mid-twentieth-century work.

A long-time reader of Schaff, I confess to have enjoyed engaging in acts of empathy as I tried to put on, figuratively, the spectacles with which this bright, well-tutored young doctor from Switzerland and Germany viewed New York City: "the evidences of civilization are here, as in the land we left behind." One wonders what he was expecting to see. One also wonders whether he would be so sure today as he was then that the coast of America and its cities were providing "the evidences of civilization." I found reasons to feel empathic when he commented on California, already then a Golden State. He saw "chaotic confusion: I would not live there for all the money in the world."

Schaff was part of the movement, in the midst of the turbulence and formlessness of modernity, nineteenth-century style, that would promote the integrity of the church. England had its Oxford and Cambridge movements; Germany had neoconfessionalism; Scotland had the Disruption of 1843. Almost everywhere a minority of Protestants and Catholics refused to succumb to the lures of those who advocated church growth of mindless sorts, and Schaff was part of such a minority in Pennsylvania, then New York, and finally through many of the states. These movements represented but one strategy. To the left of its proponents were those who advocated adapting to the world, throwing in the towel. On the right were the equally unambiguous sorts who built walls of resistance. Schaff, commuter between denominations, between continents, between disciplines, knew that neither strategy did justice to the counsels of God as he had known them. So he began to sketch a third way, a loftier, more difficult, always unfinished and ambiguous one. While doing the advocating for such a vision, he took pains to write about not what the church might become but what in many ways it already was.

Who but a mediating theologian could get into trouble as fast as Schaff did, with his inaugural lecture: he even got to pioneer in the contesting over heresy in American denominationalism! Mediators, commuters between groups of people, synthesizers who believe that the church has an organic character do not make headlines the way the new Christian right or leftish liberation theologians do. But the balanced ones may stay around longer and influence in quiet, subtle, and secondary ways. As Stephen Graham tells it, one gets the sense that, while part of his achievement is quite dated, Schaff is still around, and with this book he ought to become more available than ever. In this book we may see his mirror for world, especially America, and church — and, insofar as his theology is on target, also for ourselves. Graham holds it out with steady hand to a new generation. I hope many will receive the gift, hold it up, turn it in many angles, and be informed and delighted by what they read and thus see.

The University of Chicago MARTIN E. MARTY

Preface

Schaff's America and America's Schaff

For decades analysts have pondered the fascinating and distinctive character of religion in the United States of America. Many of them have identified the nineteenth century as a crucial time of development, of ferment and innovation in society and in religion. During that period, three particular concerns stand out as especially crucial for the distinctive character of American religion. First, the "voluntary system" of religion which originated in America has given opportunity for the rise of numerous sects and denominations which compete in the marketplace of "free enterprise" religion. Never before in history had people confronted so many religious options from which they could choose, or decide not to choose. A second issue discussed with much heat, and considerable light, was the American separation of church and state, which gives rise to controversy over the proper role of religion in a society in which civil and religious authorities are legally separated. A corollary to these discussions is the debate concerning a distinctively "American" character. This question is typified by calls by presidents and preachers for a renewal of pride in being American, and increasingly frequent assertions of the special character of the American people. These three issues will remain important elements of the debates concerning American culture for generations to come.

Many interpreters have sought to come to grips with these three characteristics of American religion and society, but most were too overwhelmed by the ferment swirling around them to see the whole picture. Only a select few were truly comprehensive in their vision and incisive in their interpretations.

As past generations wrestled with these issues, foreign observers often contributed vital insights toward a fuller understanding of the American character. In the first half of the nineteenth century Alexis de Tocqueville provided an unparalleled interpretation of the American political system and the American people in his *Democracy in America.* Interest in this book has not lessened for over a century, and as recently as 1985 a team of sociologists led by Robert N. Bellah used Tocqueville's insights to guide their penetrating study of American "individualism and commitment."[1] In a similar manner, though employing the methods of the historian rather than the sociologist, I intend to examine American culture of the nineteenth century's latter half through the eyes of an interpreter, who within his own sphere was no less perceptive than Tocqueville. In depth of insight concerning these three fundamental questions about the interrelationship between American religion and culture during the latter half of the nineteenth century, Philip Schaff has no peer.

Philip Schaff, now known as the founder of the discipline of church history in America and the most notable practitioner of that discipline in nineteenth-century America, is secure in his place as a pioneer in the history of American theological scholarship, yet little is known of his work as an interpreter of religion in America. Along with his regularly noted contributions to biblical revision, general church history, and ecumenism, Schaff should also be recognized as a distinctly gifted analyst of the development of American religion in the latter half of the nineteenth century. Many understandings of nineteenth-century American religion that are now regarded as commonplace were noted first by this astute observer.

In 1844 Schaff abandoned a promising academic career in Germany to teach in the newly founded German Reformed Seminary at Mercersburg, Pennsylvania.[2] He viewed his mission as his response to

1. Robert N. Bellah, et al., *Habits of the Heart: Individualism and Commitment in American Life* (Berkeley: University of California Press, 1985).

2. Named Philipp Schaaf at birth, he later spelled his name Schaf, but in about 1847 settled on the spelling Philip Schaff.

a desperate Macedonian call, "Come over and help us!"[3] The Pauline imagery is appropriate because Schaff saw himself as the bearer of a message of "salvation" to a people in danger of losing their souls. In his ordination sermon, which also served as a farewell address to his colleagues, he spoke of the distressed state of his countrymen in the uncivilized wilds of America. If someone did not come to their rescue immediately, they would lose every trace of their superior German heritage in culture and religion. He regretted leaving his mentors and the intellectual vitality of Germany, but in a spirit of self-sacrifice leavened with a youthful desire for adventure, Schaff accepted the challenge. The young theologian's teachers believed him to be particularly suited to the task in America because of his breadth of education and cosmopolitan interests. Born in Switzerland in 1819, Schaff received his training at the prestigious German universities of Halle, Tübingen, and Berlin. He was recommended highly for the American post by his professors Augustus Neander and F. A. G. Tholuck, as well as by the Mercersburg Seminary committee's first choice, the famous preacher F. W. Krummacher.

Remarkably, a little less than a decade after his arrival in America Schaff appeared as the stalwart defender of his adopted fatherland before an audience of his German colleagues. From a young student and professor who wholeheartedly accepted the stereotype of America as a land of backwardness and cultural chaos, Schaff had come to Europe as a destroyer of the "disproportion and caricature" of America held by his European counterparts. Throughout his career, Schaff continued his effort to interpret religious America for audiences both in his adopted homeland and abroad. While he joined a number of other commentators on various aspects of the American situation, his work is in a number of ways distinctive. Among the many foreign visitors to America who informed the world about American society and character, Schaff can be compared in his analyses to Tocqueville in depth of insight and sympathy for the subject. Due to his more narrowly defined subject matter, more exclusive audience, and lesser volume of material, Schaff's popularity did not and will not approach that of Tocqueville. The Frenchman was a genius who produced a classic; the German-

3. While in Troas, the apostle Paul had a vision of a man from Macedonia who appealed to Paul to "come over to Macedonia and help us" (Acts 16:9-10, NRSV).

American, with his focus on religious issues and his nearly half-century residence and teaching career in America, provided both a theological focus and a span of observation unrivaled among interpreters of American religion. In Schaff we find an unusually perceptive analyst whose career spanned arguably the most fascinating half-century of development in American religion. Schaff's development into an ardent defender of the new world and a champion of its ideals provides a captivating picture of an immigrant's "Americanization."

On another level, however, Schaff maintained an extraordinary constancy of vision that allowed him to conceptualize the whole of American religious and social life within the larger framework of the emerging kingdom of Christ. Within the ferment and confusion of American life, Schaff consistently discerned the continuity of God's unfolding plan in the world. The chaos was never able completely to overshadow the cosmos in his understanding. New Testament scholar J. Christiaan Beker in his work *Paul, the Apostle,* speaks of the Pauline dialectic between "authority and particularity, coherent core and contingent contextualism," that characterized the great apostle. Beker continues,

> His ability to focus in the midst of the early churches' variety of theological expressions on the one central core of "Christ crucified and risen," together with his ability to allow that focus to light up and interact with every conceivable variety and particularity of human life, is a feat that — with perhaps the exception of Luther — no other apostle or theologian has achieved.[4]

If "early churches'" is replaced with "American churches'" and the central core expanded to include Jesus' words to his followers, "I am with you always, to the end of the age," and his prayer to his Father that his disciples "may be one, as we are," this statement captures well the genius of Philip Schaff.[5] It was this distinctive vision that provides the key to understanding the life and work of Philip Schaff. While others such as Robert Baird and, later, Daniel Dorchester commented with

4. J. Christiaan Beker, *Paul the Apostle: The Triumph of God in Life and Thought* (Philadelphia: Fortress Press, 1980), 33-35.

5. Matt. 28:20; John 17:11, NRSV.

insight on the American religious situation, Schaff's unique contribution was to provide a perspective in which a cosmic schema of interpretation could incorporate the variegated data of the American experience. His view of the one and the many provided the model for much later discussion.

His dominant vision worked itself out in a number of distinctive ways, many of which were in direct opposition to the currents of American thought. While Schaff made common cause with the general Christian goals of numerous American religious leaders, he anticipated future concerns in many ways.

II

This essay covers Schaff's life and work in America, and reaches back to his early life on occasion in order to clarify issues raised by his interpretation of American religion. As an immigrant, Schaff was able to "see" religion in America from an important perspective. As a theologian and church historian, Schaff was qualified to put his observations of American religion into the perspective of the whole history of the church.

A number of volumes survey aspects of Schaff's life and work and clearly reveal his importance in the worlds of church and academy in the nineteenth century. Eight books have been published that deal substantively with Schaff. David S. Schaff published a biography of his father in 1897 which is valuable for the information it contains, including numerous quotations from his father's correspondence, yet like much late-nineteenth-century hagiography, it lacks in-depth analysis. James H. Nichols's *Romanticism in American Theology: Nevin and Schaff at Mercersburg* (1961) focuses on Schaff as theologian and places him within the nineteenth-century romantic movement which affected Christian theology in Europe and the United States. Nichols also edited a collection of the writings of Schaff and John Williamson Nevin called *The Mercersburg Theology* (1961). Klaus Penzel, the leading authority of Schaff's German background and intellectual development, has collected a number of Schaff's significant and previously unavailable writings in an impressive and valuable volume, *Philip Schaff: Historian and Ambassador of the Universal Church* (1991). This book provides an unprecedented look at Schaff's thought that represents the distillation of Professor Penzel's thirty-year study of Schaff. Henry W. Bowden discusses Schaff's theology of history in *Church History in the Age of Science* (1970), and credits him with the establishment of American church historiography as a serious discipline in its own right.

George Shriver has written in *American Religious Heretics* (1966) about the astounding state of affairs in the German Reformed Church of the mid-1840s that led Schaff to face not merely one but two heresy trials within two years of his coming to America. The best introduction for those not yet acquainted with the outlines of Schaff's career is Shriver's brief biography, *Philip Schaff: Christian Scholar and Ecumenical Prophet* (1987). While that book touches on many topics addressed in this volume, Shriver's chronological framework and brevity did not allow a thematic treatment or the depth with which they are expounded here. In 1988, Henry W. Bowden edited a collection of essays commemorating the centennial of the American Society of Church History entitled *A Century of Church History: The Legacy of Philip Schaff.* While some of the essays deal in some depth with Schaff's thought, the aim of the book is to trace developments in areas of Schaff's interest through the century since the founding of the ASCH and not to focus on developments in the ideas of Schaff himself.[6]

While all of these sources make valuable contributions to the understanding of the total life and work of Schaff, none of them approaches Schaff specifically as an interpreter of American religion and culture. The life and thought of this uniquely qualified immigrant provide

6. David S. Schaff, *The Life of Philip Schaff: In Part Autobiographical* (New York: Charles Scribner's Sons, 1897); James Hastings Nichols, *Romanticism in American Theology: Nevin and Schaff at Mercersburg* (Chicago: The University of Chicago Press, 1961); James Hastings Nichols, ed., *The Mercersburg Theology* (New York: Oxford University Press, 1966); Klaus Penzel, ed., *Philip Schaff: Historian and Ambassador of the Universal Church, Selected Writings* (Macon, Ga.: Mercer University Press, 1991); Henry W. Bowden, *Church History in the Age of Science: Historiographical Patterns in the United States, 1876-1918* (Chapel Hill: The University of North Carolina Press, 1971); George H. Shriver, ed., *American Religious Heretics: Formal and Informal Trials* (Nashville: Abingdon, 1966); George H. Shriver, *Philip Schaff: Christian Scholar and Ecumenical Prophet* (Macon, Ga.: Mercer University Press, 1987); Henry W. Bowden, ed., *A Century of Church History: The Legacy of Philip Schaff* (Carbondale, Ill.: Southern Illinois University Press, 1988).

an inviting window through which to view certain themes vital to the development of religion in nineteenth-century America. Schaff wrestled with questions which in their early forms provided the foundations for an astounding number of contemporary concerns. He developed an interpretation of the American "voluntary system" which recognized both its glaring weaknesses and its great potential. He addressed the developing relationship between church and state in a land of religious freedom and became convinced that the American way was superior to what he had known in Europe. He became an international evangelist of religious freedom. He envisioned the unity of the church while recognizing, and to a remarkable extent affirming, the growing cultural, ethnic, and religious diversity in the United States. He was more broadly ecumenical than most American Protestants in his inclusion of Roman Catholics. As an immigrant Schaff was ethnically inclusive, welcoming other immigrants with open arms, in contrast to those who desired to keep America predominantly Anglo-Saxon. He believed this unique blend of numerous ethnicities, cultures, and religious traditions would provide the context for the special destiny of the American nation.

This heir of the German "mediating theology" was theologically flexible and open to theological development in an age when a growing number could be described as theologically rigid. His mission to facilitate international dialogue and to develop a European-American theology placed him at the forefront of international scholarship and ecumenism. He was sacramentally and churchly minded in an American era dominated by sectarianism. He emphasized history and tradition in the age of revivalism. His focus on "the church question" as the most important issue of the day kept Schaff out of step with the growing number of American Christians who assumed that the salvation of individual souls should be the central concern of modern Christianity. His vision of an "evangelical catholic" church enabled him to understand how the many could be, in fact, were one. Finally, he debated the question of the role of religion in public education, and he formulated a foundational concept for theological education which would remain influential for generations to come. Thus, an analysis of Schaff's contributions to understanding nineteenth-century American religion will also illuminate the historical roots of many issues at the forefront of current religious debate.[7]

7. Seven doctoral dissertations have dealt with various aspects of Schaff's life

Schaff brought a vision to the American shore that was uncongenial to many and incomprehensible for some, and his contributions ranged from the reproofs of the angry prophet to the discoveries of the ardent seeker after truth. It is fascinating, for example, to listen to him chide Americans for their lack of "church feeling" and nearly total neglect of history, and then watch him discover the positive contributions the denominational system could make in America. The scope of Schaff's genius is revealed as he convincingly harmonizes the two. Schaff came to America with an already well-developed conception of the unity of the Christian church. Throughout his nearly half-century career as teacher, scholar, and churchman, despite an unending succession of momentous challenges to that vision that he encountered in the American situation, he maintained the essence of that vision virtually unchanged from the early 1840s to his death in 1893. Despite numerous modifications of his opinions about how and when church reunion would come about, he held tenaciously to his fundamental conviction that the church would become one in both spirit and organization. It is this interplay between an unchanging central belief and the willingness to remain flexible in its manifestations that best reveals the creativity of Philip Schaff as an analyst of and commentator on religion in nineteenth-century America. While on the one hand he was remarkably adaptable and developmental in his views of specific movements and

---

and thought and have been of value in this study. They include Theodore L. Trost, "Philip Schaff's Concept of the Church, with Special Reference to His Role in the Mercersburg Movement, 1844-1864" (Ph.D. diss., New College, Edinburgh University, 1958); George H. Shriver, "Philip Schaff's Concept of Organic Historiography Interpreted in Relation to the Realization of an 'Evangelical Catholicism' within the Christian Community" (Ph.D. diss., Duke University, 1960); Klaus Penzel, "Church History and the Ecumenical Quest: A Study of the German Background and Thought of Philip Schaff" (Th.D. diss., Union Theological Seminary, New York, 1962); John C. Meyer, "Philip Schaff's Concept of Organic Historiography as Related to the Development of Doctrine: A Catholic Appraisal" (Ph.D. diss., The Catholic University of America, 1968); Thomas J. Goliber, "Philip Schaff (1819-93): A Study in Conservative Biblical Criticism" (Ph.D. diss., Kent State University, 1976); Gary Pranger, "Philip Schaff (1819-1893): Portrait of an Immigrant Theologian" (Ph.D. diss., The University of Illinois at Chicago, 1987). See also the dissertation that provided the foundation for this study, Stephen R. Graham, "'Cosmos in the Chaos': A Study of Philip Schaff's Interpretation of Nineteenth-Century American Religion" (Ph.D. diss., The University of Chicago, 1989).

events, on the other hand his fundamental vision of the goal of God's kingdom remained constant.

III

Each of the first three chapters of this volume examines a threat to American religion that Schaff identified in his ordination sermon early in 1844. In each case, the longer he was in America, the more he realized that his initial opinions were in error. In fact, just a few months later, to an American audience on the occasion of his inauguration as professor at Mercersburg Seminary he would express ideas in sharp contrast to those in his ordination sermon. Why did this remarkable change occur? In the published and expanded version of his inaugural address, *Das Princip des Protestantismus,* Schaff presented a more complete survey of his theological program in which he identified "sectarism" and "rationalism" as the chief dangers confronting American Christianity. Romanism was still a threat, but his emphasis had changed so dramatically as to open him to the charge of the heresy of "popery." While Schaff never changed his mind about the ultimate goal of Christian unity in America, he did have to modify significantly his conceptions of the hindrances to unity found in sectarianism, Romanism, and rationalism. Chapter 1 analyzes Schaff's developing ideas toward sectarianism. The second chapter addresses Schaff's changing and apparently contradictory statements concerning the threat of "Romanism." Chapter 3 focuses on the threat of rationalism and Schaff's understanding of how Christians should meet that threat with a strategy based on a fascinating combination of German and American elements.

As his ideas about these three "threats" developed, Schaff reflected on what made American Christianity distinctive. As chapter 4 shows, he recognized that the fundamental difference between Christianity as found in the new world in contrast to the old was due to the "lively" American experiment of separation of church and state.[8] Coming from a German background but adapting quickly to the American

8. See Sidney E. Mead, *The Lively Experiment: The Shaping of Christianity in America* (New York: Harper & Row, 1963), and *The Nation with the Soul of a Church* (New York: Harper & Row, 1975).

situation, Schaff developed a particularly insightful understanding of the American system. Schaff's Americanization was illustrated, for example, by his involvement in various voluntary societies. Chapter 5 describes this characteristically American involvement and discusses the question of how this ardent advocate of the church could justify extensive work with extra-church organizations.

The final two chapters provide a summary of Schaff's fully developed thought in the areas of American nationality and evangelical-catholic Christianity. After decades of involvement in the American situation, Schaff's fundamental vision for America remained essentially the same, but he conceptualized the various forms in which the work of the kingdom would take place quite differently than when he first came to America.

When one encounters Schaff's astounding list of published materials, it becomes clear that far too little research has been done on the life and thought of this important ecumenist and scholar. Schaff understood and critiqued American sectarianism, separation of church and state, and American destiny with a depth of insight and breadth of perspective matched by few of his contemporaries. His involvement in the American Society of Church History, which he founded in 1888, and his work in the development of the American branch of the Evangelical Alliance during the 1860s and 1870s by themselves merit extensive study. Finally, Schaff established church history as a crucial theological discipline in the curricula of seminaries and divinity schools throughout the United States, and despite the general lack of concern for their own history expressed by many American Christians, he led the way to the establishment of American church history positions in many theological seminaries.

While few would want to use Schaff as a model for scientific historical scholarship today, every historian of American religion stands as a beneficiary of his pioneering work in numerous ways.[9] Fittingly, Schaff's last major address was his final call for the "Reunion of Christendom" at the World's Parliament of Religions in Chicago in 1893. Schaff died just a few weeks later, but his legacy remains. This book is an effort to bring to light a central emphasis of that legacy.

9. For an excellent analysis of Schaff's historiography see Bowden, *Church History in the Age of Science*, 31-68.

CHAPTER 1

Religious Freedom and the Threat of Sectarianism

Schaff's German Background

Philip Schaff was ordained to the Christian ministry on 12 April 1844 in the Reformed Church of Elberfeld, Germany. The circumstances of his ordination prefigured his later career, and highlighted one of his first frustrations about the religious situation in the land of his calling, America. The harbinger of things to come was the fact that Schaff was ordained as a minister in the Evangelical Union Church of Prussia — a Swiss Reformed candidate educated in Germany, ordained in a Reformed Church using the Lutheran liturgical form. This external evidence of the unity and cooperation within the Protestant Church of Germany stood in sharp contrast to the disarray awaiting him in America.[1]

The immediate occasion of Schaff's ordination was his acceptance of the call to be a professor at the newly founded German Reformed seminary at Mercersburg, Pennsylvania. Recognizing their need for an infusion of recent German theology and jealous to safeguard their German heritage and language, the representatives from Mercersburg had

1. For a discussion of Schaff's early life and his family's struggles with poverty and scandal, see Ulrich Gäbler, "Philip Schaff at Chur, 1819-1834," in *Probing the Reformed Tradition: Historical Studies in Honor of Edward A. Dowey, Jr.*, ed. Elsie Anne McKee and Brian G. Armstrong (Louisville, KY: Westminster/John Knox Press, 1989).

set their sights high. Their first choice was the famous preacher Friedrich W. Krummacher, but even had he been inclined to accept relocation to the backwoods of Pennsylvania, his prince, Frederick William IV, had no intention of losing such an outstanding leader in the German church. Frustrated thus, the Mercersburgers turned their attention to a young but highly recommended *privatdocent* at the University of Berlin, Philip Schaff. Believing his international background and adaptable personality — not to mention his impeccable academic credentials — would be of great benefit for their church, they extended their call. Quickly Schaff saw the hand of God in the offer and turned his back on a promising career in Germany to pursue his calling in the uncertainties of the new world.[2]

If one were to choose a person and a situation destined to reshape theological education and religious life in America, a less obvious candidate or circumstance could hardly be imagined. Schaff's German education, though highly regarded by his German peers in America, would cause most American Christians to view him with suspicion. In fact, many Americans regarded German theology as something of an intellectual disease — if one studied it at all, the goal was to cure its effects. Also, Schaff was to be a teacher in a relatively obscure immigrant denomination whose churches accounted for less than 1% of the churches in America, compared, for example, to over 38% for the Methodists, and by 1850, nearly 4% for the Roman Catholics.[3] In addition, Schaff would be geographically remote from the centers of influence in America. The German Reformed, with pious motive but little foresight, had decided to locate their seminary in tiny Mercersburg, Pennsylvania, in the pastoral foothills of the Allegheny mountains.

2. Though still a *privatdocent,* a status he called "literary purgatory," Schaff had every reason to expect satisfactory advancement in the German university system. In his "Autobiographical Reminiscences for My Children" he described his three years as a *privatdocent* in Berlin "among the happiest in my life." He looked forward to "the best prospects of promotion." Autobiographical Miscellaneous Box, Philip Schaff Papers, Evangelical and Reformed Historical Society, Philip Schaff Library, Lancaster Theological Seminary, Lancaster, Pennsylvania. Hereafter referred to as ERHS.

3. Statistics are from Edwin Scott Gaustad, *Historical Atlas of Religion in America* (New York: Harper & Row, 1962), 168. The Roman Catholic percentage of members would be even higher compared to the German Reformed, since each Roman Catholic church served many more persons than did most Protestant churches.

There they deemed themselves safely distant from urban evils, but they remained equally removed from urban centers of intellectual vitality and resource. It is not surprising, then, that few had any notion of the widespread impact that this young Swiss professor from this obscure denominational seminary would eventually have on religion in America.

Schaff chose Acts 16:8-10 as the text for his ordination sermon and likened his mission to the American wilderness to that of the apostle Paul who had received a "Macedonian call." For Schaff, the words came loud and clear: "*Come over to America and help us!*"[4] The call was one of utmost urgency, for as Schaff pointed out during the sermon, drawing upon all that he had heard and been taught about the new frontier of America, the religious situation there was most grim. The German Reformed congregations of America faced serious threats, and a more complete contrast could hardly be drawn than that between the civilization, harmony, strong Protestant character, and depth of culture of the old country and the barbarity, dissension, and religious chaos of the new world. It is somewhat surprising that Schaff's views of American religion and culture should be so completely negative considering his not altogether unpleasant contacts with a handful of American students and divines who had traveled to Germany to avail themselves of the latest in theological thought. Evidently the barrier of language and the marked difference in manners caused Schaff to be overly critical of his American peers. For example, Schaff failed miserably in an attempt to tutor professor Edwards A. Park of Andover Seminary in the theological system of Friedrich Schleiermacher, the father of modern theology. One can only imagine the frustration of the attempt to convey the nuances of Schleiermacher's thought by one who admittedly had a "very scant" knowledge of English to one whose mastery of German was described, probably generously, as "deficient!"[5] Schaff turned the inquiring Professor Park over to his friend K. F. August Kahnis who had little better luck, and despairing of the pupil's "many Yankee questions" exclaimed "'God forgive Christopher Columbus for having discovered America!'"[6]

4. Philip Schaff, "Ordination of Professor Schaff," *Weekly Messenger* 9 (September 4, 1844): 1870. Italics his.

5. David S. Schaff, *The Life of Philip Schaff: In Part Autobiographical* (New York: Scribner's, 1897), 65.

6. Ibid.

Later in America, Schaff became a close friend of Park and many of Park's frustratingly "Yankee" colleagues. He had a more positive encounter with George L. Prentiss while both studied with F. A. G. Tholuck at Halle. Prentiss, who evidently had a better command of the German language than Park, would often join Schaff at the home of Professor Tholuck to listen to Schaff's flute recitals and to discuss philosophy and theology.

Particularly scandalous to Schaff and his German mentors was the total fragmentation they perceived in the American religious situation. They could hardly have seen it otherwise. In all of the young scholar's travels and studies he had never been exposed to a situation where there were more than two, or at most three, recognized church bodies. In Prussia, in fact, there was strong desire among both political and ecclesiastical leaders to overcome the scandal of division between Reformed and Lutheran churches and unite them. In America, however, the chaos of numberless sects ruled, with new splits and splinter groups appearing almost daily. John Winebrenner, himself the founder of a sect which, incidentally, broke away from the German Reformed Church, included articles describing some fifty denominations in his *History of All the Religious Denominations in the United States*, published in 1849. Winebrenner also named eight "sects" that were not deemed worthy of article-length treatment. Such fragmentation violated the European passion for coherence, which was reflected in the monistic ideals of statesmen, philosophers, and church leaders who sought homogeneity in every area of life. In fairness it should be noted that of Winebrenner's fifty denominations, nearly half of them (twenty-two), were varieties of the three largest denominational families, the Baptists, Methodists, and Presbyterians. Yet in the eyes of Europeans, in American society — and particularly in the American church — there seemed to be no corrective to complete individualism and fragmentation.[7]

The evil of sectarianism, therefore, was one with which Schaff would wrestle his whole life as his thought developed and as he attempted to explain the American situation to his European mentors. Schaff had attended the prestigious universities of Tübingen, Halle, and Berlin, and in each place he had studied with champions of

7. John Winebrenner, *History of All the Religious Denominations in the United States*, 2nd ed. (Harrisburg, Penn.: John Winebrenner, 1849; original ed. 1844), 7-16.

church unity. He spoke of Tübingen as the place of the most "earnest and intense study" he witnessed during his university career.[8] The Hegelian scheme of development in history ruled supreme at Tübingen during Schaff's years there, and the leader of the "Tübingen school," F. C. Baur, used Hegel's model in his studies of the history of the church. Though he adamantly opposed Baur's rationalistic tendencies, Schaff nonetheless was strongly influenced by one of Baur's ideas: the concept of development in history. Later in his career, Schaff used this idea of development within the church as one of his fundamental arguments for the essential unity of the church in the face of empirical evidence which seemed to indicate the contrary.[9] Schaff's primary mentors in Halle were the theologians F. A. G. Tholuck and Julius Müller. Both helped shape Schaff's use of Hegelian ideas, and, more importantly, grounded him firmly in the pietism of the Württemberg revival. Müller's work on the doctrinal unity of Protestantism, which was intended to support the Evangelical Union Church of Prussia, merited the attention of all who desired church unity, according to Schaff. The pietism nurtured by Tholuck and Müller was another important foundational belief that supported Schaff's emphasis on church unity. All believers in Jesus Christ, he believed, must unite on the basis of their love for him, and then work to overcome theological differences.[10]

It was at Berlin, however, that Schaff came into contact with the scholar who was to influence him most profoundly, both personally and intellectually. While Schaff spoke highly of August D. C. Twesten, the successor to the chair of Friedrich Schleiermacher, his most glowing praise was reserved for Johann August Wilhelm Neander, the church historian. Neander, "the teacher that interested and helped me most," according to Schaff, was the one who introduced the young scholar to

8. D. Schaff, *Life*, 23.

9. See Klaus Penzel, "Church History and the Ecumenical Quest" (Th.D. diss., Union Theological Seminary, New York, 1962), 53-54. Schaff later stated that "He [Baur] gave me the first idea of historical development or of a constant and progressive flow of thought in the successive ages of the church." D. Schaff, *Life*, 20, quotes Philip Schaff, "Personal Reminiscences," which are actually titled "Autobiographical Reminiscences for My Children," ERHS.

10. See Klaus Penzel, "Philip Schaff: A Centennial Reappraisal," *Church History* 59 (June 1990): 208-9.

the "spirit of evangelical catholicity." This spirit was characterized by a sympathy for "all types of vital Christianity," and even "liberal intuitions for a free church in a free state," something Schaff would come to appreciate fully only years later.[11] Neander was also a model of "simplicity, purity, and humility" whom Schaff called "one of the greatest and best men I ever knew."[12] The fundamental ideas Schaff derived from Neander would remain basically unchanged throughout his career.

From these teachers Schaff inherited a theoretical conception of church unity; in the ecclesiastical situation in Prussia, he witnessed a physical embodiment of that ideal. The Evangelical Union Church, officially established by a decree by King Frederick William III of Prussia on 27 September 1817, was not actually the king's creation, asserted Schaff, but fell into his hands "as the ripe fruit of the age."[13] The Union Church was not wholly successful, however. Despite hopes that the time of religious dissension had passed, union was limited to various German states in which Lutheran and Reformed bodies existed in roughly equal numbers. In those areas where Lutheran or Reformed congregations predominated, union was rejected, and the upshot was that, in fact, there were now three Protestant bodies rather than just two. Nonetheless, Schaff saw the value of the attempt, and hoped that ultimately the intention of the decree would be realized throughout Germany and finally throughout the world.

According to Schaff, part of the difficulty faced by the Prussian union was that it was imposed from above by governmental decree rather than growing naturally out of the inner life of the church. Another problem was the reluctance of any of the groups (Lutheran, Reformed, or Evangelical Union), to contemplate a separation from the support of the state, and each maneuvered for a favored position in relation to it. Schaff was confident nonetheless that work toward church union "lies deeply in the wants of the church and the present age" and that it would continue. There is, he insisted, a "deep rooted tendency

11. D. Schaff, *Life,* 34.

12. Ibid. Schaff also called him "the most original phenomenon in the literary world of the nineteenth century." Philip Schaff, *Germany: Its Universities, Theology and Religion* (Philadelphia: Lindsay and Blakiston, 1857), 270. See also Schaff, "Autobiographical Reminiscences," 97a, 98.

13. Schaff, *Germany,* 183-84.

of the better spirit of the age towards a union and consolidation of Christendom."[14] "The future," he exulted, "belongs certainly to the union."[15]

A Land So Free from Restraint

After a five-week voyage Schaff viewed the American continent for the first time on 28 July 1844. His attitude about the condition of the land awaiting his arrival was hopeful, yet unsure. "I see this morning, for the first time, my future home-land. The sun rose bright upon the hills of New Jersey. A fine sight! In the evening we passed between Long Island and Staten Island by the light of the moon." He went on to add, with just a hint of incredulity, "fine homes and extensive woods are in view. The evidences of civilization are here, as in the land we left."[16] That tranquil scene was soon to be violently disrupted, however, because Schaff's portrayal of America's ills in his ordination sermon had preceded him, and raised a storm of protest from the German-American press.[17] One could hardly expect otherwise. In his sermon, in front of an audience wholly sympathetic to his ideas, Schaff's zeal for his mission allowed him to be carried away to exaggeration of the contrast between the civilization and culture of the homeland and the barbarity and boorishness of America, particularly among the German emigrants. Rising to heights of rhetorical flourish, Schaff directed his audience to

> take a full view now of this conflux of beggars, adventurers, liberty dreamers, culprits, and open blasphemers of religion, in a land so free from restraint, where all is still only in the process of formation, and where the influences and forces now present for good fall so far behind the sweeping growth of spiritual wants. View all this calmly [!] and

14. Ibid., 199.

15. Philip Schaff, *The Principle of Protestantism,* trans. John W. Nevin (Chambersburg, Penn.: Publication Office of the German Reformed Church, 1845; reprint ed., Philadelphia: United Church Press, 1964), 194. Schaff was essentially a follower of Hegel in his belief that a particular spirit dominates each age.

16. Ibid., 90.

17. See *The Principle of Protestantism,* 105, and the introduction by John Williamson Nevin, 29n.

> closely, and it will no longer seem strange to be told that our countrymen in America are in danger of being precipitated into an abyss of heathenism, even worse perhaps than that of our first ancestors; and thus may be felt the full force of the cry with which this blood-related stranger involuntarily pleads your compassion, *Come over and help us!*[18]

Schaff went on to plead that far from having nothing to do with these undesirables, this "offscouring" caught up in their "frantic infidelity," it was the Christian duty of his audience to send them the aid for which they unknowingly cried. Having thus offended his compatriots he planted his foot even more firmly in his mouth by expressing the desire that his fellow Germans would show just half the earnestness of the group least likely to have their admiration, those trouble-making do-gooders, the Puritans. One might wonder, given Schaff's negative idea about the people among whom he was to minister, why he believed there was any hope for his efforts in America at all. The answer to that question lies in his conviction that despite the degraded character of the "worthless multitude," there was nonetheless a remnant who had not bowed their knees to Baal. In fact, Schaff spoke of a "large number . . . of souls that desire to be saved" among the Germans in America.[19]

In his biography of Schaff, published in 1897, Schaff's son David explained that such negative attitudes of German America were then "current in Germany" and that when spoken, they "received the unquestioning assent of his hearers."[20] It is reasonable to assume, then, that Schaff merely echoed the sentiments of a significant segment of the German intellectual class and that his remarks, though laden with prophetic urgency and burning with missionary zeal, reflected not at all uncommon beliefs. Be that as it may, the German-American press reacted quickly and virulently. This twenty-five-year-old immigrant professor, still struggling with the language and culture of his adopted homeland, with the glamour of his missionary calling fading fast, faced

18. Schaff, "Ordination," 1869.

19. Ibid.

20. D. Schaff, *Life*, 82. David cited a letter received by Dr. Schaff in 1845 (no other information is given) which says, "I appreciate what an important mission is before you in Mercersburg, especially in view of the labyrinth and great evil of the sects and factions of which here in Germany we can form no adequate conception." Ibid., 110n.1.

denunciations as a traitor to his country and a slanderer of his own people.

Despite Schaff's ignorance and the insensitivity of his language in his ordination sermon, he did point out legitimate dangers for the German Reformed Church and the entire religious situation in America. The American church, according to Schaff, teetered on the brink of a "threefold abyss" of "HEATHENISM, ROMANISM, [and] SECTARISM [sic]."[21] One of the lamentable characteristics inherent in Protestantism, said Schaff, is its tendency to fragment. Along with the Protestant Reformation's rejection of the unifying authority of Rome and its emphasis on the ultimate authority of Scripture alone came also an undesirable yet inevitable by-product: the tendency of those who disagree about interpretation to separate. Nowhere, Schaff maintained, was that tendency to division more pronounced than in America.

The aspect of the American situation that most forcefully impressed outsiders like Schaff was the complete religious freedom they found. The Protestant impulse to divide found no hindrance in a land of such freedom. In America, Schaff told his ordination sermon audience, "there are found Reformed, Lutherans [and] Unionists," just as in Germany. But — and we can almost see Schaff pause to catch a deep breath — there are also "Episcopalians, Methodists with their various branches, Presbyterians, Congregationalists, Swedenborgians, Quakers, Hicksites, Unitarians, Shakers, Mormons, Rappists, and sects of whatever different names." What was even more appalling was the fact that they were "engaged in part in the most bitter opposition" to one another. The reason for this plethora of sects was quite simple, according to Schaff. "Every fanatic, [and in America these were unusually prevalent!] in whose brain is engendered of a night some new conceit, builds the next day a new chapel and baptizes it with his own name, as a legacy to future generations." At bottom, it was pride and vanity that produced the impulse to this "deplorable confusion" and threatened the welfare of Schaff's "sect-bewildered countrymen."[22]

In his ordination sermon, Schaff had very little good to say about America, and nothing positive to say about the "sect system" that

21. Schaff, "Ordination," 1869.

22. Ibid. Curiously, Schaff did not mention the Baptists, whose tendency to fragment was notorious.

prevailed there. America was the land of total religious freedom, and while it took Schaff some time to learn to appreciate the values of such a situation, the evils of the system were immediately obvious. The absence of governmental control over the churches made possible this "voluntary principle," as Schaff came to call it. This total lack of authoritative restraint on the excessive fanaticism of restless Americans encouraged the founding of sect after sect. Besides the danger presented to the souls of unwitting and unsophisticated people, the voluntary system was characterized by "all sorts of petty drudgery, vexations, and troubles, unknown in well endowed Established Churches." For example, immigrant pastors who were suddenly released from the restraints of government control were often unable to fill that void with essential self-control. Laypersons who were abruptly called upon to administer church property and assets, and to provide a living wage for their pastors, were frequently unable to do the former and unwilling to do the latter. The situations of many ministers were deplorable and many were forced to conduct "begging tours" to raise funds for personal support and the erection of a sanctuary.[23]

With a boldness born of a theological vision, Schaff went directly to the heart of the problem with American Christianity. Americans too easily accepted the divided condition of the church when it was obviously contrary to the teachings of Christ. With impatience and audacity Schaff readied himself to take on all obstacles in his effort to change the basic character of the religion of an entire nation. Yet even as he crossed the Atlantic the opposition gathered its forces for a counterattack.

If there were any shadows of doubt in Schaff's mind about the wisdom of his choice to come to America, they were swept away when he finally reached Mercersburg. As he journeyed through rugged mountain passes, he was reminded of his Swiss homeland. One wonders what went through the mind of this young scholar, accustomed to the bustle of the principal cities of Europe, as he first viewed this quiet village which had attained the modest status of "borough" only thirteen years before. Schaff was accorded a very warm welcome by students and faculty alike and began to feel at home in this "American Germany,"

23. Philip Schaff, *America: A Sketch of Its Political, Social and Religious Character*, ed. Perry Miller (Cambridge: Harvard University Press, 1961), 79.

as he called it.[24] A procession, led by the village band, marched Schaff down the main street, through the public square, and up the hill to the seminary, where speeches of welcome were made by students. The coming of a new professor to their seminary was a major event for the town. Not only was this young man a product of the best universities of Europe, but his presence doubled the size of the faculty. Schaff revealed a sensitive side in his journal entries about the occasion. "It was too much honor; I do not deserve it! I am humbled by it."[25]

Schaff was especially pleased to find that his colleague at the seminary, John Williamson Nevin, was unexpectedly and quite astonishingly similar in theological orientation. In Nevin, Schaff found a faithful colleague and sometime defender whose friendship he would cherish for the rest of his life. As Schaff put it, "I think I could not have a better colleague than Dr. Nevin. I feared I might not find any sympathy in him for my views of the church; but I discover that he occupies essentially the same ground that I do and confirms me in my position. He is filled with the ideas of German theology."[26] The number of theologians in America who would have been, like Nevin, so receptive to Schaff's ideas may be counted on one hand. That two such thinkers should actually find themselves united as a faculty of two in a small denominational seminary in the mountains of Pennsylvania, Schaff could attribute only to Providence. Schaff would find out before long just how fortunate he was to have been joined with Nevin.

The synod that had extended his call to the seminary also accorded Schaff a cordial welcome and asked him to give his inaugural address as professor at the synod's meeting at Reading, Pennsylvania, on 25 October 1844. Ordinarily, such an address would be the occasion for thanking those who had extended the call, cataloguing the virtues of the denomination and institution with which he would be associated, and, in general, getting things off to a harmonious start. But Schaff was a man with a mission. With not a little naïveté, Schaff plunged into his address on the "principle of Protestantism" in which he outlined his fundamental ideas of historical development and his hope for a united

24. D. Schaff, *Life*, 98.
25. Ibid., 99.
26. Ibid., 103.

"evangelical catholic" church of the future.[27] A significant part of the exposition of his concept of development was his belief that the Protestant Reformation was the natural product of the church of the Middle Ages. Schaff's appreciation of the medieval Catholic Church, apparently contradicting his views expressed in his ordination sermon just weeks earlier, caused deep unease among many of his hearers. In fact, Schaff had directly contradicted an idea expressed just a week earlier in a sermon before the synodal meeting. That sermon had affirmed a common anti-Catholic interpretation of history which denied any validity whatsoever to the church of the Middle Ages.

Had Schaff expressed such ideas in Germany his audience would have listened thoughtfully, and those most aroused would have retired to their studies to produce learned and thoughtful responses. In fact, his mentors had espoused these concepts for years without considering them at all controversial.[28] In America, however, the free interchange of ideas was not so welcome, especially within the German Reformed Church, and particularly when the subject was Roman Catholicism. When these ideas were more fully developed in the book-length *Das Princip des Protestantismus* published early in 1845, and translated into English by Nevin, including Nevin's lengthy introduction and an appendix with his sermon on "Catholic Unity," and 112 "theses for the times" written by Schaff, there was a prompt call to arms.[29] The merest hint of sympathies with the Church of Rome was all that was needed to create visions of papal empire among some of his hearers. Particularly threatening was the concept of development in doctrine. If, as Schaff claimed, Protestantism was a natural development out of Roman Catholicism, where was the violent severing of truth from error that gave

27. George H. Shriver, *Philip Schaff: Christian Scholar and Ecumenical Prophet* (Macon, Ga.: Mercer University Press, 1987), 22, notes that a half-century later Schaff said, "Here I stood fifty years ago and flung out a firebrand. However, I did it unintentionally." As Perry Miller put it, "Schaff contrived, out of an innocence that was pathetically absolute, to outrage all three of these indigenous passions — belief in the revolutionary character of the Reformation, hatred of Rome, and a hankering for revivalism." Schaff, *America,* xx.

28. For a discussion of the "high church" ideal of Ludvig von Gerlach and others of the Prussian High Orthodoxy movement, see Penzel, "Church History," 75-103.

29. *Das Princip des Protestantismus* (Chambersburg, Penn.: In der Druckerei der Hochdeutsch-Reformirten Kirche, 1845).

American anti-Catholics their identity? Some among the German Reformed had been strongly influenced by the primitivism and restorationism that characterized many American Protestant groups. Numerous groups believed that they could restore the pristine purity of the primitive church by rejecting the "corruptions" of the church in history — especially in the medieval period — and returning to "the Bible alone."[30] This was also the time of "the Protestant crusade" against militant Catholicism.[31] Schaff's ideas seemed to be a blatant sellout to the enemy.

Having withstood the buffeting of the secular press, partly through the encouragement of his German Reformed friends, Schaff now found himself faced with a heresy trial among some of those he had looked to for support. It was the Reverend Joseph F. Berg, pastor of the prestigious First German Reformed Church in Philadelphia, whose toes Schaff stepped on most painfully (Berg had preached the anti-Catholic sermon a week earlier), and who was the most vocal in condemnation of Schaff's views. Schaff could not have missed the irony that Berg's had been the first signature on the letter that first invited him to Mercersburg. Berg's strident anti-Catholicism was quite in harmony with a strong stream of social thought in nineteenth-century America. Steadily increasing immigration aroused fears of various kinds. An all-too-common response was nativism, directed against all immigrants, but Roman Catholic immigrants in particular.

Within the German Reformed Church, a small but vocal group denounced Catholics at every opportunity and buttressed their position with a view of church history that saw the true faith passed down through the centuries by small persecuted sects whose members opposed the Church of Rome. Fearful that their seminary was sliding down the slope to the abyss of Rome, the anti-Catholic group brought charges of popery and Puseyism against Schaff.

So here was Schaff, thousands of miles from home, convinced that his was a mission guided by Providence, doing exactly what he believed he was called to do (sharing the best of German thought with his

30. See, for example, Richard T. Hughes, ed., *The American Quest for the Primitive Church* (Urbana: University of Illinois Press, 1988).

31. See Ray Allen Billington, *The Protestant Crusade, 1800-1860* (New York: Macmillan, 1938).

American colleagues), determined not to suffer the shame of a return to Germany in failure, yet charged with heresy during his first months in America. Throughout the turmoil of the trial Schaff was convinced that God providentially had given him strong support in the persons of Nevin and other moderates in the German Reformed Church. In this trial over competing ecclesiologies Schaff's defense rested on the fact that fundamental objections to both post-Reformation Roman Catholicism and Puseyism were quite clearly presented in the book itself. He continued to affirm his appreciation for the church in all periods of its history, including the medieval, despite the obvious abuses and errors rampant during that time. Yet he also insisted that this position in no way compromised his firm stance alongside the Protestant Reformers. The synod of the German Reformed Church agreed and completely exonerated Schaff in October, 1845, just a few days short of a year after he gave his inaugural address.[32]

In fact, *The Principle of Protestantism* made its mark both within and beyond the German Reformed denomination. Many in the German Reformed Church applauded its ideas, and reviews of the book from outside that church were generally favorable. Charles Hodge, for example, not one to allow Romanistic tendencies to pass by unchallenged, found parts of the book with which he did not agree (and some that he admitted he did not understand), but believed charges that Schaff and Nevin tended toward "Puseyism . . . prelacy and Rome and what is necessarily connected with them," were "altogether unfounded" and completely refuted by the principle of historical development expressed in the book. Hodge concluded that "the evangelical character of the leading doctrines of his book, the seriousness and warmth of feeling which pervade it, and the high order of ability which it displays, give ground to hope that Dr. Schaf [sic] will prove a blessing to the church and country of his adoption."[33] Tayler Lewis, a layman in the Dutch Reformed Church, wrote a lengthy three-part review in the *Weekly Messenger* of the German Reformed Church and agreed that "no impartial reader can fail to be convinced of the reality, sincerity, warmth,

32. See George H. Shriver, ed., *American Religious Heretics: Formal and Informal Trials* (Nashville, Tenn.: Abingdon), 18-55.

33. Charles Hodge, "Schaff's Protestantism," *Biblical Repertory Princeton Review* 17 (October 1845): 634, 636.

and strength of their [Schaff's and Nevin's] attachment to the Protestant cause."[34] Schaff seems to have taken the controversy in stride, and true to his lifelong character, accepted both criticism and praise gracefully. It is ironic, however, that this advocate of union should have been at the center of a controversy that ultimately contributed to the failure of efforts to unite German and Dutch Reformed denominations. Berg and his party tried again to establish heresy charges against Schaff in 1846, but once again the scheme failed, and many conservatives, including Berg, left the German Reformed for the more rigidly orthodox Dutch Reformed Church.

The Protestant Principle and Sectarian Divisions

Thus far, America had not been overly kind to Schaff. In a sense, the feeling was mutual. Though he remained hopeful about the prospects for the American church, during the first few years of his residence in America Schaff was more likely to point out the nation's faults than to praise its accomplishments and possibilities. In *The Principle of Protestantism,* Schaff pointed to the two most glaring "diseases" of the church in America, rationalism and sectarianism.[35] The one characteristic of American religious life described by Schaff in his ordination sermon that was borne out most fully in his experience was the tendency toward sectarianism. Graphic illustrations of the tendency of American churches to split were the divisions over the issue of slavery in the two largest American denominations, the Baptists and the Methodists, during Schaff's first years in America. Most splits were over issues of much less moment, however, and Schaff had little good to say about this most unpleasant result of America's "free institutions and the separation of the church from the state."

Anticipating a concept that would be more fully developed nearly a century later in H. Richard Niebuhr's *The Social Sources of Denominationalism,* Schaff perceived that when established churches divided,

34. Tayler Lewis, "The Church Question," *Weekly Messenger* 11 (January 21, 1846): 2153.

35. Schaff, *Principle of Protestantism,* 129-55. More will be said about Schaff's understanding of the threat of rationalism in chapter 3.

beneath the ever-present rhetoric about the Bible and theology, their differences were in fact as often social as doctrinal. Ecclesiastical division in Germany, from the time of the Protestant Reformation, usually had been due to differences in doctrine — indeed, from the practical American perspective, differences in doctrine so minute as to seem meaningless. In contrast, American churches split over practical matters such as slavery or attitudes about revivalism. Certainly such matters had theological underpinnings, but the fact that the divisions were often regional or along class or ethnic lines shows that practical considerations loomed large. Schaff's conception of America as a "land of practicality" was reinforced by the nature of the divisions of its churches.[36]

Part of the explanation of the American tendency to divide could be found in the Anglo-American imprint on America and its primarily Reformed religious antecedents. According to Schaff, the German character, turned as it was toward the life of the mind, tended more toward the rationalistic problem of Protestantism — and this, incidentally, would help solve the sectarian problem if German thought were allowed sufficient influence in America. The Anglo-American character, however, was more practically oriented. Therefore it emphasized the organizational side of the church, and its excess was thus seen in the American proliferation of organizations. Looking deeper for the ultimate cause of sectarianism, however, Schaff insisted that the root of the matter, whether intellectual or practical, was finally due to human "sinful ambition and pride."[37] Because the church is human as well as divine, there is always the possibility that there will be "practical defects" that need to be corrected. "In almost every sect," he admitted, "we may find some particular side of the Christian life clearly and strongly marked; where as in a mirror the church should see her own defects, the wrinkles or spots that mar her visage, so as to do penance for her unfaithfulness, by which so many of her best members have been led to forsake her communion."[38]

The significance of sects, Schaff believed at this early stage of his career, was their negative role as "a disciplinary scourge, a voice of awakening and admonition by which the church is urged to new life

36. Ibid., 140-41. See H. Richard Niebuhr, *The Social Sources of Denominationalism* (1929; reprint ed., New York: Meridian, 1975), esp. 21-25.

37. Schaff, *Principle of Protestantism,* 144.

38. Ibid., 171.

and a more conscientious discharge of her duties." Grudgingly Schaff conceded that the sectarian system did, in fact, help spread religious interest and stimulate Christian zeal. Granting this, he charged that as soon as the fault within the church that gave rise to the sect was corrected, the sect must reunite with the larger body. The sect, he said, "loses its right to exist, in the same degree in which the body from which it is a secession, has corrected the faults that led to it." If it remained separated from the life-giving vine of the larger church body, it would wither and die. Sects, by their nature as correcting agents, were necessarily out of balance, and by their characteristic refusal to return to the balance of the larger body they became monstrosities which distorted Christianity. Thus, at the point in his intellectual development when he wrote the *Principle of Protestantism,* Schaff could see only a limited negative purpose in sects. Their goal should be to cease to exist.

> If sects then would be true to themselves, they must as soon as they have fulfilled their commission unite themselves again with the general life of the church, that they may thus as organic members of the body acquire new vital energy; and the church, on her side, should make special efforts to gather once more under her motherly protection and care, the children that have forsaken her and are now estranged from her bosom. To this duty the Reformed Church is specially called, as the largest part of these modern separatistic movements have sprung from her communion.[39]

For the Protestant Reformation to reach its completion, the disease of sectarianism must be overcome and a "closing act" of reunion occur to bring together the separated fragments of the body of Christ.

The problem was that with the combination of the American system's lack of restraint and the particularly innovative American character, sects naturally flourished like tares in the Christian wheat field. And due to the "unchurchly" character of most of American Christianity, that field was sorely neglected. In the *Principle of Protestantism,* Schaff's focus was on the weeds. Like Nevin, Schaff identified the immediate cause of the problem in Anglo-American "Puritanism," a type of Christianity which, he lamented, had "a zeal for God, but not

39. Ibid., 172. Italics his.

according to knowledge." The Puritans, to be sure, had exhibited "deep moral earnestness, stern self-discipline, [and] unbending force of character." Yet these inward-looking virtues led to a neglect of history, which in turn contributed to a failure to see the presence of the Lord with his church throughout the centuries, even in those centuries in which gross abuses were found.[40] By sowing the seeds of revolt against the Christian past, the Puritans reaped the disobedience of their own children whose rebellions created the ever-growing numbers of sects. The final result, according to Schaff, was the chaos of the American religious landscape. With biting irony Schaff complained that,

> anyone who has, or fancies that he has, some inward experience and a ready tongue, may persuade himself that he is called to be a reformer; and so proceed at once, in his spiritual vanity and pride, to a revolutionary rupture with the historical life of the church, to which he holds himself immeasurably superior.

Such persons had appeared in the past, but in the land of uninhibited freedom, their innovations led to numberless institutional schisms. The innovator

> builds himself of a night accordingly a new chapel, in which now for the first time since the age of the apostles a pure congregation is to be formed; baptizes his followers with his own name . . . rails and screams with full throat against all that refuses to do homage to his standard; and . . . though utterly unprepared to understand a single book, is not ashamed to appeal continually to the Scriptures, as having been sealed entirely, or in large part, to the understanding of eighteen centuries, and even to the view of our Reformers themselves, till now at last God has been pleased to kindle the true light in an obscure corner of the New World![41]

The arrogance of such a person was certainly repulsive to Schaff, but the most regrettable part of the situation was the effect such charlatans had on the common people.

40. Ibid., 145.
41. Ibid., 149.

> Thus the deceived multitude, having no power to discern spirits, is converted not to Christ and his truth, but to the arbitrary fancies and baseless opinions of an individual, who is only of yesterday. Such *con*version is of a truth only *per*version; such *theo*logy, *neo*logy; such *ex*position of the Bible, wretched *im*position. What is built is no church, but a chapel, to whose erection Satan himself has made the most liberal contribution.[42]

This was the sorry situation in which Schaff believed he now found himself. In their perverse creativity, he lamented, Americans had produced "a variegated sampler of all conceivable religious chimeras and dreams." His agitation increasing, Schaff moaned that "every theological vagabond and peddler may drive here his bungling trade, without passport or license, and sell his false ware at pleasure. What is to come of such confusion is not now to be seen."[43]

It was not just the weeds in the field that caused havoc. Even the established, more respectable denominations stood in essentially hostile relations toward one another and evinced "so little inclination or impulse toward an inward and outward union in the Lord, that one might weep to think of it." In their mad rush to gain ascendency over one another, the denominations, rather than displaying Christian charity toward their brothers and sisters in Christ, were full of "jealousy and contention, and malicious disposition," taking satisfaction in the hardships of others and discounting their merits. One is reminded of the story of the Baptist worker who exclaimed, "we won only two souls last night, but thank God, the Methodists across the street did not win any!"[44]

For Schaff, such division in the body of Christ was a source of more grief than any other conceivable earthly tragedy. Indeed, Schaff claimed that any person with a right conception of the church would not be induced by the price of the whole world to appear as the founder of a new sect. Arguments that sectarian division promoted zeal and

42. Ibid., 149-50. Italics his.

43. Ibid., 150.

44. Ibid. It would take a great deal of soul-searching and experience in the American religious context before Schaff would be able to appreciate the values of "religious populism" as noted by Nathan O. Hatch, *The Democratization of American Christianity* (New Haven: Yale University Press, 1989), 3-16.

activity and that there was unity despite denominational rivalry failed to persuade Schaff. Admittedly, the situation in America was one of intense religious fervor and widespread interest in things religious, but, Schaff insisted, "the advantage, so far as it may exist, is to be ascribed, not to the divisions in question as such, but only to God, who in his wisdom can bring good out of all evil." Ultimately sectarian division would be shown for what it was, since "in the balance of the Last Judgment . . . good works that proceed from ambition and emulation only will be found to carry but little if any weight."[45]

Although American religious innovators continually appealed to the Scriptures as the source of their ideas, Schaff argued that there could be no biblical basis for a case in favor of sectarian division. The whole tenor of the Bible was that Christ had come to bring unity, to create "one fold, under one Shepherd." Both the last command and the final prayer of the Lord expressed his desire that his followers would live in unity and harmony. Sectarians had in fact destroyed the authority of Scripture and had substituted "numberless popes . . . who would fain enslave Protestants once more to [the] human authority" of their own self-serving judgments and conceited wills. Neither could sectarians appeal to the Reformation as the ultimate source of the freedom from authority which encouraged sectarian division. If this was the legacy of the Reformation, then that movement itself stood "in direct contradiction to the holy Scriptures," and was therefore a "sinful work of man." No! thundered Schaff with as much heat as this usually temperate young scholar ever generated. "The Sect system, like rationalism, is a prostitution and caricature of true Protestantism, and nothing else." Christians must destroy pride; they must overcome this "cancerous affection." "Away with human denominations, down with religious sects!"[46] Christians must repent of their sinful selfishness and allow the Spirit of God to heal division and nourish the church as his one united body.

Whether David Schaff's appraisal was completely warranted — that "the *Principle of Protestantism* may be regarded as in its consequences the most influential literary work in the history of the German Reformed Church in the United States"[47] — it was nevertheless true that Schaff

45. Schaff, *Principle of Protestantism,* 151.
46. Ibid., 152-55.
47. D. Schaff, *Life,* 107.

sounded clearly a note of insightful criticism of the religious situation in America with which theologians and church leaders would wrestle for decades to come. For most American Christians, the church was indeed *holy, catholic* [small "c" of course!], and *apostolic,* but Schaff insisted that it also must be *one*.

It is remarkable that Schaff could continue to function — and retain his unbounded optimism — given the nearly total antagonism between his ideal of the church and the situation he found in America. In the face of this intolerable tension, in the one place in the world where it would be most difficult to realize his ideal, something had to change. Either the American religious system must undergo an immediate and drastic reform, or Schaff must somehow alter his ideal to fit the reality of the situation. Although Schaff maintained his driving passion for the unity of all Christians, he began to realize that his ideas about the means of union had to change. *The Principle of Protestantism* contained Schaff's primal vision for the church and the essence of that vision remained unaltered. The longer he lived in his adopted homeland, however, his ideas about how Christian union would be achieved developed markedly as he immersed himself in the theological, ecclesiastical, and cultural life of America.

Rich Material for a New Creation

Almost immediately Schaff began to modify his original conception of the sectarian system in America. As he read, observed, and discussed, a more accurate model of religion in America began to take shape in his mind. Schaff could claim in 1848 that "a church history of the United States is a work that has not yet been written."[48] At first glance, that statement is surprising, since Robert Baird had published his *Religion in America* just four years earlier, and I. Daniel Rupp's *Original History of the Religious Denominations at Present Existing in the United States* ap-

48. Philip Schaff, "Introduction to the Church History of the United States," *German Reformed Messenger* 14 (December 20, 1848): 2754. The "Introduction" comprised a series of articles published in the *German Reformed Messenger* from December 20, 1848, through February 21, 1849, pp. 2754, 2760, 2768, 2772, 2776, 2784, 2788, and 2792. Future references will include dates and page numbers only.

peared that same year. Undoubtedly Schaff was aware of those volumes at the time, and according to Perry Miller, Schaff was said to have admired Baird's work.[49] Even more surprising was Schaff's repetition of that opinion in 1892, four years after the publication of Daniel Dorchester's *Christianity in the United States from the First Settlement down to the Present Time*, and after the numerous publications of Schaff's own writings on American church history.

The explanation of the statements, and the reason why Schaff's mind was not changed by the nearly fifty years of writings on American Christianity, was disclosed in the source of the statement of 1892, his *Theological Propædeutic.* "The Church History of the United States has yet to be written," Schaff repeated. "Denominational and local histories we have in abundance, and the number is fast increasing." The crux of the matter was, however, that "there is no worthy history of American Christianity which represents it as an organic whole, in its genesis and growth, its connections with the mother Churches of Europe, its characteristic peculiarities, and its great mission for the future." Not only should rising scholars devote themselves to this task, but, Schaff recommended, "special chairs ought to be established in our seminaries for American Church History." In the list of literature on the church history of the United States, Schaff noted specifically why the works of Baird, Rupp, and Dorchester failed to meet his standard. Baird's *Religion in America,* Schaff noted, was "not a history, but a collection of material for history," and Rupp's book was merely a collection of short sketches on denominations and sects. Likewise, while Dorchester's work was "a considerable improvement upon the former, as an industrious collection of facts, statistical tables and maps," it neither could be considered true "history," and besides, the book was biased by the "Methodist sympathies" of the author.[50]

Interestingly, while Schaff censured Baird and Dorchester for their lack of sufficiently broad interpretive models, modern scholars have

49. Schaff, *America,* xxxi.

50. Philip Schaff, *Theological Propædeutic* (New York: Scribner's, 1894), 293. A proposed project which Schaff thought would overcome these difficulties was the *American Church History* series, whose volumes were to be written and published under the auspices of the American Society of Church History, founded by Schaff in 1888. Ibid., 294.

found the interpretations in these nineteenth-century histories to be of great value for understanding the period. For example, Henry Warner Bowden has claimed that Baird's *Religion in America* is more valuable than Schaff's work precisely because it employs "interpretational themes."[51] While Schaff surely appreciated Baird's use of the "religious character" of the colonists of various areas, the "voluntary principle," and "evangelical" and "non-evangelical" bodies as themes that helped provide explanation of much of American religious life, he argued that such treatments failed to place American Christianity within a sufficiently comprehensive framework. What Baird and others like him failed to see was that the history of American Christianity fit as an integral part in the unfolding of God's cosmic plan for the ages. The American churches must never be artificially wrenched from their place in the organic development of the kingdom of God throughout the centuries.[52] Schaff's central belief about the church was that it was one, and any interpretation that failed to take that fundamental fact into account was destined to fall into error. Bowden is correct that Baird's work "represents, in distilled and annotated form, a view of history and a sense of values that once constituted a dominant pattern in American thought." Bowden fails to note, however, that the work of Philip Schaff is all the more enlightening because this central theological vision caused him to stand against many characteristics of an "American" view of history and to call into question some of the most dearly held values of nineteenth-century American Christianity. His was an alternative view that in many respects has come to be widely appreciated only generations after he lived.[53]

51. Henry Warner Bowden, introduction to *Religion in America,* by Robert Baird (New York: Harper & Row, 1970), xiii.

52. Schaff could never accept, for example, Baird's effort to write the history of American religion "with as little reference as possible to any other country." Robert Baird, *Religion in the United States of America* (Glasgow: Blackie and Son, 1844; reprint, New York: Arno Press and The New York Times, 1969), viii.

53. Bowden, introduction to *Religion in America,* xv. Bowden also persuasively argues that few present historians do or could utilize Schaff's model of a theology of history. See *Church History in the Age of Science: Historiographical Patterns in the United States, 1876-1918* (Chapel Hill: University of North Carolina Press, 1970), esp. 65-68 where he discusses the theological foundation of the American Society of Church History and changes in that foundation following Schaff's death in 1893.

Few scholars are capable of writing comprehensive histories of a nation's religious traditions — especially those as diverse as America's — but it was an even more daunting challenge in Schaff's day when there were no interpretive paradigms with which to interact. In late 1848 and early 1849, he published a series of articles as an "Introduction to the Church History of the United States," which, he admitted, were no more than a "feeble attempt" to provide "a few fugitive hints" about the situation. A fully encompassing history of the church in America would be an extremely difficult undertaking for which one would need a breadth of vision and understanding that was truly uncommon. It was the "Sect-spirit" that had hindered the production of a complete history of the church in the United States, and previous attempts at writing an American church history had degenerated into apologies for one sect or another, according to Schaff. The difficulty (which it seems Schaff may have contemplated overcoming himself) was that a European lived too far away and was unable to "obtain a clear view of the peculiar condition of the new world." It is quite possible that the young scholar was beginning to realize that his own too facile stereotype of the American situation would not stand up under the test of experience. On the other hand, an American interested in religion was inevitably "more or less under the sect-influence," and therefore neither European nor American was in the position to be "free from the spirit of party but not destitute of interest" and able to work "in the exclusive service of truth, the whole truth."[54] It seems at this point that Schaff himself envisioned the production of an American church history, and hoped that a more lengthy residence in the United States might enable him to avoid the problems of both the far-removed European and the too-intimately-involved American. While he never succumbed to inordinate pride in his own capabilities, Schaff nevertheless had a realistic understanding of his qualifications and abilities. Just how close he came to his own ideal of the proper American church history remains to be seen.

Even he might not be able to compose such a history, Schaff fretted, given the antagonistic relationship that obtained between denominations and sects in America. In language reminiscent of that in the *Principle of Protestantism*, Schaff lamented the "rivalry and jealousy" which "throws a great obstacle in the way of a historian." For an

54. Schaff, "Introduction" (December 20, 1848): 2754.

historian in the Hegelian lineage who sought a unifying thread amidst the opposition of identifiable thesis and antithesis, the "endless variety" of the American situation drove one to humility. Even here, however, Schaff gave evidence of developing a more positive attitude toward the varied American church situation. America was, indeed, the "new world," was full of "life and activity, and provided with the conditions of a future much more full of life." He sounded this note of optimism along with the obvious exasperation of one whose deepest desire was for the unity of the church. "All the elements of the old world, all the branches of Protestantism and even of Catholicism itself, meet in renewed strength, and, possessing civil rights altogether equal and full of ardent hopes, engage in conflict with each other, the final issue of which cannot by any means now be foreseen. *This* only is unalterably fixed: the Lord of the Church is at the helm, and in his own time will secure victory to truth."[55] Schaff did not despair. American Christianity faced serious problems, to be sure, and he would identify them, yet his intention was never to scorn, but always to understand.

Schaff returned to the theme of the "puritan" character of religion in America. English Puritanism was the first dominant religious community in the new world, and, according to Schaff, it had exerted strong influence on all subsequent groups. Groups which originally had nothing to do with Puritanism, such as Methodists, Episcopalians, Lutherans, and Dutch and German Reformed, had become, he said, "more or less puritanized."[56] Puritanism, which Schaff saw as the extreme form of Calvinism "stripped of all its churchly elements" — which, Schaff argued, was not at all what the Reformer himself desired — was an "extreme, naked Protestantism" which viewed each local congregation as "a wholly independent and complete church, amenable to *no* earthly tribunal."[57] This

55. Ibid. Italics his.

56. Schaff, "Introduction" (January 24, 1849): 2776. Under the label "Puritan" Schaff and Nevin lumped together a combination of revivalistic emphases, lack of historical sense, antisacramentalism, and individualism. James Hastings Nichols, *Romanticism in American Theology: Nevin and Schaff at Mercersburg* (Chicago: The University of Chicago Press, 1961), 5ff. identifies the Mercersburgers' use of "puritan" with "evangelical." This definition fails both to identify the specific characteristics of what Nevin and Schaff opposed and to recognize that in many ways they considered themselves "evangelical." See John W. Nevin, "Puritanism and the Creed," *Mercersburg Review* (1849): 602, and Schaff, *Principle of Protestantism*, 144-48.

stereotype led Schaff to view the American denominations as duly "puritanized" and thus extremely "unchurchly" and prone to individualism. While he clearly overemphasized the "puritan" role in shaping the independent spirit of much of American Christianity, he did accurately discern its basic character. Schaff's own roots, however, were in no way "puritan," and the hills of Pennsylvania were far from New England. For him, the ideal was a church deeply rooted in history, replete with "churchly elements," strongly affirming of unity, and characterized by respect for the entire Christian tradition. Those in America who gloried in their "escape" from history mistook a vice for a virtue, according to Schaff.

Despite these flaws, America was blessed with tremendous possibilities, which Schaff recognized more and more the longer he resided in the United States. In America, said Schaff, were gathered together "all possible healthy and unhealthy elements of Europe" which created all manner of turmoil and chaos, but, on the other hand, provided "the richest material for further unconceived creations of history."[58] What was often lacking was a properly historical appreciation by Americans for their European ancestry. Worse than political nativism, said Schaff, was a sort of religious nativism in which innovators sought to establish an "*American* christianity, an *American* piety, in *hostile* opposition to all previous developements [sic]." There was some "native growth" within the field of American Christianity, but nearly all of value, in Schaff's eyes at least, had come from the old world.[59]

In the final article of the "Introduction to the Church History of the United States" series, Schaff touched upon the novelty in the American religious system that was the ultimate source of all other innovations, the separation of church and state. Schaff was beginning to see some of the benefits of such a system, though he could still insist that such a condition was not Christianity's "normal and ideal state," and that it was through such separation that "sectarianism with all its evils has obtained formal sanction."[60] This recognition of the virtues of

57. Ibid. Italics his.

58. Schaff, "Introduction" (February 7, 1849): 2784.

59. Ibid. Interestingly, Schaff would come to value highly "American" forms of Christianity as long as they were rooted in the historic traditions of Christianity. There were roses among the thorns in the new growth.

60. Schaff, "Introduction" (February 21, 1849): 2792.

the separation of church and state showed that Schaff was gradually becoming "Americanized." Just a few years earlier, Alexis de Tocqueville had noted of the Americans that "all thought that the main reason for the quiet sway of religion over their country was the complete separation of church and state."[61] Schaff himself had even come so far as to be able to advise his American audience, and whatever Europeans who might happen to be eavesdropping, that "there are yet many things that the mother [Europe] might then learn of the daughter [America] heretofore rather superciliously regarded." (And, one might add, by none more superciliously regarded than by the not-so-much-younger Schaff.) In fact, said Schaff, once again hitting the German Puritan-haters where it hurt the most, "a little more Puritanism, with its restless activity, its bold spirit of enterprize, its practical tact and talent for organization, [would] be of *very great advantage* to the German Churches."[62]

A few years earlier, Tocquéville had expressed the desire that the French people learn from the American example. Tocqueville's emphasis was on the Republican government of the United States, and although he described some of the characteristics of American religion, his focus, as his title affirms, was on *Democracy in America.* While for Tocqueville religion served as a means to support democratic government, Schaff reversed the order. Certainly he agreed that religion was necessary for the proper functioning of democratic society, but his perspective was that of a churchman, not a student of politics. For Tocqueville, government was central and religion was a very important yet complementary support. For Schaff, the development of the Christian church in history was the most important issue, regardless of the political situation in which it was found. The example of the United States was particularly crucial in Christian history, Schaff believed, because of the unique opportunity the church found in that situation for growth and influence. The political lesson that European governments could learn from America was that despite the chaotic appearance, true religion flourished in a condition of liberty.[63]

The "Introduction to the Church History of the United States"

61. Alexis de Tocqueville, *Democracy in America,* trans. George Lawrence, ed. J. P. Mayer (Garden City, N.Y.: Doubleday, 1969), 295.

62. Schaff, "Introduction" (February 21, 1849): 2792. Emphasis mine.

63. Tocqueville, *Democracy in America,* xiii-xiv, 442-49.

articles, written for a German-American audience, gave the first glimpses of Schaff's developing understanding and appreciation of the American religious situation. He had discovered unexpected "moral and religious seriousness" among the American people, and had realized that while American freedom allowed the proliferation of sects, it also permitted the "unrestrained preaching of the gospel."[64] The more severe test of trying to convince his European colleagues of the virtues of the American situation lay ahead. The opportunity to present his views to Europeans came five years later when Schaff made his first of some fourteen visits back to the old world.

America

In 1854, after a decade of strenuous labors at Mercersburg, Philip Schaff was given a leave of absence for a year of travel in Europe. According to David Schaff, his father was exhausted by the ten years of teaching and theological controversy to the extent that his eyesight was failing and he had nearly lost his voice.[65] As never before Schaff was challenged to come to an understanding of the relationship between the old and new worlds and to formulate a presentation of the American religious situation that would be comprehensible to his European audience. Called upon to produce a series of lectures on the subject of religion in America, Schaff wrote what was ultimately expanded, translated, and published as *America: A Sketch of Its Political, Social and Religious Character.* It was in this work that Schaff presented his most comprehensive understanding of the nature of nineteenth-century American religion. He believed he had overcome — by the combination of his foreign perspective and his decade of residence in America — the twin difficulties of the would-be historian of American religion mentioned earlier, and produced what Perry Miller has called, "a measured, judicious, intelligent analysis, which by its objectivity and affectionate power is as fine a tribute to America as any immigrant has ever paid."[66]

64. Schaff, "Introduction" (February 14, 1849): 2788.

65. D. Schaff, *Life,* 171. One wonders how restful the trip actually was because Schaff speaks of being "constantly on the wing in truly American style" (p. 241).

66. Schaff, *America,* xxxv. This reprint edition of *America,* published over a

The significance of this work for understanding religion in nineteenth-century America is difficult to exaggerate. Written by the foremost church historian of mid-nineteenth-century America, these lectures provide a brief but by no means superficial survey of most of the major characteristics of American religion. Somewhat similar surveys had appeared from the pens of foreign travelers and denominational promoters, but Schaff's perspective allowed him to avoid the superficiality of the former and the bias of the latter. In addition, his academic pedigree gave him a hearing with his European audience that few others could expect. As a pioneer reflector on the American religious situation, he had few peers. The lectures were lively and to the point. Once again looking at America from across the ocean, Schaff had the perspective necessary to focus on what was important. The natural suspicions of his audience and his concern for historical objectivity forced him to provide both a balanced presentation of the flaws of the American situation and a judicious appraisal of its virtues. His persuasive skills were tested severely in his attempt to correct false conceptions of America.

By the time *America* was ready for publication, and despite the situation in America that threatened to split the nation in two, Schaff provided his European and American hearers and readers with a portrayal that did not avoid strong indictment of American problems, but at the same time gave a highly optimistic forecast of what could be in that land of opportunity. In a supplement to the preface for the English translation of *America,* "to the American reader," Schaff noted developments in America subsequent to the publication of the original work in Berlin and admitted that they "seem to contradict the highly favorable views of this book on the present condition and future prospects of our country, and to justify the fear that it is rotting before it is ripe." "Still," he insisted, "I would not on this account retract any sentiment publicly expressed at Berlin and at Frankfort, and several other cities of Europe."[67] Indeed, Schaff had become hopeful about the

---

century after the original, shows that the work is still recognized by scholars as a valuable contribution to understanding nineteenth-century American religion. The lectures were first published as *Amerika: Die politischen, socialen und kirchlich-religiösen Zustände der Vereinigten Staaten von Nord-Amerika mit besonderer Rücksicht auf die Deutschen, aus eigener Anschauung dargestellt* (Berlin, 1854; revised and expanded editions, 1858, 1865).

67. Ibid., 20.

American situation to an extent that some of his European hearers criticized him for being "too favorable to the land of my adoption."[68] Given the prevailing European views of the American scene, though, it is quite possible that anything less than a total indictment would have failed to satisfy them.

Be that as it may, it is nonetheless evident that Schaff's attitude about the land of his adoption had developed significantly since his first expressions about it in his ordination sermon. Philip Schaff was — or at least was becoming — an admiring and insightful adopted son of America. He tried to be objective, according to the best historical standards of his training in Germany, insisting, "I would appear neither as the unqualified eulogist of the Americans, nor as an unsparing censor of them, especially behind their backs."[69] Charges by some Europeans that America was nothing but a "grand bedlam," "a barbarian country" where the dregs of European society had settled, Schaff considered unnecessary to refute. His own notions to that effect had been corrected through painful experience. It was important, however, "to remove, or at least to soften, certain widespread prejudices, which I have already had frequent occasion to notice during my short visit here." It is indicative of Schaff's concern for the truth (and probably a strong desire to avoid repetition of the controversy among Americans that his ordination sermon had generated) that he was willing to change significantly his views about particular relationships in American religion. His duty, as he saw it, was to convince his mentors that his core convictions about the church had not changed, but that direct exposure to the American religious circumstance had demanded reevaluation of some specifics. Thus, part of his goal in his European lectures on America was to overcome the "disproportion and caricature" of America held by those of the old world.[70] On the other hand, Europeans were correct in identifying "slavery, materialism, radicalism, and sectarianism" as "the

68. Ibid., 3. In a letter to his wife Mary (13 October 1854), Schaff spoke of the good reception of his lectures. "As a general thing however my views on America seem to be too favorable. But I would think it very ignoble and ungrateful to run down my adopted fatherland abroad. What I have to object to the Americans I better tell them to their face at home." Philip Schaff papers, ERHS.

69. Schaff, *America,* 5.

70. Ibid., 25, 81.

chief deformities of the United States." Even so, the country contained enough "soundness and vitality" to overcome these very serious problems.[71]

As in earlier writings, Schaff continued to insist that the "SECT SYSTEM is certainly a great evil" because it contradicted the fundamental idea of church unity. And America was, Schaff admitted, "the classic land of sects."[72] But, he continued, the situation was inevitable given the universal freedom of religion and worship that prevailed in America and which, he added, was making progress even in Europe. So far Schaff had said nothing especially new or threatening, but his changed ideas and strong advocacy led him to challenge his hearers' prejudices. Not only did he insist that religious freedom was vital to the future of Christianity in America, but, in an even more astounding claim, Schaff declared that the advantages of such a system on the whole outweigh the disadvantages of a state church with its "police force and dead uniformity." Recapturing an insight from his mentor Neander, Schaff insisted that religion could not be coerced, and compulsion produced only "hypocrisy and infidelity."[73] In dramatic contrast, the vitality of religion in America, "the most religious and Christian country in the world," was precisely the result of the equality of all its churches and sects and the voluntary system of membership and support.

A parallel that Schaff used as an illustration of the presence of both good and evil in the sect system (and, incidentally, one which certainly carried more weight in Europe than in America), was that of the medieval papacy. Both contained within them an anti-Christian

71. Schaff, *America*, 5, 6. Schaff also expressed satisfaction with the knowledge of some Europeans about the American situation. In a letter to his wife Mary he said, "I am surprised to find some people here s[o] well informed about America and entertaining such intelligent and liberal views about our affairs. Especially a rich and pious merchant, Mr. Grafe, with whom we took supper, talked as if he had lived there for years." Philip Schaff papers, ERHS. Perry Miller spoke of this stereotype of American life among the European population. "This was the attitude that generally prevailed among the cultivated of Berlin, most of whom by then sadly concluded that the German churches of America had fallen into the American pit and were unreclaimable." Schaff, *America*, xv.

72. Schaff, *America*, 10, 96. Emphasis his.

73. Ibid., 10. See also Philip Schaff, *Saint Augustine, Melanchthon, Neander* (New York: Funk and Wagnalls, 1885), 147, and Penzel, ed., *Philip Schaff*, lvi-lvii.

element, but, Schaff insisted, diseases such as these in the Christian body became in God's providence "*negative conditions* precisely of her [the church's] *progress*."[74] According to his providential view of history, the "distractions and fermentings of Protestantism" which were most graphically portrayed in America were part of a "necessary transition state to a far higher and better condition, to a free unity in spirit and in truth, embracing the greatest variety of Christian life."[75]

Schaff is perhaps most recognized by twentieth-century readers because of his description of the American church as a "motley sampler of all church history." But taken out of the larger context in which it is found, the statement fails to disclose Schaff's essential optimism about the American future. Certainly he lamented the "present distracted condition of the Church in America," and insisted that it "must yet be regarded on the whole as unsatisfactory and as only a state of transition." But the point is that it *was* a state of transition to "something higher and better," and the motley sampler merely reflected "the results it has *thus far* attained." A few lines further Schaff could speak of America as "the Phenix grave not only of all European nationalities . . . but also of all European churches and sects," and maintain that "out of the mutual conflict of all something wholly new will gradually arise." He continued, "all the powers of Europe, good and bad, are there fermenting together under new and peculiar conditions. All is yet in a chaotic transition state; but organizing energies are already present, and the spirit of God broods over them, to speak in time the almighty word: 'Let there be light!' and to call forth from the chaos a beautiful creation."[76] Enemies of American religious freedom like the Roman Catholics might exult in their evident opportunity to overcome a divided Protestantism, but the final result of the ferment would be "something far more grand and glorious than Catholicism ever presented in its best days." In America, Schaff avowed, "the cosmos lies in the chaos."[77] The ferment was only

74. Philip Schaff, *What is Church History? A Vindication of the Idea of Historical Development* (Philadelphia: J. B. Lippincott, 1846); reprinted in *Reformed and Catholic: Selected Historical and Theological Writings of Philip Schaff*, ed. Charles Yrigoyen, Jr. and George M. Bricker (Pittsburgh: The Pickwick Press, 1979), 116 [100]. The page number from the original edition will be noted in brackets.

75. Schaff, *America*, 13-14.

76. Ibid., 80-81. Emphasis mine.

77. Ibid., 102-3.

that which preceded an act of creation. The future of Christianity in America was indeed bright.

> The history of the kingdom of God in America has already entered upon the dawn of a new era, and will unfold itself, under circumstances and conditions altogether peculiar, not indeed beyond Christ — for he is Alpha and Omega of church-history, and before Him the Americans bow with the deepest reverence as before the highest and holiest name in the universe — but beyond all that has hitherto existed in the ecclesiasticism of Europe.

To his skeptical audiences he declared that "in America the most interesting experiments in church-history are now made."[78]

In order to understand Schaff's rejection of the sect system as an evil, even though God could use it for good, it is important to note his refusal at this point in his career to distinguish between sects and denominations. The distinction between "church" and "sect" was not helpful in America, Schaff said, because, since there was no national established church, there could be no dissenting sects. Likewise, "the distinction between confessions or denominations (as the word is there) and sects is therefore likewise entirely arbitrary."[79] Both groups were atomistic in their focus on the salvation of individual souls rather than the organic unity of all Christians in the body of Christ. If one's conception of Christianity were based totally on the faulty model of mere conversion of individuals, then, Schaff admitted, the American sect system was highly successful, driven as it was by competition to that end. On the other hand, if the true model for the Christian church was a more proper conception of the organic body of Christ in which all members worked in peace and harmony for the building up of the common whole, the sect system was weighed in the balance and found wanting. The model for the church, Schaff insisted, must be Jesus' description of himself and his followers as "one flock [and] one

78. Ibid., 213.

79. Ibid., 97. Klaus Penzel says that in order to be able to appreciate the significance of denominations and some sects, Schaff had to adjust his conception of historical dialectic to include both "great dialectics" and "small dialectics." Penzel, "Church History," 349-50.

shepherd."[80] The unchurchly character of American Christianity was therefore at best a caricature of the model intended by Christ.

Denominations vs. Sects

Despite the ever-worsening situation of American society in the late 1850s with its rumors of civil war, Schaff retained his optimism about the future of religion in America. He returned from his year in Europe feeling "almost ten years younger in body and spirit," and eagerly immersed himself in his work, including numerous literary and ecclesiastical duties. He laid the groundwork for his series of volumes on the *History of the Christian Church* and published the first volume in 1858. In his desire to promote mutual influence between Germany and America, and as a companion to the volume on America, Schaff prepared a book for American readers in 1857 entitled *Germany: Its Universities, Theology and Religion.* Schaff tapped the deep American curiosity about German thought and wrote to "guide . . . the English and American student through the luxuriant forest of Teutonic systems and opinions." This was his first major effort at writing in English and, as such, was a clear example of his hope to bring "the German and American mind into closer union and friendly cooperation for the advancement of sound Christian literature, theology, and religion."[81]

While Schaff remained faithful to the limited circles of the German Reformed denomination through his work at Mercersburg Seminary and various denominational duties, during the decade after his journey to Europe he became increasingly involved in the broader world of American Christianity and worked with an ever-widening circle of colleagues and institutions. Schaff's desire to meet people was insatiable and during this period, as throughout the rest of his life, he sought to stay in touch with the developments in American Christianity through acquaintance with its most important leaders. Here was no denominationally bound professor limited to contacts and issues within his ethnic group. In fact, tensions began to build between Schaff's desire to be a part of the most

80. John 10:16, RSV.

81. Schaff, *Germany*, 9-10. A more complete discussion of Schaff's concern to unite German and American scholarship is found in chapter 3.

significant happenings in American Christianity and his "captivity" in the backwoods of Pennsylvania. Schaff felt keenly the isolation of the seminary at Mercersburg and hoped that the school might soon be moved to a city more accessible and congenial for one who sought to remain in the mainstream of scholarship and religious life. "Sometimes," he lamented, "I confess, I can hardly endure longer the dreary separation from the springs of life and exile from congenial intercourse." He tolerated the situation as long as he did due to a deep loyalty and because of his expectation that the seminary would soon relocate to a more central place. "What folly," he exclaimed, "to put the institutions of the church away from the centre of population to an inaccessible outpost! What will be thought of such a penny-wise, pound-foolish policy in 1900?"[82]

In 1857, Schaff prepared a report for the Evangelical Alliance meeting in Berlin on "Christianity in America." Schaff was unable to attend the meeting himself, but his paper was presented and later published in the *Mercersburg Review.* The purpose of the report, according to Schaff, was to show "*characteristic features of American Christianity as distinct from the European.*"[83] The most striking difference was the existence in America of numerous denominations coexisting in a situation of religious liberty. Schaff shaped this presentation, before a group whose very reason for being was the promotion of Christian unity, quite differently than he had formulated his European lectures on denominations and sects three years earlier. To this audience of leaders from various Christian groups, Schaff said nothing about the evil of sectarianism. Instead, he confined his attention to benefits that had come from denominational distinctions within the church. First, it was the coexistence of the religious refugees who formed various denominations in the new nation of the United States that forced the founders of the nation to separate church and state. Separation of civil and religious authorities could be called "the sweet fruit of the bitter European, especially English intolerance and persecution" which had helped cause the rise of many denominations.[84] In addition, though Schaff still in-

82. D. Schaff, *Life*, 197.

83. Philip Schaff, "Christianity in America," *Mercersburg Review* 9 (October 1857): 499; reprinted in Yrigoyen and Bricker, *Reformed and Catholic*, 351.

84. Ibid., 360.

sisted that division in the church was caused by "human guilt," he was able to see the purpose of God in it all and could maintain that "when each division, be it Protestant, or Roman, or Greek, shall have fully accomplished its separate mission, the hidden unity of life will also visibly appear arrayed in the beauty of infinite variety." Schaff could see God's purpose in denominational distinction, yet the ultimate plan was still for "the invisibly omnipresent power of divine love . . . to unite the most distant parts of Christendom, for which it bled on the cross, into one, holy, catholic brotherhood of faith and love."[85]

Denominations and sects were once again on Schaff's mind as he presented another series of lectures during 1865 in Germany and Switzerland. He called his work on the subject of the Civil War and Christianity in North America "the best service he was able to do at that time to America and Germany."[86] His presentations were attended by "immense crowds" and hundreds had to be turned away due to lack of room. While generally well accepted, Schaff's advocacy of the Union cause, his "cordial presentation of American institutions," and rejection of slavery were offensive to the aristocracy and, in fact, may have cost him an invitation to the chair formerly occupied by Neander at Berlin.[87] An indication of the extent of Schaff's devotion to the land of his adoption is the strong probability that he would have rejected the offer of that prestigious chair, even though he was at that time contemplating resigning from his position at Mercersburg.[88] He was becoming thoroughly Americanized and his German colleagues became quite uneasy about his democratic notions in both politics and religion. Schaff had, for example, become quite an admirer of the "Western plebeian" Abraham Lincoln in his rise from obscurity to the presidency.

Schaff revealed similar "democratic" tendencies through his changed attitude toward the American denominational system in his lectures on the Civil War. He could still speak of the perception of

85. Ibid., 390.

86. D. Schaff, *Life,* 241 quotes a letter written by Schaff. The lectures were later published as *Der Bürgerkrieg und das christliche Leben in Nord-Amerika* (Berlin: Berlag von Wiegandt und Grieben, 1866). An English translation by C. C. Starbuck was published in the *Christian Intelligencer* 37 (March 1–May 17, 1866). Both references will be given, the *Christian Intelligencer* will be noted as *CI.*

87. D. Schaff, *Life,* 241.

88. See Shriver, *Philip Schaff,* 41.

America as "the classic soil of an indefinite and injurious subdivision of Christianity," but he shifted the blame from the new world back to Europe, insisting that the various groups of Christians found in America were nothing more than the extension of divisions already accomplished in the old world. Growing ever bolder to declare the virtues of American Christianity, he asserted that these American extensions could boast of firmer adherence to the general concepts and fundamental teachings of orthodox Christianity than their parent European churches.[89] Schaff maintained that all the churches of America, with the exceptions of the Roman Catholic, Unitarian, and especially the Latter-day Saints, were true representatives of proper religious life. From his original concept of a large-scale dialectic in which the entire American church as a monolithic entity would play the part of the antithesis to the thesis of European Christianity, Schaff modified his ideas to include a multiplicity of smaller-scale dialectics working within the American situation and including numerous essential elements. The American church as a whole would make its contribution to the universal progression of world history, but internally, its character would be shaped by the interaction and complementary work of various denominational and other voluntary bodies. Few of the groups were superfluous. According to Schaff, "we must thank God and rejoice that he has sent so many workers into his American vineyard, and appointed to each a special field that they and no others can successfully cultivate."[90]

With more negative language, Schaff had hinted at such ideas as early as 1845 in his *Principle of Protestantism.* Sects appeared, he asserted, because of the presence of evil within the church. As late as 1855, in *America,* Schaff rejected the idea of distinction between "sects" and "denominations." By 1865 and his lectures on the Civil War, however, he had come to appreciate more fully the positive contributions of the various Christian groups. Schaff's work in the period following 1865 reflects his growing awareness of the value of denominational diversity within cooperative Christian unity. Having resigned his professorship at Mercersburg and moved to New York City in 1865, Schaff became increasingly involved in interdenominational agencies, and accepted an appointment at Union Theological Seminary. His initial appointment

89. Schaff, *Bürgerkrieg,* 38-39; *CI* 37 (April 5, 1866): 1.
90. Ibid., 40.

there — he would eventually occupy four different chairs — revealed his breadth of interest and ability. He was appointed in 1870 as Professor of *Theological Encyclopedia* and Christian Symbolism.[91] One colleague quipped that since Schaff covered theological encyclopedia, none of the other faculty seemed necessary!

At the end of the 1870s, Schaff set forth a more fully developed concept of the positive contributions of denominations, as opposed to his still negative view of sects. Rather than throw up his hands in resignation to the divided and divisive condition of American Christianity or turn cynical about American religion and society, Schaff came to believe that since the denominational pattern had cut so deeply into the fabric of American religion, the system must contain something of value. Something vital would be lost if it were destroyed, if the wrong kind of organic union were forced upon it too soon. His optimism about the future of the church in America caused him to rethink his model for the church and led him to a remarkable solution. In an address to the Evangelical Alliance conference at Basel in 1879, Schaff made his first significant theological distinction between denominations and sects.[92] In contrast to the transitory nature of sects, whose members should work to correct a specific temporary distortion within the universal church and then allow themselves to be reincorporated into that body, the functions of denominations were much more enduring. Denominations, said Schaff, "represent historical phases and types of Christianity, which must be fully developed and finish their mission before there can be a free reunion." Unlike the temporary divisions brought about by sects, denominational division, though likewise representing a "transition state," could conceivably await the second advent for final reunion.[93]

In that same year, Schaff published an article in the *Princeton*

91. Emphasis mine.

92. Thus, at the beginning of debate on this issue that continues to merit discussion within the church we find Philip Schaff establishing the groundwork for the dialogue. See Russell Richey, ed., *Denominationalism* (Nashville: Abingdon, 1977); Sidney Mead, *The Lively Experiment: The Shaping of Christianity in America* (New York: Harper & Row, 1976), esp. chapter 7.

93. Philip Schaff, "Religion in the United States of America," in *The Religious Condition of Christendom: Described in a Series of Papers Presented to The Seventh General Conference of the Evangelical Alliance, Held in Basle, 1879,* ed. J. Murray Mitchell (London: Hodder and Stoughton, 1880), 90.

Review on the "Progress of Christianity in the United States of America" which revealed the continuing development of his thought. In opposition to his earlier assertion that when the work of a sect was completed — that is, when the problem in the larger body that gave rise to the sect was corrected — the sect should reunite with the church, Schaff admitted that some bodies which originated as sects had become denominations themselves, for example, the Methodists and the Baptists. On the other hand, he affirmed his distinction between "denominationalism" and "sectarianism," and maintained that the former was compatible with "true catholicity of spirit" while the latter was nothing but "extended selfishness."

Schaff did not make clear exactly how the one may legitimately develop into the other, but part of the answer to this process may be located in a change in attitude among adherents to a sect. Those who were able to overcome selfishness, who avoided proselytism, and who, to some extent, cooperated with other Christian groups could be classed as legitimate denominations. Others who failed to mature in this manner became what Schaff called "petrified sects" who had "no right to exist except as antiquarian curiosity shops."[94] Those who cooperated in such ventures as the Sunday School Union, the Evangelical Alliance, and various missions and charitable institutions, on the other hand, provided a strength and vitality through "unity in diversity" that was of immeasurable benefit to the American church and nation.

He expressed similar ideas in an address to the Evangelical Alliance conference of 1884 in Copenhagen. His presentation was published in 1885 as a chapter on "The Discord and Concord of Christendom; or, Denominational Variety and Christian Unity," in a collection of his writings called *Christ and Christianity.* Rather than expecting an immediate reunion of all Christians, Schaff admitted that the "tendency of Protestantism to division and multiplication of denominations is not yet exhausted."[95] Christianity would be united, he was still able to affirm,

94. Philip Schaff, "Progress of Christianity in the United States of America," *The Princeton Review* 55 (September 1879): 231.

95. Philip Schaff, "Discord and Concord of Christendom, or Denominational Variety and Christian Unity," in *Christ and Christianity: Studies on Christology, Creeds and Confessions, Protestantism and Romanism, Reformation Principles, Sunday Observance, Religious Freedom, and Christian Union* (New York: Scribner's, 1885), 293.

but union must not be forced through "a crusade against the denominations." As elsewhere, he insisted that the evil of division was not to be found in denominational diversity, but in sectarian selfishness. Denominations had grown out of "the diversity of divine gifts" whereas sectarianism "is evil and evil only."[96]

Schaff had modified his goal of church union to fit more properly the American situation. First of all, he said, one must distinguish between "Christian union and ecclesiastical or organic amalgamation." His emphasis had shifted from an ideal of the latter to a conception of the former which allowed widespread diversity of ecclesiastical organizations while it required a unity of spirit and purpose. He cited the diversities found in nature and history and noted the parallel diversity in Christianity where "every Christian church or denomination has its special charisma and mission, and there is abundant room and abundant labor for all in this great and wicked world." One must not desire all denominations to conform to any one of them. The cause of Christ would be "marred and weakened," he said, "if any one of the historic churches should be extinguished, or be absorbed into another."[97]

While he remained adamant as "no champion of sects and schisms," Schaff had developed his conception of church unity in diversity to the extent that he could say that "none of the leading denominations of Christendom which faithfully do their Master's work, could be spared without most serious injury to the progress of the gospel at home and abroad." In fact, "we should thank God that he has raised so many agencies for the defence and spread of his kingdom of truth and righteousness throughout the world."[98] The unity that now obtained in Christianity was spiritual, not outward and visible, and it actually never had been otherwise. In a significant modification of his earlier language, Schaff asserted that the Scriptures promised "one *flock* and one shepherd," but not "one *fold*." There could be many visible folds in which were sheltered members of the one flock.[99] Lest this shift appear a disingenuous case of special pleading, Schaff supported his change of understanding by noting the erroneous translations of John

96. Ibid., 298.
97. Ibid., 299-300.
98. Ibid.
99. Ibid., 302.

10:16 found in the Latin Vulgate and the Authorized Version, and defended his use of the term "flock" rather than "fold" on the basis of the Greek original and the translation of the Revised Version.

Denominational diversity was at worst a "*necessary* evil," he insisted, and it was "far better than a dead or tyrannical and monotonous uniformity." Schaff's vision of organic unity had not dimmed, however, because ultimately the Lord would bring about such a union; he would, in an absolute sense, "bring cosmos out of chaos, and overrule the discord of Christendom for the deepest concord."[100]

The advocate of Christian union revealed the complete development of his views concerning denominations and sects in the year of his death, 1893. During that year he attended the World's Parliament of Religions during the Columbian Exposition in Chicago. Schaff had been warned by physicians that the trip to Chicago would damage his already fragile health, but he was determined to give one last witness for the cause of Christian union at this, the best forum possible for his lifelong message. At the Parliament, as never before in history, religious leaders gathered from around the globe. Not for a moment did Schaff think that the common platform signified an equal value of religious traditions. Instead, this opportunity was the ultimate pulpit for the presentation of the Christian gospel and the oneness of all Christians. His address, which he called "the sum of my life and of my theological activity, and my testament to the church and to my contemporaries," he entitled appropriately "The Reunion of Christendom." Schaff dealt at length with the American voluntary system, the resulting profusion of Christian groups, and prospects for Christian union.[101] As before, he claimed to see "the hand of Providence in the present divisions of Christendom." He noted the "great difference" between denominationalism and sectarianism, calling the latter "a curse" and the former "a blessing."[102] There were sects that had fulfilled their missions and ought to cease, but the "historic denominations" were "permanent forces" and

100. Ibid., 303.

101. Quoted in D. Schaff, *Life*, 483.

102. Philip Schaff, *The Reunion of Christendom: A Paper Prepared for the Parliament of Religions and the National Conference of the Evangelical Alliance Held in Chicago, September and October, 1893* (New York: Evangelical Alliance Office, 1893), 311. See also the reprint of Schaff's address in Penzel, ed., *Philip Schaff*, 302-40.

worked to supplement each other. Schaff illustrated his point by a parallel he drew between plural denominations and plural gospel accounts in the New Testament. Just as the life of Christ "could not be fully exhibited by one gospel, nor his doctrine fully set forth by one apostle, much less could any one Christian body comprehend and manifest the whole fulness of Christ and the entire extent of his mission to mankind." None of these "historic denominations" could be spared "without great detriment to the cause of religion and morality, and without leaving its territory and constituency spiritually destitute."[103]

Still, the situation in America did not match the ideal of one church. Schaff lamented the "sin of schism," but always with the assurance that God was providentially active within every situation and that all divisions would ultimately be eliminated in a totally harmonious union. Schaff was not consistent in his assertions about when and how this final reunion would take place. In some places he said that it might not occur until the second advent of Christ, while elsewhere he spoke as if it might take place immediately if only persons within the various denominations would swallow their pride and recognize their oneness with other Christians. Schaff seems to speak of two different types of union which he did not always distinguish clearly in his writings. First, the union that will take place after the second advent will be a total elimination of differences in doctrine, polity, and all other denominational distinctives. Christ will be head of the church and it will be visibly one without any divisions. Early in his career, Schaff seemed to have desired this kind of unity in the temporal church, although he was realistic about the difficulty of attaining such a union.

As his career developed, however, Schaff began to realize that a more attainable goal was a more exclusively spiritual and cooperative union in which denominational distinctives would continue to provide diversity within the one Christian church, but where there also would be a common understanding of the oneness of all Christians in Christ, and a recognition that denominational distinctives were not themselves essential elements of the faith. To force union which would "destroy all denominational distinctions" would be to "undo the work of the past," the work that God had accomplished through the centuries in preparation for the final reunion of all Christians. In fact, late in his life Schaff

103. Ibid.

affirmed that variety was *essential* to unity. "Variety," he insisted, "in unity and unity in variety is the *law of God* in nature, in history, and in his kingdom. . . . There is beauty in variety." On a practical level, Schaff instructed each denomination to prepare a "short popular and irenic creed of the essential articles which it holds in common with all others." This creed could be the basis for Christian fellowship and cooperation while larger questions could be reserved for professional theologians "whose business it is to investigate the mysteries and solve the problems of faith." Although the denominations were "a blessing," although unity in variety was God's pattern, complete reunion was God's will and "each denomination must offer its idol on the altar of reunion."[104] This reunion was one compatible with the American voluntary system; freedom brought diversity, but it also created the possibility of cooperation in a deeper unity.

Schaff's career revealed significant developments in his theory of the nature of American Christianity. Particularly illustrative was his evolving conception of the value of diversity in America. Beginning with views that were shaped by the teachings of his mentors in Germany and by the actual situation of institutional unity among German Christians, he came to modify some specifics of his original vision because of the realities of the American situation. Although he never despaired of the final unity of all Christians and retained the coherent core of his beliefs, as he became more and more "Americanized" he came to see that there could be diversity in unity, and that such a situation was, in fact, a blessing of God for the upbuilding of God's kingdom on earth. Schaff developed a widely inclusive view of Christian cooperation in America that threatened the ideals of many of his Protestant colleagues. Virtually all Protestant denominations were included, and as the following chapter will show, the Roman Catholic Church played a significant — and for his fellow Protestants astonishing — role in Schaff's conception of the church of the future.

104. Ibid., 313, 315, 323. Italics mine.

CHAPTER 2

Religious Freedom and the Threat of Romanism

Ecumenism on Trial

Schaff's ideal of united Christianity faced a considerable challenge in the presence and increasing activity of Roman Catholics in America. If his conception of Christian union were to make sense in the American situation, Schaff had to locate this increasingly large Christian group in his scheme of reunion. Could authentic Christian union be realized if Roman Catholics were shunned as non-Christian, as many of his Protestant peers desired? How could Schaff express his appreciation for the Catholic heritage in his American setting and still avoid condemnation as a crypto-papist?

Klaus Penzel argues persuasively that Schaff's background in the German "mediating theology" provided the "unity underlying his whole life's work."[1] Schaff attempted to find a mediating position, in this case, between German *Lehrfreiheit* (complete unhampered freedom) and a system of ecclesiastical rule which forced conformity and demanded unqualified assent to all details of a particular confession of faith.[2] His

1. Klaus Penzel, ed., *Philip Schaff: Historian and Ambassador of the Universal Church* (Macon, Ga.: Mercer University Press, 1991), xxvi.

2. David S. Schaff, *The Life of Philip Schaff: In Part Autobiographical* (New York: Scribner's, 1897), 432-33.

efforts to walk this tightrope reveal both his debt to his German training and his accommodation to American Christian patterns. Though his opinions about particular actors within the voluntary system evolved throughout his half century of labor, Schaff's search for an intermediate position continued. In 1888, he could still insist that "the dangers of liberty are great," but at the same time he asserted that they are "no greater than the dangers of authority." America's lot was cast with freedom, and the nation and its churches "must sink or swim, perish or survive with it."[3] In Schaff's opinion, religious freedom was the distinctive and indispensable condition that allowed the American experiment to take place. He marvelled at the unique character of the American situation where "all nations, all churches and sects, all the good and the evil powers of the old world" were gathered together in this place of unparalleled freedom, yet they were able to coexist — as never before — "without blows or bloodshed."[4]

It took Schaff some time to realize that this was indeed the case in America. In his ordination sermon, for example, the young scholar used highly militaristic language to rally the forces of Protestantism against those of the Church of Rome, "the enemy, ever waxing stronger," who "now is mustering his legions for war."[5] These combative metaphors revealed a militant opposition to the unceasing efforts of the Roman Catholic Church to "win" the American territory.

In this age of ecumenical tolerance, it is difficult to grasp the hatreds between Catholics and Protestants that characterized the nineteenth century. Especially in the new world, Protestants feared a Romanist conspiracy to capture the land and rule its people. The sometimes violent anti-Catholic movement known as nativism spread as a result of those fears. For various religious and social reasons, Protestants of all stripes took alarm at the growing waves of Roman Catholic immigrants. Antagonism had been building since colonial days. Those of Anglo-Saxon heritage remembered a long history of strident anti-

3. Philip Schaff, *Church and State in the United States, or The American Idea of Religious Liberty and Its Practical Effects with Official Documents* (New York: G. P. Putnam's Sons, 1888), 82.

4. Philip Schaff, *America: A Sketch of Its Political, Social and Religious Character*, ed. Perry Miller (Cambridge: Harvard University Press, 1961), 17.

5. Philip Schaff, "Ordination of Professor Schaff," *Weekly Messenger* 9 (September 4, 1844): 1869.

Catholicism in Great Britain and had lingering mistrust of Catholic religious and political designs. For all their optimistic rhetoric in the new world, they continued to harbor deep suspicions that Catholics were aligned with European monarchs in a conspiracy to overthrow both their Protestant religious heritage and their democratic form of government. Even though American anti-Catholic sentiment was sometimes hidden for reasons of political alliance, such as when the Roman Catholic French were needed to aid in the Revolution, the strong current was never far from the surface.

Modern Americans often are unaware of the numerous anti-Catholic laws passed in the colonial period which were designed to limit Catholic political and social influence, even though some were still in force well into the nineteenth century. Nor do they remember the myriad periodicals, founded in the eighteenth and nineteenth centuries, whose primary or sole *raison d'être* was to promote anti-Catholicism. These were not just scandal sheets published by fanatics on the fringes, though many of them did engage in sensationalism. Centers of education and culture were also involved, such as Harvard University, where a lecture series was founded in 1750 by the anti-Catholic promoter, Paul Dudley, "for the detecting and convicting and exposing of the idolatry of the romish church: their tyranny, usurpations, damnable heresies, fatal errors, abominable superstitions, and other crying wickedness in her high places."[6] The lectures were continued until 1857 when a lack of funds caused their cancellation until 1888. On a more commonplace level, popular activities reflected anti-Catholic sentiment, such as a favorite New England game called "Break the Pope's Neck," and the "popular American holiday," Pope Day, during which a parade culminated in burning an effigy of the Roman pontiff.[7]

The early 1800s saw some of the most violent confrontations over religious matters in American history. In Charlestown, Massachusetts, antagonisms between Protestants and Catholics erupted in violence that led to the burning of an Ursuline Convent in August, 1834. Tensions

6. Ray Allen Billington, *The Protestant Crusade, 1800-1860* (New York: Macmillan, 1938), 16.

7. Ibid., 16-18. George Washington forbade celebration of Pope Day during the Revolution to avoid offense to Catholic French Canada, from whom the colonies hoped to gain aid against England.

had smoldered for a number of years, and many circumstances contributed to the outbreak. Supposed "escaped nuns" appeared with stories of atrocities committed in the convent, which confirmed rumors many Protestants had heard about such institutions. Ethnic and social antagonisms were strong. One of the most damaging contributions to the Charlestown situation was a series of sharply anti-Catholic sermons preached by the popular minister Lyman Beecher of nearby Boston. In the sermons, Beecher described how Catholicism and despotism were allied against American republican freedoms, and called for action against popery. While the burning of the convent would probably have taken place regardless, rioters took such sermons as justification for violent action in their righteous crusade against the Antichrist.

A few years later, the most bloody religious riots in American history took place in Philadelphia. Radical anti-Catholics saw confirmation of their opinion that Catholics hated the Bible in Bishop Francis Kenrick's demand that Catholic children be allowed to use their own version of the Bible in public school religious exercises, and that they be excused from other religious instruction. While such issues are discussed today with vigor, there is always the expectation that dialogue will remain civil. Such was not the case in the 1840s. When the school board granted the request, a storm of protest, encouraged by the American Protestant Association, broke in Philadelphia. Anti-Catholic sermons and inflammatory pamphlets increased the tensions, and confrontations between Protestants and Catholics became more and more frequent. Finally, on 6 May 1844, the inevitable happened. Several thousand anti-Catholics marched menacingly through an Irish neighborhood, shots rang out, and one of the marchers was killed. Over the next two days, anti-Catholic mobs rioted and burned until at last the police restored order. Relief was short-lived, however, and when the riots finally ended two months later a total of thirteen Philadelphians had been killed and more than fifty others wounded. New York Catholics avoided similar disturbances due to the determination and actions of Bishop John Hughes, who posted armed guards around Catholic properties in that city and threatened to defend them regardless of the cost.[8]

8. Ibid., 220-37. Billington records that a riot nearly broke out in St. Louis when news of the Philadelphia clashes reached there. The problem in St. Louis was exacer-

Otherwise levelheaded men such as Samuel F. B. Morse joined Beecher in proclamations of nativist bigotry. Morse became convinced that foreigners indeed plotted to overthrow the American system through papal conspiracy with anti-democratic governments. Morse was particularly important for the nativist cause due to his plausible linking of Catholicism and immigration as complementary threats against American religion and liberty. Beecher also took up the cudgel against what he perceived as a particular Roman Catholic threat against the western territories of North America. In his widely popular *A Plea for the West*, written in 1835, Beecher agreed with Morse that the despotic governments of Europe had joined with Rome in the diabolical attempt to crush American republicanism and Protestantism. Beecher's particular angle was that education was the primary weapon of the Catholics, so their efforts must be offset by establishing Protestant schools and colleges. Both Beecher and Morse attracted wide followings and prompted a number of lesser known combatants to enter the fray.

The extent of anti-Catholic propaganda knew few bounds. The Pope intended to establish the Inquisition in America, nativists claimed, and already Catholics had built their churches with torture chambers in subterranean dungeons, and stockpiled weapons in anticipation of the Pope's signal to attack.[9] In the 1830s and 1840s, various denominations felt compelled to speak strongly against those who sympathized with Rome. Presbyterians concluded more than a decade of debate — not over whether to accept Roman Catholics as fellow Christians, but over how strongly to condemn them — with passage of a resolution in 1845 rejecting the validity of Roman Catholic baptism. Methodists were urged by their leadership in 1844 to awaken and address the growing Roman Catholic threat, and Congregationalists in that same year agreed that the danger was greater than at any time since the Reformation. Episcopalians fought the battle at their own doorstep with the emergence in the 1830s of the Oxford, or "Anglo-Catholic" movement, or

---

bated by careless students at a Jesuit college and medical school who "had left sections of human bodies and other anatomical specimens lying about the college grounds where they were seen by passers-by." Those who saw the body parts started the rumor that they were the remains of Protestants dismembered as part of the Catholic Inquisition! A mob formed, but was dissuaded from destroying the school by an armed force of Irish who surrounded the buildings.

9. Ibid., 122-27.

as some American Protestants called them, "papists in disguise." Episcopalians became so polarized that choices were limited to being nativistic and against the Oxford movement, or high-church and pro-Catholic. Most joined their peers in other denominations and chose the former. As Ray Allen Billington put it, "by the middle of the 1840s, the American churches were able to present a virtually united front against Catholicism." American Christians were so inundated with anti-Catholic sermons and literature that "wherever the church-going, evangelical Christian of that day looked, he found arguments and invective against Rome."[10]

The German Reformed Church had its own notable anti-Catholic agitators, the most prominent of whom was the Reverend Joseph F. Berg. By the time of Schaff's arrival in America, Berg had already published five anti-Catholic books, with titles such as *The Great Apostasy Identified with Papal Rome* and *Oral Controversy with a Catholic Priest*. When Schaff lambasted Roman Catholicism in his ordination sermon, his audience, both within the German Reformed denomination and throughout American Protestantism, could affirm with a vigorous "amen!" Berg must have been delighted in his expectation to join forces against Rome with this most impressive and eloquent ally.[11]

Berg's hopes, however, were almost immediately dashed. The actual situation Schaff found in America caused him to reconsider his positions on a number of issues, including the place of the Roman Catholic Church. And the hyperbolic rhetoric of his ordination sermon had exaggerated Schaff's true beliefs. Romanism was indeed a threat and that spirit must be stoutly resisted. But Catholicism was more than the Romanist perversion. In one of his first published essays, Schaff had explored this difference and had affirmed his respect for Catholicism and, to a significant degree, the Roman Catholic Church, while at the same time absolutely condemning the abuses of Romanism.[12]

10. Ibid., 171-85.

11. See ibid. and E. E. Y. Hales, *The Catholic Church in the Modern World: A Survey from the French Revolution to the Present* (Garden City, N.Y.: Doubleday, 1960), 148-68.

12. Philip Schaf, "Katholizismus und Romanismus," *Literarische Zeitung* (Berlin), no. 40 (1843): 633ff.; no. 61 (1843): 969ff.

The Catholic Union with the Past

It is uncharacteristic that the language of Schaff's ordination sermon was so highly belligerent and punctuated with inflammatory statements about the "insidious poison of the Jesuite [sic] morality," and the poor souls "already in the grasp of the Romish wolves" who operated with "serpent cunning."[13] These extreme views perhaps had been shaped by a visit to Rome Schaff had made at the age of twenty-three while serving as a tutor to a young Prussian nobleman. After preaching at the German Embassy chapel on Palm Sunday, 1842, Schaff went to St. Peter's to witness the festivities there. While impressed by the pageantry, he concluded that "the whole service makes an impression of the decided worldliness of the Catholic Church," and made the characteristically Protestant observation that "a plain pungent sermon on the atoning sufferings and death of Christ would be of much more worth than all this gay and perishable pomp."[14] Schaff witnessed self-scourging by a number of poor people from the "lowest class" who, he insisted, were "certainly not the worst offenders in this Babylon." He also gained an audience with Pope Gregory XVI and noted the pontiff's kindly "gray eyes," and "the nostrils of his large nose [which] were soiled with snuff." He found it difficult to kiss the pope's red slipper, but managed to endure the humiliation. After a short interview in which the pope was surprised to find out that he was a Protestant with no intention of converting, Schaff received his blessing and left reflecting that "he is certainly a good man."[15] Later in America, the young scholar would have to explain why a good Protestant would be at all interested in having such a meeting.

At his ordination, Schaff lamented the "extraordinary progress"

13. Schaff, "Ordination," 1869.

14. Philip Schaff, "Rome Fifty Years Ago," *Homiletic Review* 29 (January 1895): 3-9; 29 (March 1895): 195-204; 31 (May 1896): 469-73. Also quoted in D. Schaff, *Life*, 46. There are some interesting differences in the quotations in the biography and the articles in the *Homiletic Review.* For example, the statement that the "service makes an impression of the decided worldliness of the Catholic Church" was translated in the biography as "the whole service makes strong appeal to the senses and the imagination." In a preface to the translation in the *Review,* David Schaff mentioned that the original journal was written in "fine German characters which Dr. Schaff found it difficult to decipher on his last visit in Rome in 1890," and which David had to use a magnifying glass to read.

15. D. Schaff, *Life,* 54.

of the Roman Catholic Church in America, progress which was facilitated by the condition of religious freedom. In addition, freedom produced divisions among the Protestants which were a source of malicious laughter for the Roman Catholics, who seized the opportunity to profit from such confusion. It must have been incomprehensible to those who heard that sermon when they learned only a few months later that its speaker faced a heresy trial — on the charge of Roman Catholic sympathies. While the synod eventually deemed the charge unfounded and totally exonerated Schaff, it is necessary to examine closely his *Principle of Protestantism,* which was the source of the charges, in order to discover how this changed perception of Schaff's opinions came about and to measure the extent of his change of mind.

To begin with, Schaff asserted that of the three challenges he addressed in his ordination sermon, the most serious challenge to American Protestantism was rationalism and *not* Roman Catholicism as many of his American colleagues believed. Certainly, he insisted, orthodox Protestants have much more in common with moderate Catholics than they do with rationalistic Protestants like Strauss and Feuerbach. Indeed, were the Reformers Luther and Calvin alive in his day, Schaff believed that they would focus their energies on combatting this "purely negative pseudo-Protestantism, as something altogether worse than popery itself."[16] It must have seemed strange to his American audience that Schaff would concentrate on this admittedly real but obviously (they thought) secondary threat to Protestant religion in America. There were free thinkers in America, many of them among the German immigrants, but to consider them a greater danger than the Roman Catholic menace must have struck Schaff's hearers as highly unusual. It was in Germany, not America, that rationalists like Strauss and Baur had made their mark. The issues they had raised would not be widely debated in America for decades.[17]

16. Philip Schaff, *The Principle of Protestantism,* trans. John W. Nevin (Chambersburg, Penn.: Publication Office of the German Reformed Church, 1845; reprint ed., Philadelphia: United Church Press, 1964), 134-36. Klaus Penzel has noted the cooperation between Roman Catholics and Protestants that was part of Schaff's milieu during his time as a student in Germany. See "Church History and the Ecumenical Quest: A Study of the German Background and Thought of Philip Schaff" (Th.D. diss., Union Theological Seminary, New York, 1962), 90-94.

17. See Mark A. Noll, *Between Faith and Criticism: Evangelicals, Scholarship, and the Bible in America* (San Francisco: Harper & Row, 1986), 11-31.

Identifying Roman Catholicism as the "lesser-of-the-two-evils" might have proved more acceptable to the anti-Catholics in the German Reformed Church had not Schaff gone on to proclaim boldly the positive virtues of the Roman Church, even in the period just prior to the Reformation. The source of the work of Luther, for example, was not something foreign to medieval Catholicism, but was, on the contrary, found in the "very center of the religious life of the Catholic Church." As the Law in Judaism was necessary to show humans their inability to please God, so the "mortification of the flesh and . . . legal wrestlings after righteousness with God, by the noblest spirits of the Middle Ages" provided the basis for what was to come later with the Protestant Reformation. Thus, rather than being a movement foreign to medieval Catholicism, as many of the anti-Catholics tried to maintain, Schaff made bold to claim that "*the Reformation is the legitimate offspring, the greatest act of the Catholic Church.*"[18]

While noting the organic connectedness of medieval and Reformation Christianity, Schaff could also offer an objective critique of Catholicism based on his theology of history. The problem was that "*the Church of Rome, instead of following the divine conduct of history, has continued to stick in the old law of commandments, the garb of childhood, like the Jewish hierarchy in the time of Christ, and thus by its fixation as Romanism has parted with the character of catholicity in exchange for that of particularity.*"[19] While such statements strike the ecumenical sensibilities of most Christians today as being quite harsh, they had the opposite effect on many of Schaff's hearers. For those occupying the trenches against the Romanist onslaught, Schaff's ideas seemed wholly too sympathetic to the enemy. Some of them had recently abandoned their homelands for the promise of American freedom and unconditionally refused to allow the encroachments of Rome to jeopardize their liberty.

Schaff's theory of development in history allowed him to affirm the value of every period of history and to maintain that the purpose of the Reformation was not to overthrow and reconstruct the entire church, but was instead to "carry forward and complete that work"

18. Schaff, *Principle of Protestantism*, 73. Italics his. These ideas were affirmed by Schaff's teacher Ludwig von Gerlach. See Penzel, "Church History," 91.

19. Ibid., 73-74. Italics his.

which had been begun by the general councils of the church and transmitted faithfully by ancient and medieval Christianity to the time of the Reformation. The Reformation continued the process, and proceeded "to define and settle what had not yet been made the subject of action, in the same positive style." The medieval Roman Catholic Church was therefore not a total perversion of Christianity, but "*the legitimate bearer of the Christian faith and life.*" Schaff fearlessly declared that he did not "question the presence of the gospel in the communion of the Roman Catholic Church," despite the fact that the predominant spirit of that church was legal rather than one that emphasized the gospel of grace. In this way, he was able to emphasize the "retrospective aspect of the Reformation" and its "*catholic union with the past.*"[20]

Schaff cited the promise of the Lord that he would be with the church to the end of the world, and insisted that the strident anti-Catholic arguments of some of his peers were, in effect, a denial of that promise. "Let us never forget," he urged, "the much that we hold in common with the Roman Church, the bond of union by which she is joined with us in opposition to absolute unbelief. . . . Let us first with united strength expel the devil from our own temple, into which he has stolen under the passport of our excessive toleration, before we proceed to exorcise and cleanse the dome of St. Peter."[21] Excessive toleration! How could one use such language who himself opened the gates of the Protestant citadel to admit the Trojan horse of Rome? Schaff's brief experience in America, however, had convinced him immediately of the foolishness of conspiracy theories — including those he had voiced only a few months before — and led him to identify the battle for the mind as the more serious conflict in American Christianity. In his view, American Christians expended their energies on a futile effort to escape from their history while all the time the foundations of their faith were being eroded by unbelief. The young professor rose boldly to confront them with the folly of their ways.

Yet Schaff also went on to describe the fundamental error of Roman Catholics who refused to recognize legitimate development at the time of the Reformation. The Catholic Church, within the providence of God, had created a legalistic way of salvation, and when one

20. Ibid., 78. Italics his.
21. Ibid., 137.

as scrupulous as Luther immersed himself in that system he was inevitably driven to rely on the grace of God. Out of this struggle — of Luther and others — developed the "*life principle*" of the Reformation, "the doctrine of the *justification of the sinner before God by the merit of Christ alone through faith.*" The problem with Roman Catholicism and with movements such as Puseyism was that they lacked a true conception of historical and theological development within the church. Both were guilty of "*utter misapprehension of the divine significance of the Reformation, with its consequent development, that is, of the entire Protestant period of the church.*"[22]

Despite Protestant dominance in America, Roman Catholicism remained a threat even though its hierarchical system of authority was truly foreign to American freedom. "Who would have thought twenty years ago," Schaff mused, "that popery was ever to acquire importance in the land of freedom?" Schaff remained optimistic, however, that Protestantism would emerge victorious despite the "mighty advances of the Romish Church, stalking forward through the motley crowd of our sects." Schaff was confident enough about the essentially Protestant character of united Christianity that he could insist that "we may not exclude the Romanists themselves" from the kingdom of God. In fact, "Protestantism cannot be consummated without Catholicism," and "the consummation of both will be at the same time their union."[23]

In *The Principle of Protestantism* Schaff redirected Protestant concerns from a focus on Catholicism to attention to the greater threat of rationalism. Yet he also recognized that the Church of Rome remained a significant challenge to American Protestantism. While many of his Protestant peers were offended by his refusal to condemn Roman Catholicism completely, even greater changes were beginning to take place in Schaff's mind, and the darkest fears of the anti-Catholics in the German Reformed Church in America were to be realized as Schaff sought to include Roman Catholics in his vision of a fully united church.

22. Ibid., 80, 160. Italics his.
23. Ibid., 213, 215-16.

The "Semi-Popish Doctrines" of the Tractarians

After he received and accepted his call to America and set the tone of his attitude toward that country in his ordination sermon, Schaff began a leisurely journey to the United States. He spent six weeks in England, whose church and society he viewed as something of a middle point between the highly developed intellectual and cultural life of Germany and the wilds of America. Schaff was impressed by the practicality of English Christianity and the rhetorical abilities of English speakers. Their most evident flaw, at least according to Schaff's Germanic sense of propriety, was their tendency to gush on and on with compliments. He attended a meeting of the Wesleyan Missionary Society in London and wryly noted that "An English digestion is necessary to assimilate the sweet things that are said by and to the chairman."[24] Schaff visited both dissenting and established churches, preferred the preaching in the former and the liturgy in the latter, and thus got his first taste of the pattern of diversity that he would find even more manifest in America.

While at Oxford, Schaff sought out leaders of the Tractarian movement, who had stirred urgent debate within the Anglican church. Schaff had been influenced by the high doctrine of the church of the jurist and lay theologian Ludwig von Gerlach while in Berlin, but that background does not fully explain his interest in the Anglo-Catholics.[25] A more satisfying explanation for Schaff's willingness to risk censure in order to find out more about the feared and despised Tractarians is his insatiable curiosity and desire to learn firsthand about every religious movement. At a time when few German thinkers deemed events and movements in the church outside their homeland worth their attention, Schaff was amazingly perceptive and alert to anything, anywhere that might be influential in the church. He plunged eagerly into a lengthy and enlightening interview with E. B. Pusey, who, knowing Schaff's ultimate destination, denounced the sectarian divisions of the church

24. D. Schaff, *Life,* 83.

25. James Hastings Nichols, *Romanticism in American Theology: Nevin and Schaff at Mercersburg* (Chicago: The University of Chicago Press, 1961), 71-74, discusses the theological ideas of Gerlach and his influence on Schaff. See also Penzel, "Church History," 86-89.

in America and lamented the neglect of the doctrine of apostolic succession there and elsewhere.[26] Already suspected by the heresy hounds in America who sniffed the stench of German rationalism, Schaff compounded the problem by tainting his garments with the unmistakable odor of Tractarian incense. Episcopal Bishop Eastburn of Massachusetts had only recently called the *Tracts* a "work of Satan" concocted by "followers of the Scarlet Woman."[27] Robert Baird, an evangelical Presbyterian interpreter of American religion, reflected the contempt of most Protestants for the "semi-popish doctrines" of the Tractarians, but he was sure that they would have little influence in America.[28]

Unaware of the repercussions his meeting with this extreme Anglo-Catholic would have later in America, but true to his widely inclusive perspective, Schaff tested his concept of the continuing development of the church against Pusey's insistence that "we dare not go outside the first six centuries," and defended German theology against Pusey's attacks by citing Neander and Tholuck as its best representatives.[29] These events give a foretaste of the later career of Schaff, who would eventually become truly American himself and would spend the next half-century attempting to infuse America with the best that the old world had to offer. He would also eventually come to see that within the chaos of the American wilderness was much that could be of positive influence on the rest of the world. This youthful scholar was always courteous and respectful, but also boldly sought meetings with the leading theologians and churchmen of his day and refused to back down when his views were challenged. There is an innocence of character in this young man who desired the unity of all Christians but who failed to realize that consorting with people like Pusey, whom Schaff's German peers might view as an amusing anachronism, would be met with strong condemnation by some in America who believed Anglo-Catholicism was among the greatest perversions of Christianity in history. Before many weeks passed he would be confronted with the error of his ways.

26. For more on the historical and theological context of the Tractarian movement and Schaff's interactions with its leaders, see Nichols, *Romanticism*, 77ff.

27. Quoted in Sydney E. Ahlstrom, *A Religious History of the American People* (Garden City, N.Y.: Doubleday, 1975), 2:67.

28. Robert Baird, *Religion in the United States of America* (Glasgow: Blackie and Son, 1844; reprint ed., New York: Arno Press, 1969), 506.

29. Pusey's statement is quoted in D. Schaff, *Life*, 89.

Schaff outraged opponents when he affirmed the positive aspects of the Oxford movement, calling it "*an entirely legitimate and necessary reaction against rationalistic and sectaristic pseudo-Protestantism, as well as the religious subjectivism of the so-called Low Church Party.*"[30] In fact, the Anglo-Catholic movement as a whole had many characteristics that were attractive to Schaff. It emphasized the significance of the church, sacraments, and tradition, which were sorely neglected by many American Christians. On the other hand, charges against Schaff were generally unfair, because in this as in all other cases he pointed out weaknesses as well as admirable characteristics. The most crippling defect of Anglo-Catholicism, and one that would absolutely prohibit Schaff from joining its ranks, was the movement's "*utter misapprehension of the divine significance of the Reformation, with its consequent development, that is, of the entire Protestant period of the church.*"[31] Such a position, which totally contradicted Schaff's philosophy of development within the history of the church and the resulting value of every era, set Anglo-Catholicism at variance with the very core of his conception of the church, despite the many characteristics of the movement that he admired.

Professor Schaff's Poisonous Popery

On one level, Schaff made dramatic shifts in his attitudes about the American religious situation. While his ultimate goal of total church unity remained constant, his changing conception of the relationship between Roman Catholicism and Protestantism in America is a prime example of the development in his understanding of how that union might be realized in the complex American situation. In *America,* Schaff dealt specifically with the status of the Roman Catholic Church in America and various attitudes toward it. Having been in the United States for a decade, Schaff was well aware of the relatively significant number of groups dedicated to anti-Catholicism. The ten years he had spent in America were notable for the tremendous influx of immigrants, many of whom were Roman Catholic. During the 1830s, for example, 600,000 Catholics immigrated to America. The next decade would see

30. Schaff, *Principle of Protestantism,* 158. Italics his.
31. Ibid., 160.

that number swell to 1,700,000 more, and as many as 2,600,000 more immigrated during the 1850s.[32] Despite such growth, Schaff maintained that Roman Catholicism would never be able to attain a position of dominance in North America, "the most radically Protestant land." The divisions that were the necessary evil of American Protestantism, though they gave hope to Roman Catholics for an ultimate victory, did not mean that Catholicism would come to dominate. According to Schaff, a return to Catholicism would be "a relapse to a position already transcended in church history," and "such an annulling of the whole history of the last three centuries, is, according to all historical analogy, impossible."[33] Besides, Romanism was "extremely unpopular" and stood in contrast to "the ruling spirit of the nation, and its institutions, and the power of public opinion," which were "thoroughly Protestant." Roman Catholicism, with its "mediaeval traditions, centralized priestly government, and extreme conservatism" was incompatible with American ideals of freedom and innovation.[34] The Roman Church, said Schaff, maintained the view of "everything for the congregation, nothing by the congregation." But by this very principle it stood in direct opposition to the national genius of America, which, in religion as in politics, followed the maxim, "Everything for the people, nothing without the people."[35] Nonetheless, the Roman Catholic Church shared the "spirit of enterprise" inherent in American Christianity and therefore "promises itself a glorious future in America," even though it would never realize its dreams of domination.[36]

When Americans read Schaff's published lectures, many of them agreed wholeheartedly with his description that Catholicism was opposed to the "ruling spirit of the nation." One of the clearest examples of this opposition was the dispute over trusteeism between lay Catholics and the hierarchy. Traditionally in the Roman Catholic Church, all church property was controlled by the bishops. In democratic America, however, many lay Catholics deemed it more appropriate that a committee of their peers be appointed as trustees, and some took the

32. T. Maynard, *The Story of American Catholicism* (New York: Macmillan, 1942), 277.

33. Schaff, *America,* 102.

34. Ibid., 193, 181.

35. Schaff, "Christianity in America," 385.

36. Schaff, *America,* 88.

democratic principle so far as to demand the prerogative to appoint and dismiss their priests. In fact, in some cases the lay trustees were supported by civil legislation passed to guard against control of American property by a foreign power, the pope, who exercised ultimate authority over the bishops. For some bishops, most notably Archbishop John Hughes of New York, such a situation was intolerable. Hughes used his influence to have a bill introduced before the New York legislature in 1852 which would have overturned a law of 1784 that forbade ecclesiastical authorities to hold title to church property. Protestants, already angry with Hughes for his militant promotion of Catholic expansion, saw this move as one more attempt to impose papal control in free America. The Protestant outcry led the legislature to defeat the bill, and, in reaction, to pass legislation which demanded lay ownership of all church property. Other states followed suit, and though these laws were never strictly enforced, further damage had been done to the Roman Catholic image in America. Ray Allen Billington labeled the trustee controversy one of the Catholic Church's "blunders" in the period 1850-54, and summarized clearly the effects of the disputes.

> Actually the church suffered less from these laws — which were never enforced — than from the controversies that inspired them. With trusteeism again before the public, nativists had an excellent chance to preach the undemocratic nature of a religion which refused to allow the people control of their own churches and to decry the manner in which Popery sought to evade American laws.[37]

Schaff may have been thinking of the trusteeism controversy when he expressed his opinions about the incompatibility of Roman Catholicism with American democracy. Yet whereas Protestants like Beecher and Morse would close the doors to further immigration of Catholics and legislate against those already in America, Schaff was more optimistic. Roman Catholic immigrants, he believed, could be assimilated into American life, and, in fact, could make necessary contributions to the development of American religion and society. On the one hand, Schaff lamented the "injustice, deception, misrepresentation, and passion" which was so common in the journalistic battles between Roman

37. Billington, *Protestant Crusade,* 295-300.

Catholics and Protestants, but on the other hand, he admitted that the "last decisive engagement" between the two would occur on American soil.[38] His conception of the character of this engagement is what is interesting. Again utilizing his Hegelian conception of development, Schaff envisioned a church emerging from the conflict superior to either of the two antagonists alone. Catholicism in America would become, of necessity, a more liberal and tolerant version. Even if the Roman Catholic Church were to be victorious in America and absorb "German, English, and Anglo-American Protestantism" (an outcome Schaff in no way anticipated), the result would be "a complete regeneration and rejuvenation of Catholicism itself."[39] What would result in any case was an "evangelical Catholicism," a Catholicism shorn of papacy, saint and relic worship, the spirit of persecution, and any form of tyranny over conscience.[40]

Schaff sought a mediating position between legitimate affirmation of the Catholic heritage and criticism of what he called "Romanist" abuses. Once again, however, a position that was compatible with Germany's greater freedom of academic expression and long-standing cohabitation of Catholics and Protestants proved highly inflammatory in the tense American situation. His attitudes were far from acceptable among the violently anti-Catholic members of the German Reformed Church. During the first decade of his career in America, Schaff regularly had to combat accusations that he was headed toward Rome. When, for example, Roman Catholic journals and others that supported the high-church Anglo-Catholicism of E. B. Pusey favorably reviewed Schaff's *Principle of Protestantism*, antagonists took that as additional proof of his Catholic sympathies. An article that appeared in the *Weekly Messenger* of the German Reformed Church in 1845 attempted to prove that the Roman Catholic Church was the Antichrist, and contrasted the Protestantism of Mercersburg with that of the German Reformed Church and the Bible. The Mercersburg professors had "lifted high" the "floodgates of error" and allowed "muddy and bitter waters" to pour into the

38. Schaff, *America*, 195, 191.

39. Ibid., 187; Philip Schaff, "Religion in the United States of America," in *The Religious Condition of Christendom: Described in a Series of Papers Presented to the Seventh General Conference of the Evangelical Alliance, Held in Basle, 1879*, ed. J. Murray Mitchell (London: Hodder and Stoughton, 1880), 99-100.

40. Schaff, *America*, 191-92.

church.[41] In fact — with a blow that must have hurt Schaff acutely — the author insisted that Schaff's writings, far from promoting catholic unity, had produced the opposite effect. The persistent Joseph F. Berg even went so far as to send incognito to Mercersburg a former Roman Catholic priest who had been converted to Protestantism. Berg's spy contrived a report of the "Romanizing poison" in the teachings of Nevin and Schaff.[42]

The controversy reached its climax in the early 1850s when antagonists published a number of tracts against the supposed Roman Catholic sympathies of the Mercersburg theologians. The most outspoken critic was J. J. Janeway, a Dutch Reformed minister who in 1852 published *A Contrast Between the Erroneous Assertions of Professor Schaf, and the Testimony of Credible Ecclesiastical Historians, in Regard to the State of the Christian Church in the Middle Ages.* After quoting a lengthy passage from Schaff's *Principle of Protestantism,* Janeway went to significant lengths to document the opinions of "CREDIBLE AND FAITHFUL ECCLESIASTICAL HISTORIANS" concerning the complete corruption of the medieval church.[43] Two years later Janeway generously offered an *Antidote to the Poison of Popery in the Publications of Professor Schaff.* This book contained arguments from Scripture against the primacy of Peter and again listed various anti-Christian abuses found in medieval Christendom. At one point, Janeway let nativism creep into his argument and blasted Schaff as "a *German Professor* and *historian,* who looks down upon us Americans, as if we understood neither theology, nor history." At the end of the pamphlet, Janeway magnanimously noted that if a reprint of his work was called for, he would include some of Schaff's notes "and thus save the trouble of referring to his bulky volume of 678 pages, and the expense of purchase, to those who do not wish to possess it."[44]

41. SR, "Protestantism of Mercersburg Contrasted," *German Reformed Messenger* 11 (October 15, 1845): 2096. See also George H. Shriver, ed., *American Religious Heretics: Formal and Informal Trials* (Nashville: Abingdon, 1966), 31-40.

42. Schaff later met Berg at a meeting in Philadelphia and told him, "I have not gone to Rome yet and do not mean to; but I did want to go to Jerusalem, but was not able." D. Schaff, *Life,* 199. The spy incident is recorded in *Life,* 115.

43. J. J. Janeway, *A Contrast Between the Erroneous Assertions of Professor Schaf and the Testimony of Credible Ecclesiastical Historians; in Regard to the State of the Christian Church in the Middle Ages* (New Brunswick, N.J.: Terhune and Son, 1852), 5-7. Emphasis his.

44. J. J. Janeway, *Antidote to the Poison of Popery in the Publications of Professor Schaff* (New Brunswick, N.J.: Terhune and Son, 1854), 42, 50. Emphasis his.

In 1853, Reverend Jacob Helfenstein entered the fray and preached a sermon on "A Perverted Gospel; or, the Romanizing Tendency of the Mercersburg Theology." Finally, in 1854 Professor J. W. Proudfit of Rutgers College published extensive reviews of Schaff's works in which he insisted that Schaff had progressively moved toward Roman Catholicism and that his theory of historical Christianity was "thoroughly Papal in all its essential features and tendencies." In fact, Proudfit growled, if Schaff's works were used as texts in Protestant seminaries as had been suggested by some, it would be necessary to "apply to the 'General of the order of Jesus' to send us over professors to teach it," since Protestants would feel "some awkwardness in laying down the primacy of Peter as the foundation of the church of Christ."[45]

The situation was made more complex by the vacillations of Schaff's colleague John Williamson Nevin. Whereas Schaff was of irenic personality and sought to avoid strife, Nevin relished theological conflict and wrote with a style calculated clearly to separate supporters from opponents. In addition, it seems that Nevin seriously contemplated conversion to Roman Catholicism during the early 1850s.[46] In part due to serious health problems and his exasperation with the attacks on himself and Schaff, Nevin spent much of 1851-52 in convalescence and solitary reflection, all the while carrying on a fascinating correspondence with the celebrated convert to Catholicism, Orestes Brownson. Schaff used various means to persuade Nevin to remain true to Protestantism. Besides direct encouragement and prayer, the historian indirectly chided his colleague through published statements about Roman Catholicism. In fact, some of Schaff's harshest language about errors and abuses within Roman Catholicism came during this period. In the German edition of *America*, for example, Schaff blasted the Roman Catholic Church for its "frightful presumptiousness and impenitence."[47] Finally, Nevin emerged once again as a staunch champion of Protestantism,

45. J. W. Proudfit, "Dr. Schaff's Works on Church History," *New Brunswick Review* 1 (May 1854): 1-63, esp. 8, 61. See also J. W. Proudfit, "Dr. Schaff As a Church Historian," *New Brunswick Review* 1 (August 1854): 278-325.

46. For a fascinating discussion of the relationship between Schaff and Nevin during this period, see John B. Payne, "Schaff and Nevin, Colleagues at Mercersburg: The Church Question," *Church History* 61 (June 1992): 169-90.

47. Philipp Schaff, *Amerika: Die politischen, socialen und kirchlich-religiösen Zustände der Vereinigten Staaten von Nordamerika* (Berlin: Verlag von Wiegandt und Grieben, 1854), 253.

though never a hater of Catholicism. Nevin admitted, probably correctly, that much of the animosity directed against Mercersburg was due to his personal conflicts and Schaff's guilt was mostly by association. The battles were real, however, and Schaff supported his colleague as he had been supported by Nevin in past years, despite encouragement by friends that he distance himself from Nevin.[48]

There are hints that Schaff's admiration of aspects of Catholicism troubled those nearest to him. During his European travels Schaff had the opportunity to visit important bishops and cardinals, and his letters reporting those visits to his wife Mary repeatedly assure her that despite cordial discussions with these leaders, he was "as good a Protestant as before," and that the effect of these meetings was "to increase my confidence in Protestantism and in America." He also noted the "immense contrast between Catholic and Protestant worship" and assured her that he much preferred the latter.[49]

Following a visit to Italy in 1854 Schaff wrote to Mary that

> I have seen nothing here that would induce me to alter my views on Romanism; nothing which would confirm the Puritan condemnation of it as the synagogue of Satan or its own claims to be the only church of God. . . . I will answer Dr. Nevin's lst letter and say to him that my respect for Romanism has not increased and my confidence in Protestantism has not been weakened by my visit to Europe. . . . I shall return a better Protestant and a better American than I left and yet full of filial veneration for good old Europe.[50]

Schaff revealed in the letter that this was much more to him than merely an academic issue. He continued,

48. For example, Charles Hodge advised Schaff to separate himself from Nevin so that charges against one would not hinder the work of both. D. Schaff, *Life,* 200; Shriver, *Philip Schaff,* 28. For a discussion of Nevin's life and work, including his correspondence with Brownson, see James Hastings Nichols, *Romanticism in American Theology: Nevin and Schaff at Mercersburg* (Chicago: The University of Chicago Press, 1961), 192-217; and Theodore Appel, *The Life and Work of John Williamson Nevin* (Philadelphia: Reformed Church Publication House, 1889).

49. Letter of Philip Schaff to "My Dear Mary," 5 June 1854, Philip Schaff papers, ERHS.

50. Quoted in D. Schaff, *Life,* 188.

> At mass I knelt and prayed fervently that God might keep and confirm me in the simplicity of the evangelical faith, in the knowledge of His holy Word, in living communion with Christ, in the confidence of his atoning sacrifice on the cross and in love for all his people.[51]

The controversy finally subsided after its peak in the mid-1850s and Schaff continued to describe himself as "a child and servant of Protestantism and an admirer and friend of Catholicism."[52] Nevin had resigned from his position at the seminary in 1852, and Schaff recalled many years later that following Nevin's resignation he "had to stem the current toward Romanism . . . as gently and considerately as I could." While he and Nevin agreed on "the development theory," Schaff noted their basic difference in perspective. Nevin, he said, "looked backward and became Romanizing" while Schaff described his own position as always looking "forward to new and higher developments." In fact, Schaff believed that the Mercersburg Theology "took a wrong and reactionary turn with Nevin's 'Anglican Crisis' and articles on Cyprian, etc."[53]

Later Schaff wrote to Theodore Appel concerning Appel's forthcoming biography of Nevin and expressed the hope that Appel had not "identified me too closely with Dr. Nevin's theology. I was never Romanizing and tried to check that tendency without producing a split."[54] Given Schaff's position at the Presbyterian Union Theological Seminary in New York — which faced serious problems of its own — it is not surprising that he wanted to avoid digging up the old controversy.

51. Ibid.

52. D. Schaff, *Life,* 200-201. This comment was quoted from a letter to the editor of a Roman Catholic journal and Schaff affirmed that "I gladly extend to you and to every pious Catholic the hand. It may seem strange to you, if it does not appear to be an inexplicable inconsistency, that one can be at one and the same time a child and servant of Protestantism and an admirer and friend of Catholicism."

53. Letter of Philip Schaff to "Dear Friend" (probably Theodore Appel, Nevin's biographer), 13 February 1889, Philip Schaff papers, ERHS.

54. Letter of Philip Schaff to "Dear Dr. Apple [sic]," 18 June 1889, Philip Schaff papers, ERHS. In his diary of 1873, Schaff noted, "Saw Dr. Nevin. Interesting conversation about Papal infallibility and Old Catholics. He is taking the back track. A providential escape." Entry for 13 May 1873, Box IV, The Philip Schaff Manuscript Collection, The Burke Library, Union Theological Seminary, New York. Hereafter UTS.

Despite the charges against him of Romanism and the perceptions of enemies that he traveled the road to Rome, Schaff avoided the anxiety which beset Nevin and never considered abandoning Protestantism.

On the other hand, rather than an all-out effort to convert Roman Catholics to Protestantism, as was the goal of most Protestants of his time, Schaff believed that people should usually remain in their denominations and bring revitalization from within. For example, speaking of the popular preacher Père Hyacinthe Loyson of the Notre Dame cathedral in Paris, Schaff described him as "on the bridge between Protestantism and Catholicism," and maintained that "he ought to remain in the Catholic Church (as the Apostles did in the synagogue), so long as his liberal testimony against Ultramontane tendencies is tolerated."[55]

Schaff's relationship with Charles Hodge is instructive concerning attitudes about the Roman Catholic Church. Hodge was the leading theological warrior at the citadel of Presbyterian orthodoxy, Princeton Theological Seminary, for half a century until his death in 1878. He and his colleagues gloried in their conservatism and insisted that they maintained the true Reformation teachings of John Calvin in contrast to those who attempted to modernize the faith. Hodge condemned "the errors of Popery," which were "the most dangerous form of delusion and error that has ever arisen in the Christian world."[56] Here was no friend of Rome. Schaff was less strident than Hodge in his criticisms of Rome, and spoke strongly in support of Hodge and others in the Presbyterian Church who stood against the declaration in 1845 of their General Assembly that Roman Catholic sacraments, including baptism, have no validity.[57] On the other hand, Hodge deemed the Mercersburg theology mystical and anti-Protestant, and urged Schaff to distance himself from Nevin in order to avoid censure. As a loyal colleague and friend, Schaff continued to support Nevin (though he did try to moderate some of Nevin's tendencies), and insisted on the values of both the Oxford movement and Roman Catholicism in America. In the late 1850s Schaff spoke to Hodge about Nevin. "'And how is Dr. Nevin?' he [Hodge]

55. Quoted in D. Schaff, *Life,* 251.

56. Charles Hodge, "Is the Church of Rome a Part of the Visible Church," *Biblical Repertory and Princeton Review* 18 (April 1846): 344.

57. Philip Schaff, "Princeton and Mercersburg," *Weekly Messenger* 13 (June 7, 1848): 2650.

said. I [Schaff] replied, 'He is building a house, not in Rome, but at Lancaster.' 'But Rome is ubiquitous,' said Dr. Hodge. 'Yes, but Calvinists do not believe in the ubiquity of the body,' was my answer."[58] The relationship between Princeton and Mercersburg became more and more strained.

Some of the most obvious signs that Catholicism was clinging to outdated forms in both religion and society were the social, economic, political, and religious differences between North and South American countries. The Catholic system had served its function by "Christianizing and civilizing the barbarians of the Middle Ages," but by refusing legitimate historical development it had forfeited the benefits of the modern world. Compare, for example, the United States with Mexico. The contrast, Schaff noted, is one between "national prosperity and misery, progress and stagnation, life and death." In Roman Catholic Mexico one finds nothing but "priest craft and military despotism, ignorance and superstition, revolution and anarchy in unbroken succession." The contrast could not be greater with "the unexampled external and internal development of the United States of North America [which] is the wonder of modern history."[59]

Romanism or Catholicism?

Having suffered through the conflicts within the German Reformed Church over his views of Roman Catholicism, Schaff maintained his balanced opinion of the Catholic Church, but for many years turned to other, less controversial topics. In 1874, however, he returned to the subject of the relationship between "Protestantism and Romanism" and placed both branches of the church into his overall scheme of church history. The conflict between the two was prefigured by the confrontation between Peter and Paul at Antioch, which Paul recorded in his epistle to the Galatian churches.[60] With language that revealed the

58. D. Schaff, *Life,* 200, 205. See Hodge's review of Schaff's *History of the Apostolic Church,* in *Princeton Review* (1854): 148-92. More about the relationship between Mercersburg and Princeton is found in chapter 3.

59. Schaff, "Christianity in America," 348-49.

60. The confrontation between Peter and Paul is found in Gal. 2:11-15.

influence of thirty years of absorbing American ideals, Schaff insisted that Protestantism, as a type of Pauline or "Gentile Christianity . . . is modern Christianity in motion." It is "the religion of freedom . . . of evangelism and spiritual simplicity . . . the Christianity of the Bible . . . progressive and independent." In contrast, Romanism, which represents the Petrine or "Jewish type of Christianity," is "medieval Christianity in conflict with modern progress . . . the religion of authority . . . of legalism . . . of tradition . . . of outward institutions."[61]

Here for the first time since 1843, with a nuance that few of his Protestant peers could embrace, Schaff insisted that a crucial distinction be made. Romanism was *not* the same as Catholicism. While this distinction had been a part of his thinking for nearly his entire career, he had not explicitly outlined it since an article published prior to his move to the United States.[62] Catholicism might be reconciled with the core Protestant affirmation of salvation through the grace of God in Christ alone; in fact, that affirmation had always been a part of true catholic theology. But Romanism (which he also called "Popery") was foreign to the gospel. The recent decree of papal infallibility (1870) was, for Schaff, a prime example of popery. In fact, the decree represented the "consummation of hierarchical pride [and] may be the beginning of its downfall." The final end of that process could well be "the destruction of Popery . . . [and] the emancipation and reformation of Catholicism."[63]

This distinction allowed Schaff to affirm the value of the catholic principle in history, and at the same time denounce abuses by the hierarchy of the Roman Catholic Church. It also allowed him to recognize the Christianity of individual Catholics in the face of the evident corruption of the "Romanist" system. As Schaff became increasingly Americanized, he wrestled with the tension in American Christianity between individual and corporate religion. This modest shift to an increased emphasis on individual Christianity was scarcely recognizable when Schaff made it, but it carried far-reaching implications for his conception of church union. As he conceded the unlikelihood of attaining his initial ideal of institutional

61. Philip Schaff, "Protestantism and Romanism," *Reformed Church Messenger* 40 (March 11, 1874): 2-3.

62. Schaf, "Katholizismus und Romanismus."

63. Schaff, "Protestantism and Romanism," 2-3.

church union, he derived some comfort from efforts at union, such as the Evangelical Alliance, which celebrated the cooperation of individual Christians from various denominations.[64] The distinction between "Romanism" and "Catholicism" fit well with his developing conception of church union as based on personal piety rather than institutional unification. The hierarchy at Rome might never become a part of the "evangelical catholic" church of the future, but multitudes of pious Catholics could make valuable contributions to the emerging united church. Old visions die hard, however, and Schaff persistently avoided complete exclusion of the Catholic hierarchy from his conception of the united church, infected though it was with a spirit of "Romanism." The final goal of total union remained fundamental, but it might have to be postponed.

The Roman Catholics were one of three major groupings of Christians in the United States ("Roman Catholics," "Evangelical," and "Heterodox") in Schaff's 1879 report to the Basel meeting of the Evangelical Alliance. Although these categories are similar to types used by Robert Baird in 1844 ("Evangelical" and "Unevangelical"), there is one significant difference. While Schaff provided a separate category for Roman Catholicism, Baird included that church in the "Unevangelical" type. Baird insisted that by doing so he in no way intended to identify the Roman Catholic Church too closely with, for example, Unitarians, since the Roman Catholics at least maintained the essential doctrines of salvation, albeit "buried amid the rubbish of multiplied human traditions and inventions, as to remain hid from the great mass of the people." Yet his message was clear. A wide gulf was fixed between the Church of Rome and the evangelical Protestant churches.[65]

64. For more on Schaff's involvement in the Evangelical Alliance see chapter 7. See also Philip D. Jordan, *The Evangelical Alliance for the United States of America, 1847-1900: Ecumenism, Identity and the Religion of the Republic* (New York: Edwin Mellen Press, 1982). While Schaff did not envision the Alliance as inherently anti–Roman Catholic as some of his colleagues did, he recognized its capability to strengthen Protestantism. In 1870, after a year of preparation and indefatigable work to insure international attendance at the meeting scheduled for that year in New York, Schaff was deeply disappointed when forced by the Franco-Prussian War to postpone the meeting. He took heart, however, and noted in his diary the pending defeat of Napoleon III and "perhaps also the temporal power of the pope. God is dealing harder blows now to Rome than the Gen[eral] Conf[erence] of the Alliance [could]." Entry for "Mon. Aug. 8, 1870," Box IV, Philip Schaff Manuscript Collection, UTS.

65. Baird, *Religion in the United States of America*, 612. Other than the Roman

True to his lifelong work toward Christian union, Schaff tried to bridge that gulf, yet he wrestled with what he perceived to be areas of serious incompatibility between Catholicism and American society. Surprisingly unaware of how deeply the American situation had affected Catholicism, Schaff told his audience at Basel "I need not describe [the Catholic] church, since it is the same in America as in Europe." The "Evangelical" churches were the largest numerically and had the greatest influence on American religion and society, but he had to admit that "Romanism" had made more numerical progress during the last half century due to immigration and the acquisition by the United States of predominantly Catholic territories. Still, he hoped that the "thoroughly Protestant atmosphere" of America would exert a liberalizing influence on the Catholic Church. His disappointment was clear when he was forced to admit that "no sign of such a change has appeared yet." He retained his optimistic view, however, and insisted that "history never moves backward, and the open Bible and Protestant freedom are making faster and deeper progress than Romanism."[66]

Schaff continued to affirm the validity of the Roman Catholic denomination and to work with various leaders within that communion. His hope that true "Catholicism" would emerge from the false shell of "Romanism" seems to have faded during the late 1870s, and he once again spoke little of that distinction. Instead, he believed that the hierarchical church could itself be shaped by events in the modern world to become more evangelical. Most likely, Schaff was encouraged by the reversal of the conservative policies of Pius IX by his successor Leo XIII, who had immediately proposed a plan of reform upon his election in 1878. Schaff even went so far as to admit that the honor of being the organizing center for the emerging evangelical-catholic church would have to be conceded to either the Greek Orthodox or the Roman Catholic communion. Schaff confessed that Protestant union with

---

Catholic Church, the lists of churches in the "heterodox" and "unevangelical" categories are virtually the same. There is a difference of treatment, however, as Schaff regularly spoke more charitably about the members of that group than did Baird.

66. Schaff, "Religion in the United States of America," 91, 99-100. It was only two to three decades later that most scholars would regard American Catholicism as truly distinctive. Schaff said little about the "heterodox," but insisted that he used that label "without disrespect."

Rome would be more difficult in the aftermath of the decrees of "papal absolutism and papal infallibility declared by the Vatican Council in 1870." Yet papal decisions were and should be binding on all Roman Catholics, he believed, though they have no force at all with non-Catholics.[67]

Schaff was by his own admission "an inveterate hoper," and even the Vatican Council decrees did not destroy his ability to provide creative suggestions for reunion. "What if," Schaff dreamed, "the pope, in the spirit of the first Gregory and under the inspiration of a higher authority, should infallibly declare his own fallibility in all matters lying outside of his own communion, and invite Greeks and Protestants to a fraternal pan-Christian council in Jerusalem, where the mother-church of Christendom held the first council of reconciliation and peace?"[68] How seriously Schaff made this suggestion is hard to judge. There had been some hopeful signs coming from the pontificate of Leo XIII, but for Schaff to imagine that he would actually consider calling such a conference was extremely idealistic, even for him. On the other hand, papal actions have occasionally been quite unexpected. Schaff went on to praise the virtues of virtually every part of the Christian family, from Greek Orthodoxy to Roman Catholicism, from Lutheranism and the Reformed to Universalism and the Salvation Army. Why could not all of these, he asked, be shorn of their errors and abuses through an exercise of extraordinary humility and join in the chorus of exaltation of their common Lord? He concluded, "there is room for all these and many other churches and societies in the Kingdom of God, whose height and depth and length and breadth, variety and beauty, surpass human comprehension."[69] Schaff had a truly cosmic vision of the possibility of a worldwide united church. It was this vision of what could be that led him to see in the midst of American social and religious confusion a providentially designed order that would overcome all difficulties and create order out of the chaos.

Schaff's most fervent desire was the unity of the Christian church,

67. Philip Schaff, *The Reunion of Christendom: A Paper Prepared for the Parliament of Religions and the National Conference of the Evangelical Alliance Held in Chicago, September and October, 1893* (New York: Evangelical Alliance Office, 1893), 28.

68. Ibid. More discussion of Schaff's conception of the places of Roman Catholicism and Greek Orthodoxy in evangelical-catholic Christianity is found in chapter 7.

69. Ibid., 45.

and with that end in mind he came to America. Upon his arrival a process began through which he would grow in understanding of the merits of the American voluntary system. As he became more "American" himself, he developed insights into the American situation that in many cases were unpopular at the time, but later became parts of the standard interpretation of religion in America. In the face of a prevalent American desire to deny the Roman Catholic heritage of all Protestants, Schaff counseled moderation and historical appreciation of the Christian heritage through all ages. In the face of American nativism, Schaff insisted that unbelief was a greater danger than Catholicism, and that the Catholic Church in America had something significant to offer to the one evangelical-catholic church for which Schaff longed.

Schaff's American peers already regarded him suspiciously because of his deep appreciation for Christianity's catholic principle. But his views developed even further to the point of including Roman Catholicism among the acceptable denominations that could contribute to evangelical-catholic Christianity. Romanism was not the threat he originally thought, Schaff realized, because the American people steadfastly demanded freedoms that papists could never allow. The American religious environment was fraught with dangers for Christianity, but that context could also shape Catholicism in positive ways. In addition, Schaff's conception of the development of Christianity both softened the threat of Catholicism — since knowledge of origins helps destroy unfounded fears — and allowed him to critique the legitimate Catholic weakness of failing to recognize development in Christianity.

Schaff refused to reject Catholicism completely, as many of his Protestant peers did, and his half century of exposure to the American situation made him realize that institutional union could not happen during his lifetime. His solution to both problems was an understanding of Catholicism that appreciated all that it had to offer to evangelical-catholic Christianity in the present, with the assurance that the Christian church would finally and fully become one.

There was also a negative side to development. Schaff once again drew on his training in Germany to identify and fight those who would take the principle of development too far. Along with sectarianism and Romanism, the threat of rationalism challenged American Christianity. Despite the complacency of many of his American Christian peers, Schaff was convinced that this threat might well be the most serious one of all.

CHAPTER 3

Religious Freedom and the Threat of Rationalism

The Abyss of Heathenism

In 1847, the minister of Hartford's North Congregational Church, Horace Bushnell, lamented the sorry state of American culture in his book *Barbarism the First Danger.* His colleagues who directed their energies against the menace of Roman Catholicism, he maintained, had failed to recognize the most potent danger in their midst. Like Lyman Beecher, Bushnell argued that if the "good manners and Christian refinement" that were necessary for the development of the American Republic were to be formed in the American people — particularly those in the West — great effort had to be focused on promotion of educational institutions. In fact, Bushnell believed that the danger of barbarism was so great that the common attitude of anti-Catholicism should be overcome and Protestants should cooperate with Catholics in educating the American people. Common schools, thought Bushnell, should not be "Protestant" schools, but "Christian" schools. "Let us draw our strange friends as close to us as possible," Bushnell argued, "not in any party scramble for power, but in a solemn reference of duty to the nation and to God."[1]

1. Horace Bushnell, *Barbarism the First Danger: A Discourse for Home Missions* (New York: American Home Missionary Society, 1847), 27, 31-32, quoted in

A few years earlier, Philip Schaff had expressed remarkably similar ideas about threats to American society and religion. He lamented the loss of culture among German immigrants, and agreed wholeheartedly with Bushnell and Beecher about the need for improved education in America. Schaff's attention was naturally drawn to higher education, however, since his teaching was on that level, and coming from Germany he perceived the intellectual dangers America faced in a different light than did his pastor colleagues. He believed America needed rigorous higher education to combat rationalism. In fact, rationalism was, in the immigrant's eyes, the greatest threat to religion, both in America and throughout the world. It is not surprising that he should have that opinion. Just a few years prior to Schaff's arrival at Tübingen to pursue theological studies, David Strauss's *Life of Jesus* had plunged that school, and much of German theology, into turmoil by denying the historicity of the miracles recorded in the Gospels.[2] Schaff had been nurtured in the atmosphere of Württemberg pietism, which stressed spiritual renewal and represented a conscious break with the rationalism of the German Enlightenment. The reaction of most within that movement to Strauss's work had been to change their emphasis from awakening sinners to fighting against the powers of unbelief represented by Strauss and the leader of the so-called Tübingen School, Ferdinand Christian Baur. Schaff had attended Baur's lectures while at Tübingen and expressed deep admiration for Baur's theological brilliance. Baur was strongly influenced by Hegelian philosophy and sought to understand Christianity as a synthesis that grew out of the conflict between Petrine and Pauline versions of the faith. The result was that, according to Baur and his followers, most of the New Testament was a product of the period of synthesis, and therefore had little of historical value to say

---

Lawrence A. Cremin, *American Education: The National Experience, 1783-1876* (New York: Harper & Row, 1980), 48.

2. Klaus Penzel has carefully analyzed both Schaff's background in the pietistic revival in Württemberg and his opposition to the Tübingen School. See "Church History and the Ecumenical Quest: A Study of the German Background and Thought of Philip Schaff" (Th.D. diss., Union Theological Seminary, New York, 1962), 10-27, 43-44. See also Walter H. Conser, Jr., *Church and Confession: Conservative Theologians in Germany, England, and America, 1815-1866* (Macon, Ga.: Mercer University Press, 1984), 28-38, and James Hastings Nichols, *Romanticism in American Theology: Nevin and Schaff at Mercersburg* (Chicago: The University of Chicago Press, 1961), 64-83.

about the first century. Schaff believed that this innovative example of Baur's brilliance was disastrous for understanding the historical foundations of Christianity. Traditional theology in Germany fought for its life against the "destructive work of criticism" by this "latest form of infidelity."[3]

Schaff recognized that America lagged behind Germany in intellectual matters (later he would be shocked to find just how far behind!), and the attitude about the American situation that prevailed among the intellectual elite of Germany saw the situation in America as exceedingly grim. Such attitudes pervaded both Schaff's ordination sermon and the exhortations given by his mentors. Schaff was sent off as an intellectual champion charged to battle the evil forces of rationalistic perversion in America, where such forces had heretofore met little resistance. Dr. Friedrich W. Krummacher, one of the most famous preachers in Germany — who had himself turned down the mission for various reasons — urged Schaff to fight "the many-headed monster of pantheism and atheism, issuing from the sphere of German speculation, as it has there become flesh and broken forth into actual life, in concrete form, spreading desolation and terror." Utilizing imagery from the Hebrew Scriptures, Krummacher called upon Schaff to meet this giant, protected only by the "armor of the shepherd boy of Bethlehem and to smite [him] with incurable wounds."[4] The forces of good that would accompany Schaff also took on human form. As Krummacher reminded him, "you are called to transport German theology in its thoroughness and depth and its strong, free life together with the various branches of learning that stand related to it as a family of full-grown daughters."[5]

Given the German concept of intellectual and ecclesiastical propriety, there was little to commend the American situation. It is humorous, though not altogether surprising considering the battles they had been fighting in Germany, that American unbelief in all its forms should

3. Philip Schaff, *Germany: Its Universities, Theology and Religion* (Philadelphia: Lindsay and Blakiston, 1857), 158-59. Interestingly, as early as 1851 Schaff had predicted the decline and disappearance of Baur's "Tübingen School." Philip Schaff, *History of the Apostolic Church with a General Introduction to Church History*, trans. Edward D. Yeomans (New York: Scribner's, 1854), 290.

4. Quoted in Philip Schaff, *America: A Sketch of Its Political, Social and Religious Character*, ed. Perry Miller (Cambridge: Harvard University Press, 1961), xvii-xviii.

5. Ibid., xvii.

have been considered such a formidable enemy. Nonetheless, it was this specter, real or imagined, that Schaff girded himself to battle. In his ordination sermon of 1844, he put it quite clearly. The German Americans to whom he would go stood on the edge of the "threefold abyss" of "HEATHENISM, ROMANISM, [and] SECTARISM," into which they were bound to fall if aid did not reach them immediately. Their main weakness was due to character flaws. Though some suffered from the external hardships of unemployment and poverty, most were "adventurers and vagabonds . . . the friends of lawless freedom." Even the poverty-stricken put the welfare of the body above that of the soul and engaged in the "vain pursuit" to "become rich and to lead a life in all respects agreeable to the flesh." Many had fled the old world to escape punishment for crimes, and some because of their "direct hatred of the gospel."[6]

It was this last group that presented the greatest challenge to Schaff's mission. Their "black art," their "infidel science" had reached its climax in the "Mythen*strauss*," which had "laid hold of the most precious, and sacred, and true, and well authenticated history, that has ever been known, the life of the Son of God, and transformed it into a withered garland of fables." This was the fruit of the new heathenism, the "rationalism" that most gravely threatened American religion and culture. Schaff's rhetoric knew few bounds as he impressed upon his hearers the gravity of the situation.

> She [rationalism] has turned the future into the present, and sunk heaven down to earth, and impudently reasoned away the whole invisible world, which at the same time however bears up the visible. And over these ruins of all that is high and holy, she has uttered no cry of distress, shed no tear of sorrow, but only exclaimed with frozen heart and satanic pride: "Humanity is God. No longer fall down before the Unseen, but before the heroes of Art and science, partaking of your own nature; that is, worship yourselves!"[7]

It was as if the prophecies concerning the "Man of sin, the son of perdition," were being fulfilled. The situation was exacerbated in Amer-

6. Philip Schaff, "Ordination of Professor Schaff," *Weekly Messenger* 9 (September 4, 1844): 1869.

7. Ibid.

ica, where freedom to publish one's opinions met with no restraint whatsoever. "Take a full view," Schaff exhorted, "of this conflux of beggars, adventurers, liberty dreamers, culprits, and open blasphemers of religion, in a land so free from restraint." Little wonder, then, that "our countrymen in America are in danger of being percipitated [sic] into an abyss of heathenism, even worse perhaps than that of our first ancestors." Those who showed any interest in religious things were in danger of being snapped up by a zealous Roman Catholic or sectarian proselytizer, but most would be lost to unbelief if not rescued immediately. Schaff was headed, he believed, to "a people and . . . a land which seem to have become estranged from the deeper life of the soul in the pursuit of that which is material and outward." Part of his concern was to maintain the riches of the German heritage. "All that remains of the German art and life," he warned, "if it be not speedily rescued with powerful help, must be shortly swallowed up in a foreign nationality."[8] Thus, Schaff was faced with the task of maintaining the benefits of German culture and religion in a land where such things were not valued. It is fascinating to watch him as he wrestled with the process of cultural assimilation common to immigrant groups, and to analyze how Schaff himself changed, as well as to see what he believed must be maintained from the German heritage and incorporated into the American situation.

Quite obviously, Schaff's initial approach lacked a great deal in tact, and he found himself attacked by German Americans in both the secular and religious presses. German papers from New York to Missouri attacked Schaff as "a traitor to his country and a slanderer of his country men," and warned parents against sending their young people to Mercersburg.[9] Even though it took years for Schaff to overcome the distrust and prejudice aroused among the German-American population, he quickly recognized the errors in his portrayal. It did not take him long to realize that he had been too sweeping in his generalizations about the character of the immigrant Germans, but he remained troubled by the lack of depth in the American system of education. For that problem, he thought, German scholarship had the answer. Part of the difficulty lay in the fact that Americans were so action oriented.

8. Ibid.

9. David S. Schaff, *The Life of Philip Schaff: In Part Autobiographical* (New York: Scribner's, 1897), 105.

Schaff's observations in *The Principle of Protestantism* about America's "busyness" were not original, but his insights into the effects of this characteristic on the life of the mind are instructive, especially as he applied them to the church. American Christians were so concerned for utility that they had little time to develop higher culture. The guiding questions for American society evaluated every practice on the basis of immediate usefulness. "What has it accomplished for the souls of men or their bodies? Can it fill an empty pocket or an empty stomach? Has it ever manufactured a steamboat or so much even as a pin?"[10]

The attitude revealed by such questions had been a major influence toward creating the anti-intellectualism Schaff found in many American church bodies. Schaff immediately recognized the situation later described by Richard Hofstadter in *Anti-Intellectualism in American Life.* While there had always been a tension in Christianity between the life of the mind and practical outworking of the faith, in America the situation was weighted dramatically in favor of action. In addition, Hofstadter insisted that since "the American mind was shaped in the mold of early modern Protestantism," what took place within the church had profound repercussions in American society as a whole.

> At an early stage in its history, America, with its Protestant and dissenting inheritance, became the scene of an unusually keen local variation of this universal historical struggle over the character of religion; and here the forces of enthusiasm and revivalism won their most impressive victories. It is to certain peculiarities of American religious life — above all to its lack of firm institutional establishments hospitable to intellectuals and to the competitive sectarianism of its evangelical denominations — that American anti-intellectualism owes much of its strength and pervasiveness.[11]

The church should provide leadership in all areas of life and thought, Schaff believed, but in America the church had become a

10. Philip Schaff, *The Principle of Protestantism,* trans. John W. Nevin (Chambersburg, Penn.: Publication Office of the German Reformed Church, 1845; reprint ed., Philadelphia: United Church Press, 1964), 196.

11. Richard Hofstadter, *Anti-Intellectualism in American Life* (New York: Vintage, 1963), 55-56.

slavish follower, and had allowed itself to be shaped unduly by the American ethos of practicality and action. Schaff wryly noted that his description of one of the threats to America in his ordination sermon had not been completely accurate. Unbelief had not progressed in America to nearly the extent it had in Europe, and the reason was clear: "where a man does not think, it requires no great skill to be orthodox." Such a condition was far from desirable, however, since "orthodoxy that includes no thought, is not worth a farthing."[12]

Actually, Schaff pointed out, rationalism was no more than the flip side of the sectarian coin. Both grew out of the same principle: "a one-sided false subjectivity, sundered from the authority of the objective." In fact, "rationalism is theoretic sectarianism; sectarianism is practical rationalism."[13] In an explanation that probably mystified many of his Bible-believing readers, Schaff went on to explain that both sectarianism and rationalism violated aspects of the objective Christian tradition. Sectarianism, despite its claims to be based on the highest authority, the Bible, actually denied the objective character of the church throughout the world and throughout history, and, in effect, rejected the affirmation of Christ that he would always be with his church.[14] The rationalists, on the other hand, denied the objective authority of Holy Scripture and treated it as just another book. In addition, having thus jettisoned the authority of the Bible, they proceeded to cast aside its central message of salvation by divine grace alone. Rationalism, said Schaff, exalts a "general idea of humanity" and proclaims it "the creator, preserver, and redeemer of all things."[15] This emphasis of Protestant rationalism made it similar to Roman Catholicism, according to Schaff. Both are fundamentally

12. Schaff, *Principle of Protestantism,* 137.

13. Ibid., 155. It was not until the 1960s, when Sidney Mead used this insight into the relationship between rationalism and sectarianism to help explain the separation of church and state in America and the adoption of religious freedom, that the concept received its due. See Sidney Mead, *The Lively Experiment: The Shaping of Christianity in America* (New York: Harper & Row, 1963), 38, 61-62. Mead relabeled the components "rationalism" and "pietism," but their emphases are quite similar to those of Schaff's "rationalism" and "sectarianism." Although Mead did not cite Schaff as his specific source for this idea, he did acknowledge his debt to Schaff for the basic motifs of these essays.

14. "I am with you always, to the end of the age" (Matt. 28:20, NRSV).

15. Schaff, *Principle of Protestantism,* 133.

Pelagian in their stress on the human contribution to salvation, and neither relies enough on the final authority of Scripture. For Roman Catholics, the "tradition principle" is determinative, and the "reason principle" rules among rationalists. The latter is still the greatest threat, however, for at least the Roman Catholic Church is only "*half* Pelagian and *half* rationalistic."[16]

To combat this danger, Americans should seek to bolster their intellectual abilities. The most obvious and valuable way to do that, according to Schaff, was to avail themselves of German powers of thought. Rationalism and the German answer to it would both play a vital shaping role in the development of American theology, Schaff foresaw. The problem was not exclusively religious, however, since rationalism had also infected secular thought in America. German secular periodicals, for example, had become "organs more or less expert, to the service of infidelity, with the worst influence on the more common class especially of our immigrant population."[17] At the same time, however, Schaff was troubled to find that "even in the liturgies and hymnbooks of the German American Churches rationalistic elements are by no means rare, without being perceived by those who use them."[18] The American situation had created dangers that were not found even in Germany. The sad result of rationalistic thought in the free and chaotic religious situation of America was that clergymen who had been educated in the rationalistic systems of Germany, but who had also been protected by the piety of German evangelicalism, had spread their ideas to common folk in America who did not have a similar pietistic safeguard. In other words, Schaff maintained that pious faith built on a solid theological foundation was the strongest defense against rationalism, and while the two were often found together in Germany, in America separation between them was common, and weak faith usually gave way to the rationalistic onslaught.

Rationalism had also served a positive purpose, however, through the "purifying power" of its "severe criticism and grammatico-historical exegesis." Part of the positive result, from Schaff's point of view at least, was that the "absolute despotism of the metaphysics of Locke is in a

16. Ibid., 135-36.
17. Ibid., 138, 134n.
18. Ibid., 138.

measure broken." While there were dangers involved — for example, Thomas Carlyle's pantheistic "hero worship, which reaches even to Muhammad" had developed out of Anglo-American rationalism — such results were the exception rather than the norm.[19] In fact, orthodoxy would only be strengthened by the free interchange of ideas. Despite Locke's downfall, which for many was tantamount to the destruction of orthodoxy, Schaff was able to affirm that

> the old faith has sustained in this way no loss. It remains essentially the same. It has come forth from the critical fire, improved only in its form and argument, and cleared of all sorts of dross. It has lost nothing in living power, inwardness, and depth, while it has gained in freedom and solid scientific strength.[20]

Nonetheless, Schaff warned his readers not to underestimate this threat against which there was little defensive preparation in America. The sorry condition of American intellectual life had, as yet, provided "no scientific antidote" for the poison of rationalism. Americans must "stand on our guard . . . and prepare ourselves beforehand for the crisis that may come."[21] Both aspects of the defense, deep piety and intellectual competence, needed strengthening in America, but as Schaff got to know America and its people better, he viewed the situation with increasing confidence.

Educating America

After a decade of residence and work in America, Schaff had moderated his views somewhat. It was not fair, he told a European audience in 1854, to expect a young country such as America to attain the level of culture in just a few decades that it had taken the old world centuries to develop. Instead one should marvel that the Americans had pro-

19. Ibid., 170, 206. Schaff wrote of Mercersburg's attack on "the popedom of the philosophical system of Locke and rationalizing ultra-Protestantism." See D. Schaff, *Life*, 140.

20. Schaff, *Principle of Protestantism*, 170.

21. Ibid., 138-39.

gressed as far as they had. Indeed, if the German Americans had shown the liberality of their New England Puritan countrymen, they could already have established a full-fledged German university in Pennsylvania. America had in fact become a "land of colleges" during the nineteenth century. Legislation, such as the Northwest Ordinance of 1787 and the Morrill Act of 1862, nurtured a proliferation of colleges.[22] Schaff cautioned his hearers against being misled by the sheer number of institutions, however.

Education in America was different from that to which his European hearers had grown accustomed. In the ferment and freedom of American society education tended to be spread broadly in numerous institutions. The main weakness was a lack of depth. Many American professors were quite superficial as scholars, yet ironically seemed quite puffed up with "learned vanity and magniloquence." Schaff decried the liberal bestowing of honorary degrees to the extent that they became virtually meaningless. "There are," he fretted, "American doctors of divinity, who, however distinguished they may be as men and as preachers, have not done science the least service, and can hardly read the New Testament in the original text."[23]

Though his observations were accurate, Schaff's condemnation of American professors was a bit unfair. In many colleges, especially the newer and smaller ones, professors were often expected to teach the entire range of the curriculum, and their images of themselves and their work were not conducive to depth of scholarship. Normally they saw themselves as "generalists rather than specialists and as pedagogues rather than scholars."[24] By the 1840s and 1850s, some American

22. Cremin, *American Education*, 400, lists statistics. In 1831, there were some 46 colleges, 22 theological seminaries, 16 medical schools, and 7 law schools. By 1850 the numbers had grown to 119 colleges, 44 theological seminaries, 36 medical schools, and 16 law schools. In 1876, the United States Bureau of Education reported 356 colleges and universities, 124 theological seminaries, 78 medical schools, and 42 law schools. Clinton Rossiter, *The American Quest, 1790-1860* (New York: Harcourt Brace Jovanovich, 1971), 166, points out, however, that while the nine colleges founded before the Revolution were joined by another 175 by 1860, more than 500 others had been founded and then "withered away" during that same period.

23. Schaff, *America*, 61. Schaff had himself received a number of honorary degrees and valued them highly. Particularly meaningful was the one conferred by the University of Berlin in 1854. See D. Schaff, *Life*, 184.

24. Cremin, *American Education*, 407.

scholars had begun to adopt the German ideals of specialization and scholarship, but the process of acceptance was painfully slow and uneven. Critics lambasted even the most distinguished educational institutions in America for their deficiencies. Louis Agassiz, the famed scientist who had come to Harvard from the continent, complained that even that august institution was no more than a "respectable high school where they taught the dregs of learning."[25]

On a different level, the system had advantages, however, and faith in education as the cure for all social ills became a common creed in America. The benefit of the number of public schools in America was that virtually everyone had at least the possibility of obtaining some education. In addition, as Alexis de Tocqueville noted, common schools took on increased importance in America where education outside the home was more common than in Europe. Schaff also noted the increasing role of common schools in American society and became, like many of his Protestant peers, concerned about the limited religious education such schools provided. The Sunday schools helped make up this lack, and Roman Catholics and some Protestants had decided to establish parochial schools that would insure religious education, but these institutions did not affect most of America's school-age children. For decades, debate had raged over the proper relationship between religion and education. Nearly all agreed that for the American Republic to endure, general education was necessary. The problem lay in the fact that for centuries people had assumed that the moral standards that would make education effective in promoting democratic ideals were based on religion, specifically Christianity. But how was the role of religion to be defined in state-sponsored schools when religious and civil authorities were legally separated?

Enthusiasts like Horace Mann, secretary of the Massachusetts Board of Education and one of the prime movers behind the development of public education in America, insisted that "*the common school is the greatest discovery ever made by man.*" Mann also took a stance that would become more controversial when he identified the moral elevation brought about by the schools as the particular product of nondenominational Protestantism. To his diary he confided, "the fundamental principles of Christianity may and should be inculcated [in the common

25. Quoted in Rossiter, *The American Quest*, 166.

schools]. . . . After this, each denomination must be left to its own resources, for inculcating its own faith or creed."[26] Tocqueville had noticed the common morality preached by all the Protestant sects, and most other Protestants also recognized this "Protestant common denominator" that allowed them to cooperate in support of state-sponsored public education.[27] The general Protestant morality of the immensely popular McGuffey readers, for example, was viewed by Protestants throughout the country as acceptable, even necessary, for the moral education required by citizens of the Republic.[28]

In a country where Christianity was so dependent on literate adherents, where the Bible was such a central part of religion and society, education was obviously crucial. Schaff recognized the need for Christian consensus in the education of America's youth, yet he also sensed the tension created by the growing diversity of beliefs in America and tried to recognize the rights of all Americans to freedom of conscience. During the year of Schaff's coming to the United States, Horace Mann had conducted a survey of Massachusetts public schools which revealed that of 308 schools, only three had answered negatively when asked if they regularly used the Bible.[29] Schaff never mentioned this survey, but it is clear that he would have been encouraged by its findings. He spoke approvingly of the "time-honored custom" of Bible reading in the schools which, however, was being "violently and persistently assailed by infidels, Jews, and especially by Roman Catholics."[30]

In order to understand Schaff's views rightly, however, this rather uncharacteristic condemnation must be put in context. First, he was well in step with religious thinkers of his time in his belief that reli-

26. Quoted in Cremin, *American Education,* 137, and in William Bean Kennedy, *The Shaping of Protestant Education: An Interpretation of the Sunday School and the Development of Protestant Educational Strategy in the United States, 1789-1860* (New York: Association Press, 1966), 28.

27. Alexis de Tocqueville, *Democracy in America,* trans. George Lawrence, ed. J. P. Mayer (Garden City, N.Y.: Doubleday), 290; Robert T. Handy, *A Christian America: Protestant Hopes and Historical Realities,* rev. ed. (New York: Oxford, 1984), 34.

28. Publishers sold some 100 million copies of the McGuffey readers between 1836 and 1890. See Kennedy, *Protestant Education,* 29.

29. Herbert M. Kliebard, ed., *Religion and Education in America: A Documentary History* (Scranton, Penn.: International Textbook Co., 1969), 6.

30. Philip Schaff, "Progress of Christianity in the United States of America," *The Princeton Review* 55 (September 1879): 227.

gionless public education was the bane of church and society. Not unlike many of his contemporaries, Schaff insisted that "an education which ignores religion altogether would raise a heartless and infidel generation of intellectual animals, and prove a curse rather than a blessing." Also, education in and of itself could never be a sufficient foundation of society. As a good student of the Reformation, Schaff scorned those who in their idealization of education forgot "the inborn depravity of human nature."[31] Education in morality — which for Schaff necessarily implied religious values — was essential for maintenance of the political and social freedoms enjoyed in America. The key distinction, then, was between education that was religious, but not necessarily Protestant, and that which was non- or anti-religious. The former might have been acceptable in some instances while the latter could never be.

Schaff's protests against Jews and Catholics was tempered by his desire for ecumenical cooperation and his recognition of religious pluralism in America. Here as elsewhere "sectarian animosities" were the plague of society and one of the primary goals of common public education was "to check and moderate them and to raise a homogeneous generation." Schaff admitted that "absolute uniformity seems impracticable and undesirable in a country where the States are independent, the population heterogeneous, and the public sentiment divided." Yet the goal of consensus must always remain uppermost, and the consensus should be based on Protestant Christianity.[32]

A problem that appeared in Schaff's reasoning at this point was his failure to explain adequately precisely how the Jews would fit into this consensus. On the one hand, he respected their right to reject overtly Christian religious education. While the general flavor of the education in public schools was Protestant — and this was unavoidable due to the dominant Protestant character of the nation itself — Schaff was willing to recommend separate explicitly religious education based on free choice by parents. He discussed various plans of religious education, including a "general scheme of religious instruction which shall be confined to the essentials held in common by all." The "all" he had in mind included the various Protestant denominations, Roman Catholics, and Jews. But this sensitive ecumenist was forced to admit that

31. Ibid., 214.
32. Ibid., 228-29.

such a plan, though theoretically acceptable, was probably impractical since "the Roman Catholics are not likely ever to agree with the Protestants on any religious formula. And the conscience of the Jews must likewise be respected." Rather than offend the religious sensibilities of those of other beliefs, Schaff proposed what he called a "German" model which, as it turned out, was similar to that adopted on occasion in America. "Let religious instruction be separately given in appointed hours by special teachers chosen for the purpose by the different churches; the parents to be free to send their children to the teacher they prefer, or to excuse them from attendance."[33]

In their rejection of overtly Protestant religious instruction, including the exclusive use of the King James Version of the Bible, Roman Catholics were being "conscientious and consistent" with their overall point of view, Schaff admitted, since prolonged Protestant influence would "gradually free the Catholic youth from exclusive influence of the priesthood, and put them on a more liberal track."[34] Schaff did not try to hide his hope that Catholic youth would be "liberated," and in fact he believed their "emancipation" was inevitable. Such "liberalizing" of Roman Catholicism would help bring about the evangelical catholicism that he envisioned as the future form of Christianity in America.[35] Even if the Catholics remained intransigent and succeeded in removing the Protestant Bible from the public schools, the victory of evangelical-catholic Christianity was assured, according to Schaff, since the churches would be spurred to "greater zeal in training the young for usefulness in this world and happiness in the world to come."[36]

The combination of inherently but not overtly Protestant public schools, confessional parochial schools, and the work of Sunday schools assured the continued Protestantization of the America people. Schaff, then, seems to fit the pattern of those nineteenth-century leaders whom Thomas G. Sanders has labeled "theocrats." According to Sanders, these Protestants did in fact develop the public school, but in a "dis-

33. Ibid. It should be noted that Schaff expressed this attitude in 1857 while he was still in Mercersburg, and long before he had come into close contact with the large Jewish population in New York City.

34. Ibid., 227; Schaff, *America*, 197.

35. For more detailed examination of Schaff's conception of the blend of Roman Catholic and Protestant elements in "evangelical catholic" Christianity, see chapter 7.

36. Schaff, "Progress of Christianity," 229.

guised Protestant form." They sought a "middle-ground" somewhere between establishment, which they agreed should not obtain in this land of religious freedom, and neutrality, which could never provide the necessary moral supports for such a free society.[37]

With the enormous influx of Roman Catholic immigrants in the mid-nineteenth century, however, the situation became increasingly complicated. Catholics chafed under the overtly Protestant religious teachings and practices of the common schools, and sought various alternatives. Two proposed options that particularly raised the ire of Protestants were attempts to replace the King James Version read by students with a Catholic version for Catholic students, and requests for public funds in support of parochial schools. At the forefront of these battles was Archbishop John Hughes of New York. In 1852 Hughes's official paper, the *Freeman's Journal,* carried articles calling on Catholics throughout America to unite in demanding public money for the support of their own schools, or, failing that, the passage of laws forbidding the reading of Protestant versions of the Bible in state-supported schools. Protestant reaction was swift and strong. Catholic rejection of the King James Version was interpreted as confirmation of the hierarchy's hatred for the Bible, of whatever version. Under threats from their predominantly Protestant constituencies, legislators passed statutes in various states which forbade use of public funds for sectarian institutions, and required Bible reading in all state schools.[38] Though defeated at that time, Catholics made similar efforts during the latter decades of the nineteenth century, and though never successful in gaining public funds to support their schools, they did manage to start a process that eventually broke the Protestant hegemony over the public schools.

Scholarship and the Church

The American religious situation also created serious difficulties for the possibility of establishing a full-fledged university in the German

37. Thomas G. Sanders, *Protestant Concepts of Church and State* (New York: Holt, Rinehart and Winston, 1964), 255.

38. Ray Allen Billington, *Protestant Crusade, 1800-1860* (New York: Macmillan, 1938), 292-95.

sense. Since there were so many churches and sects in America, Schaff noted, it would be impossible to provide a coherent theological faculty, and without a theological faculty a university would lack "its animating soul and its ruling head."[39] In the absence of university theological departments, the myriad denominations and sects had established theological seminaries and schools to meet their needs. Once again, the profusion in number stood in inverse proportion to quality. In fact, some of the seminaries could hardly be considered academic institutions, and many struggled financially. Schaff's own experience at Mercersburg had shown him this negative side of the separation of civil and religious institutions in America. He deplored having to go on "begging tours" to bring in necessary funds and resources to conduct proper seminary education. Instead, he insisted, "a few first-class institutions would be better than many poor ones which spread a superficial culture at the expense of depth and solidity." He was hopeful for some sort of cooperation and union of institutions, but for that to happen, sectarian feeling must be overcome. "The vast extent of the country and the rivalry of sects stimulate the multiplication. There are institutions where one or two professors must teach all branches of learning, and spend the vacation in the humiliating business of collecting their own scanty salary."[40] While Schaff never openly complained about his teaching load or his salary, that account exactly described his situation at Mercersburg![41]

Schaff's criticisms of the American situation during his visits to Europe confirmed his hearers' prejudices about the sorry condition of American education. Schaff did not allow them to become too comfortable, however. Although these problems were serious, they could be remedied by an infusion of the best of German thought and theology, and it was the duty of the churches of the old world to help provide that assistance. There were also benefits to the American situation that Schaff came to appreciate and tried to convey to his European friends.

39. Schaff, *America*, 59.

40. Schaff, "Progress of Christianity," 232.

41. Schaff did, however, on the occasion of his inauguration at Mercersburg, point out to his audience that "a professor of theology and a pack horse are not exactly the same thing." Philip Schaff, "Conclusion of Dr. Schaf's Address," *Weekly Messenger* 10 (April 23, 1845): 2. Schaff's depth of scholarship and level of productivity are all the more remarkable considering the breadth of topics he covered in teaching and writing.

For the Germans, academic theology was a scientific discipline which in practice could be separated from the church. In America, however, the situation was reversed. As Schaff put it, "theology is the daughter of the church and should not rebel against the mother."[42]

Significant differences distinguished the European and American situations. In America, there was no separation between theology and the church, and little between theology and society. In contrast, while German theologians worked in universities funded by the state, their theologies were separated from the church and had little immediate impact on society. This, then, was the dilemma Schaff faced in his attempt to promote highest-level scholarship in a country that separated religious and civil authorities. Certainly European government support promoted scholarship, but often at the expense of piety and the church. Religious freedom, on the other hand, because of its focus on practicality, kept theology and church closely united, but also encouraged the multiplication of sectarian institutions to the neglect of scholarly depth. Neither of the situations was ideal, but Schaff was guided by a vision in which both rigorous scholarship and personal piety in service to the church could be united. Schaff retained a concern for highest-level scholarship throughout his career, but late in his life he emphasized more and more the importance of piety of life in addition to rigor of academics. He dwelt on the subject at length in a letter written during his last visit to Europe in 1890.

> In a German university a theological professor is appointed by the state, supported by the state, responsible to no creed, and expected to teach and promote science. The state looks only at theoretical qualifications, and cares little or nothing about the orthodoxy and piety of the candidate. The church, as such, has nothing to say in the matter. The result is that a professor may teach doctrines which are utterly subversive to the church, and disqualify the student for his future work. This is an unnatural state of things. It may be favorable to the freest development of theological science and speculation, but very dangerous to the healthful and vigorous development of church life.[43]

42. D. Schaff, *Life,* 471.
43. Ibid. There is no reference to the person to whom the letter is written.

Schaff sought a mediating position in which an institution could promote both academic freedom and highest scholarship. Yet this would be done always in the service of the church through the safeguards of piety of life, depth of faith, and the essentials of traditional orthodoxy. His move to Union Theological Seminary in 1870 must be seen as an attempt to realize this ideal. The tension remained, however. His remarks during the heresy trials of Union's Charles A. Briggs (1891-1893) reveal a deep commitment to academic freedom. "There is such a thing as Presbyterian as well as Prelatical and Roman popery. 'Presbyter is priest writ large.' There must be elbow room for development, and liberty of investigation; or we may as well shut up our Seminaries." Yet the safeguard of true piety must guide scholarly investigation. As Schaff had put it in an address to the graduating class of Union in 1871, "scholarship is good, virtue is better, holiness is best of all."[44]

The principles of Schaff's scholarship, then, may be described as follows: (1) Scholarship should be pursued in the most rigorous fashion possible. Schaff had no place for anti-intellectualism within Christianity, no matter how pious sounding it was. (2) Theology must never be divorced from the church. The whole point of theology is better understanding of human redemption by God, and the church as the body of Christ is the organic community in and through which that redemption is accomplished. Therefore, appointments to academic theological posts must take into account the commitment of the candidate to historical Christian beliefs as enunciated in the catholic creeds of the church. Schaff fought for scientific study of theology in the context of faith, in contrast to a study of theology that considered its work merely a science like others. (3) The theologian, in order to do his or her work properly, must be a believer. "The very first condition of all right knowledge," Schaff insisted, "is a pre-existing sympathy with the object to be known." This is particularly important for Christian theology, since Christianity is the highest knowledge. That is, the Christian will understand at least the basics of other religions and philosophies because Christianity, being at the center of the world's life, "throws the clearest light on all other history." The reverse is not true, however. Since in Schaff's opinion

44. Letter by Philip Schaff to "My Dear Brother," 7 April 1892, Correspondence, Box II, Philip Schaff Manuscript Collection, The Burke Library, Union Theological Seminary, New York. Hereafter UTS. See also D. Schaff, *Life,* 438, 293.

non-Christian religions and philosophies in no way attain the heights of Christian knowledge, there is a gulf of darkness in the understanding of unbelievers. Thus, "the church historian, to do justice to his subject, must live and move in Christianity." The church historian who does not believe what he studies academically "can only set before us, at best, instead of the living body of Christ, a cold marble statue, without seeing eye or feeling heart."[45] Finally, (4) it is religious experience rather than rational proof that provides the final apologetic for Christianity and its strongest defense against rationalism. For Schaff, concerning Christianity, one believes in order to understand, and where evidence is not conclusive, one must accept in faith the traditional wisdom of the church. "Faith," he insisted, "is the most fruitful mother of knowledge."[46] He advised young ministers facing the critical problems of history and theology to realize that ultimately experience and not intellect was the best antidote for agnosticism, skepticism, and infidelity. Faith would lead them to understanding.

According to Klaus Penzel, this concept became basic for those like Schaff nurtured by the Württemberg Awakening:

> In the Awakening religious experience was promoted to the rank of a scientific principle of cognition which itself was no longer subject to any other authority whatsoever. Schaff made this standpoint wholly his own and remained true to it to the end of his days.[47]

Schaff made common cause with "rationalistic supernaturalists," such as the Princeton theologians, in their concern to safeguard the truth and authority of Scripture, but his emphasis was different. Rather than basing belief in the authority of Scripture on a rationally developed theory of inspiration logically constructed from passages of Scripture, Schaff stressed the witness of the Holy Spirit which assured the believer of the unique character of the apostolic age and the apostolic writings. This is not to imply either that Schaff neglected the assertions of the

45. Philip Schaff, *History of the Apostolic Church with a General Introduction to Church History*, trans. Edward D. Yeomans (New York: Scribner's, 1854), 35, 101.

46. Philip Schaff, *Theology for Our Age and Country* (New York: Rogers and Sherwood, 1872), 14.

47. Penzel, "Church History and the Ecumenical Quest," 46.

Bible or that the Princetonians failed to rely on the Holy Spirit. Both are present in each system, but levels of emphasis are different. Schaff concluded, "We must come to the conclusion that Christianity is life and power and independent of critical questions on the extent of the canon and the mode of inspiration."[48]

Here was the boundary to Schaff's reliance on "scientific" historical and biblical criticism. In his opinion, the first century was a unique period of time and the documents of Scripture were unique religious writings. Their supernatural character demanded a different type of treatment than other eras or documents. Schaff's defense of such a position was simply that the uniqueness of the apostolic age and apostolic writings became evident to anyone who cared to examine them with an open mind and receptive spirit, and a source of certainty to the believer through the witness of Christian experience.[49] Schaff insisted that the scholar should follow "science" (that is, critical scientific methodology in biblical studies and history) as far as possible, but must always keep in mind that the final judge between the findings of modern science and foundational Christian beliefs should be religious experience.[50] Schaff was convinced that the experience of "knowing" Christ and the witness of the Holy Spirit were the most objective evidences possible. His definitions of "rationalism" and "reason" are instructive here. "Rationalism," he insisted,

> arrogates to itself the title of rationality or reason as specially its own. In truth, however, it moves not at all in the sphere of reason, but only in that of the abstract understanding, the region of mere finite thinking, entangled in contradictions and external appearances, the standpoint of reflection. Reason, on the contrary, is the power of perceiving the supernatural, the infinite, the harmonious unity, the essence of things, the primal idea of the absolute. It is the longing of the spirit after its true country, its home-drawing toward God and the revelation he has made of himself in Christ; just as conscience is the

48. D. Schaff, *Life*, 503. Nichols, *Romanticism in American Theology*, 3, uses the term "rationalistic supernaturalism" to describe the Princeton theology.

49. Philip Schaff, *The Person of Christ: The Perfection of His Humanity Viewed as a Proof of His Divinity* (New York: American Tract Society, 1882), gives testimonies of believers and nonbelievers that affirm the uniqueness of Christ and the Bible.

50. Penzel, "Church History and the Ecumenical Quest," 157-58.

> point of contact between the human will and the ground of all will in God. Reason, then, in its inmost nature, is a receptive faculty that must go beyond itself for its contents.[51]

Schaff utilized the principles of Friedrich Schleiermacher and his emphasis on Christian piety, but modified them to include traditional affirmations about the authority of the Bible.

> But the *full* and *unconditional* reverence for the holy word of God, in which the whole Schleiermacherian school is more or less deficient, requires, wherever science cannot clear away the darkness, an humble submission of reason to the obedience of faith, or a present suspension of decisive judgment, in the hope that farther and deeper research may lead to more satisfactory results.[52]

He based the final defense against rationalism, therefore, on the Christian experience of the believer.

> The best authority against Strauss is an honest soul filled with Christ, whose life of faith hid with God knows that Christianity is not an idea hanging in the air, but that forth from the prophet of Nazareth there continues to go power which overcomes the world and also life for all sympathetic hearts.[53]

Schaff's emphasis on Christian experience caused strained relations between him and the Princeton theologians, particularly Charles Hodge. Although the personal relationship between the two men was always cordial and Schaff spoke of Hodge as "a saintly man," their differences in theological method caused friction between them on occasion. Much of the difference may be attributed to the difference between a German idealistic philosophical foundation and that of Scottish realism.[54] Utilizing

51. Schaff, *The Principle of Protestantism,* 134n.
52. Schaff, *History of the Apostolic Church,* 101.
53. Quoted in D. Schaff, *Life,* 24.
54. See Mark A. Noll, ed., *The Princeton Theology, 1812-1921* (Grand Rapids, Mich.: Baker, 1983), 155-64; Mark A. Noll, ed., *Charles Hodge: The Way of Life* (New York: Paulist Press, 1987); and Bruce Kuklick, *Churchmen and Philosophers: From Jonathan Edwards to John Dewey* (New Haven: Yale University Press, 1985). Schaff spoke

the insights of Scottish commonsense realism, Hodge viewed the Bible as a "storehouse of facts" which could be clearly understood by the unbiased interpreter. God had revealed himself in such a way that would allow the Bible reader logically to formulate precise, exact conclusions about the divine nature. In contrast, Hodge viewed German idealism as engaged in unwarranted a priori speculation. The organicism of the Mercersburg men, as well as their emphasis on historical tradition and development, caused some of their ideas to be virtually incomprehensible to Americans in the commonsense tradition. Hodge reviewed Schaff's *Principle of Protestantism* in the *Biblical Repertory and Princeton Review* and stated at the outset that the book was "not easy to understand." German writers, he said, have many faults, not the least of which "they are seldom very intelligible." Nonetheless, even though there was much in the book attributable "to the peculiar philosophical and historical training of the writer; much that we do not understand and much with which we cannot agree," Hodge concluded with a "hope that Dr. Schaff will prove a blessing to the church and country of his adoption."[55]

In 1848, Schaff felt compelled to respond to Hodge's scathing review of his Mercersburg colleague John W. Nevin's *The Mystical Presence.* Relations to that time had been strained but cordial, but "now," Schaff insisted, "the visor has fallen. The men who heretofore, at least, extended to us the left hand, stand forth now openly as our decided opponents." What really irritated Schaff was what he perceived as Hodge's arrogant attitude. Hodge had allowed Nevin's work to lay on his desk unread for two years, until a "'stimulus of a special necessity'" forced him to read and review it "'within a fortnight.'" Disagreement was one thing; condescension was quite another.

> If one scholar is able in a fortnight, with borrowed authorities, to overthrow the positions of another, who has devoted himself with the most earnest industry for a full year at least to the study and inves-

---

of the theological faculty at Princeton in 1848 as "if it be not the very best, [it] is without doubt one of the best in America." Philip Schaff, "Princeton and Mercersburg," *Weekly Messenger* 13 (June 7, 1848): 2650.

55. Charles Hodge, "Schaff's Protestantism," *Biblical Repertory and Princeton Review* 17 (October 1845): 626-36; Noll, *Princeton Theology*, 155-64.

tigation of the sources themselves, and who has furnished the material for his reviewer; — then this is quite a natural conclusion — either the latter must be wanting in all healthy comprehension, or the former be gifted with sharp-sightedness far beyond the usual lot of mortals.[56]

Princeton and Mercersburg continued to exchange salvos in the years to come, but the rivalry between the two institutions was not without humor for Schaff. Once when a student was asked of the home of Luther's hard-headed adversary John Eck, Schaff himself quipped, "Princeton." After the applause had subsided he corrected himself. "No, he came from Ingolstadt; I make that correction authoritatively." Some time later, while looking through an archive of sermon manuscripts at Princeton, "he thanked God he had come on the excursion if for no other reason than that he would henceforth know one dry place to flee to at the next deluge."[57]

International Theological Nuncio and Mediator

The most serious threat to American religion, then, was rationalism, and the main problem Schaff found was the American lack of depth of thought, which made self-correction of the problem next to impossible. For Schaff, theological ignorance was certainly not bliss and if American Christians were to solidify their faith, they must improve their capability to think on the highest academic levels. The solution was not, however, the kind of orthodox rationalism found at Princeton. Instead, the answer came from across the sea in the form of German evangelical theology. The mediating theology that nurtured Schaff during his youth must infuse American thought with the best of its characteristics. In addition to saving the culture of the ordinary German immigrants, Schaff's mission included creation of an "Anglo-German" school of theology, and his first published works were purposely directed to that end.[58]

Schaff was qualified, perhaps uniquely so, to act as a theological

56. Schaff, "Princeton and Mercersburg," 2650.

57. D. Schaff, *Life,* 265, 291, 274.

58. Ibid., 163-64. See, for example, Schaff, *Anglo-Germanism,* 14-24; and Schaff, *Germany,* 10.

mediator between America and Germany. His breadth of interest and appreciation for the good in nearly every system of thought led him to seek harmony between American and German schemes. His dialectical understanding of the flow of history allowed him to reconcile systems that seemed to be antagonistic, even antithetical. When conflict did arise within the church, he was able to see it as birth pains preceding the emergence of something better than either of the two conflicting systems. His irenic personality and deep piety earned him and his thought respect in situations where similar ideas accompanied with less cordial presentation — the case of Charles A. Briggs comes immediately to mind — might have alienated rather than brought unity.[59] Finally, his impeccable academic credentials in the finest universities of Europe coupled with his warm appreciation of the values of the American religious situation gave him a hearing that few others could boast. Schaff understood his work as a "providential mission . . . to labor as a sort of international theological nuncio and mediator."[60] As his Union colleague Marvin R. Vincent put it in reference to the work of Schaff and Henry Boynton Smith, they had both been trained in the leading schools of Germany and were therefore well equipped to "keep steady hands on the floodgates through which, a little later, the tide of German thought came pouring into the square enclosures of New England metaphysics and theology."[61]

The floodgate metaphor also fits Schaff's conception of his mission because he recognized in the powerful flights of German theological ability some great dangers which he had no desire to transplant in America. The theologies of David F. Strauss, Ludwig Feuerbach, Bruno Bauer, and others of that type were characterized by "keen penetration," but such authors "have no more spiritual apprehension than a horse." "A theologian without faith," growled Schaff, "is like a sky without a star, a heart without a pulse, light without warmth, a sword without edge, a body without soul."[62] The theology that Schaff sought to transplant, in contrast, was that which had been described as "pectoral" or

59. Schaff lamented in a letter to his son David that "B[riggs] makes it very hard for his friends to defend him," due to his abrasive personality. Letter of Philip Schaff to "Dear Son," 25 May 1891, The Philip Schaff Manuscript Collection, UTS.

60. D. Schaff, *Life,* 409.

61. Marvin R. Vincent, "Address Commemorative of PS," Delivered at The Century, December 30, 1893, 7.

62. D. Schaff, *Life,* 69; Schaff, *Principle of Protestantism,* 132.

heart theology, characteristic of the best of the German mediating theologians. "The truth," Schaff insisted, "lies not in the extremes, but in the *middle,* or the *deep* rather, in which they may be said to meet! The very nature of an extreme is, that it pushes one side of a truth into prominence at the cost of another."[63] Examples of the mediating principle were common in the history of the church. The Chalcedonian Definition, for example, was not just a "mish-mash," or a form of "loose eclecticism," but an expression of the deep truth which was being distorted by the extreme positions on both sides of the argument.

The distinguishing mark of the evangelical German theology was its Christocentrism. According to Schaff, each period of history must formulate its own theology, which emphasizes a particular aspect of the Christian message to meet the particular needs of the time. For the late nineteenth century, that aspect was the "great mystery of God manifest in the flesh, the divine-human personality and atoning work of our Lord."[64] In order for the church to progress, theology must progress, and the way for American theology to develop, according to Schaff, was to infuse itself with the best that Christocentric German thought had to offer. There was a "believing German theology" that had "resuscitated" orthodoxy, but it was not a stagnant inflexible orthodoxy. On the contrary, it was a "true, positive theology" that was in tune with the development of the church in the modern world. Those who would blindly reject all that was German because of the great heresies that had been developed by German theologians were out of touch with the flow of history. Admittedly, the heresies of Strauss and those like him were extremely dangerous and must be rejected, particularly their denial of the divine-human character of Christ. On the other hand, such flights of intellect deserved grudging respect, since, Schaff conceded, "only an archangel can become a devil."[65]

63. Philip Schaff, *What is Church History? A Vindication of the Idea of Historical Development* (Philadelphia: J. B. Lippincott, 1846); reprinted in *Reformed and Catholic: Selected Historical and Theological Writings of Philip Schaff,* ed. Charles Yrigoyen, Jr. and George M. Bricker (Pittsburgh: The Pickwick Press, 1979), 112 [96]. Page numbers in the original edition hereafter will be noted in brackets.

64. Philip Schaff, "Consensus of the Reformed Confessions," in *Christ and Christianity: Studies on Christology, Creeds and Confessions, Protestantism and Romanism, Reformation Principles, Sunday Observance, Religious Freedom, and Christian Union* (New York: Scribner's, 1885), 169, 172.

65. Schaff, *Principle of Protestantism,* 187-89, 202.

Yet the good in German theology was only accentuated by the contrast. The errors were only the "negative side" of a process that advanced "toward higher and more solid ground than [was] occupied before." "No modern education," Schaff concluded, "can be complete which does not include some acquaintance with German learning." In fact, the solution to the problem of rationalism (as well as the problems of sectarianism and the Romanist threat) could be largely solved if believing German theology were "transplanted into our midst" and made to "enter organically into our religious life."[66]

What Schaff hoped for was a "higher order of theology" that would result from the combination of German depth of thought and American practicality and activity.[67] America was the place where it could happen. "The United States may be expected, at no distant day, to make important contributions to historical theology, proceeding mainly from a combination of the English and German mind, and serving the interests of a sound evangelical-catholic Protestantism."[68] Schaff stood in a distinctive position to help bring about that development. He came to be recognized as a "theological mediator between the East and the West" and was compared by the theological faculty of the University of Berlin to the great sixteenth-century Reformer Martin Bucer, who had been a bridge for Reformation ideas between Germany and England.[69]

Three major projects of Schaff's career stand out as examples of his work as a theological mediator. All three were international efforts that served to facilitate the exchange of ideas and contacts between scholars from Europe and America. Through all three, Schaff hoped to pave the way for the flow of ideas in both directions. From his initial conception that Americans would sit as pupils at the feet of their European — read German — masters, the "American by adoption" had come to see that the new world had much to teach the old. The first project was the massive effort of translation and adaptation of Lange's *Commentary on the Holy Scriptures: Critical, Doctrinal, and Homiletical.* The second effort, the *Schaff-Herzog Encyclopedia,* also involved translation and adaptation but on a much smaller scale. Both of these

66. Ibid., 203-4, 209, 231.
67. Schaff, *Theology for Our Age and Country,* 20.
68. Schaff, *History of the Apostolic Church,* 315.
69. *Semi-Centennial of Philip Schaff* (New York: privately printed, 1893), 10.

undertakings involved the transmission of German scholarship to the new world and its adaptation to the American context. The third project involved Schaff's association with the Evangelical Alliance, an organization of ecumenically minded Christians with chapters in many European countries and the United States. Through the Alliance and especially its New York Conference in 1873, Schaff believed the advantages of American Christianity could provide important lessons for Europeans.

As Schaff became increasingly "American" it was natural that he should turn his attention to the preeminent place of the Bible in American culture. His editorial work with Lange's *Commentary on the Old and New Testaments* was a significant part of his little-recognized but highly significant contribution to biblical studies in the United States.[70]

John Peter Lange, who died in 1884, had served as general editor of a series of biblical commentaries which reached gargantuan proportions. Written over a period of twenty years through the labors of nineteen scholars, the German edition was completed in 1877. Schaff had corresponded with Dr. Lange as early as 1858, when the first German volumes had been available for only one year, with the object of producing an English version of the commentaries. Schaff organized a committee of translators and served as general editor. The committee gave Charles Scribner authority to publish the English version, and after the interruption of the Civil War, the translators began their work. After an exhausting sixteen years, the scholars had produced twenty-five volumes, containing some fifteen thousand double-column pages. The seemingly interminable process had given rise to the saying — which Schaff frequently feared true — "All things come to an end, but Lange."[71]

Schaff's adaptation to his adopted homeland and its language and customs were evident both in his taking on the project in the first place, and more particularly in his directions to the contributors of the individual volumes. Schaff accorded considerable latitude to the translators who, he believed, should do "justice to the thoughts of the author," but at the same time should always keep in mind the "language of the

70. See Thomas J. Goliber, "Philip Schaff (1819-1893): A Study in Conservative Biblical Criticism" (Ph.D. diss., Kent State University, 1976).

71. D. Schaff, *Life*, 233.

reader." The commanding vision was to be an "evangelical catholic spirit" which would combine the "scholarship and piety of Europe and America."[72] In the preface to the series Schaff spoke of both the purpose and spirit of the work. It was to be "a commentary learned, yet popular, orthodox and sound, yet unsectarian, liberal and truly catholic in spirit and aim."[73]

An interesting example of "Americanization" in the commentary series was Schaff's addendum to his translation of the commentary on Matthew 22:20-21. In that passage, the Pharisees confronted Jesus with the question of Jewish loyalty to the Roman government. Jesus asked for a coin and whose image was stamped on it. Upon receiving the answer "Caesar's," he instructed his hearers to "Render therefore unto Caesar the things which are Caesar's; and unto God the things that are God's." Lange interpreted the passage as instructing Christians to be obedient in "all the obligations to the State," yet to remember that "this obedience must ever be conditioned by obedience to God." Schaff agreed with that interpretation, but added the distinctly American notion that the civil and religious authorities "ought to be kept distinct and independent in their respective spheres without mixture and confusion, and yet without antagonism, but in friendly relation in view of their common origin in God, and their common end and completion in the *Basileia tas doxas* [kingdom of glory], where God shall be all in all."[74]

A much smaller but more enduring work was the *Schaff-Herzog Encyclopedia.* Originally published in German and arranged and edited by Johann Jakob Herzog, the American edition was begun by John Henry Augustus Bomberger and taken over by Schaff in 1879. He carried the project to completion and published the *Schaff-Herzog* in three volumes in 1882-84. As with other projects of this nature in which Schaff became involved, this effort became more complicated than he had originally envisioned. The original publisher, Scranton and Company of Hartford, had recruited Schaff for the project, but withdrew its support when costs

72. Ibid., 231-32.

73. John Peter Lange, *A Commentary on the Holy Scriptures: Critical, Doctrinal, and Homiletical, with Special Reference to Ministers and Students,* trans. and ed. Philip Schaff (New York: Charles Scribner, 1864-1880), 1:viii.

74. Ibid., 1:396-97.

ran over their original estimates. Ever the optimist, Schaff continued the research at his own expense, including the work of two research assistants whom he paid out of his own pocket, and searched until he found another publisher. His correspondence with various publishers reveals his anxiety to complete the work as soon as possible. In addition to the ongoing expense of salaried research assistants, Schaff noted that "time is flowing rapidly, and what I am to do yet in this world, I must do quickly."[75] To another publisher he complained that a suggested delay "may put off the completion of the reunited work to the day of resurrection when Cyclopedias will be needed no longer."[76]

Schaff was tenaciously devoted to the work as an important cooperative effort to bring together German and American scholarship. He described his goal to produce for theological students who could not afford more expensive sets a useful work that would introduce them to theological work "as much Anglo-American as German."[77] His original plan to complete the work in two years was frustrated by the troubles with publishers and the inevitable delays involved in working with numerous contributors. Schaff lamented his "heavy pecuniary loss" and realized that only a very large sale of the work would allow him to be reimbursed. Yet he did not regret his efforts. He anticipated that it would become "a very useful book of reference," and foresaw its increasing use as "sectarian prejudices pass away." He provided for revisions of the volumes by stating in his will that the copyright should go to his son David and Samuel M. Jackson, his assistants in the project.[78]

Jackson carried out Schaff's wishes for the *Encyclopedia* to be kept up to date, and the mediator's prophecy proved true. "A good Encyclopaedia, if kept abreast of the times becomes an institution. The

75. Philip Schaff, Letter to "My dear Friend" [Thomas Clark of Edinburgh, Scotland], 13 February 1878, Philip Schaff papers, ERHS.

76. Philip Schaff, Letter to "Mr dear Mr. Harper," 8 February 1878, Philip Schaff papers, ERHS.

77. Schaff, "Autobiographical Reminiscences," 52-53.

78. Ibid., 64-65. The delay in completion of the work was no doubt exacerbated by personal difficulties which he called "the severest affliction which has befallen my family, severer than the deaths of our five children." During the year, Schaff's eldest son, Anselm, suffered a breakdown which Schaff blamed on "a most ungenial and unhappy marriage," including the institutionalization of his wife. Anselm's breakdown caused him to be admitted to the same "Lunatic Asylum at Bloomingdale."

German Herzog will no doubt likewise renew its youth after the present edition is exhausted. Individuals die, but institutions live on."[79]

Despite the assertion of Schaff's biographer and son David that his father had been a "warm advocate" of the Evangelical Alliance from its beginning in 1846, Schaff initially rejected the Alliance. Ironically, the ecumenist condemned this ecumenical group as not inclusive enough. The original purposes of the Alliance incorporated many of Schaff's deepest concerns: championing Christian unity and religious liberty and fighting modern unbelief. Schaff's rejection of the group with these apparently noble goals was due to the staunchly anti-Catholic stance of the movement's founders. As late as 1853, Schaff blasted the Alliance as a "total failure" and though recognizing the admirable goal of Christian union, felt constrained to call the Alliance's attempt to limit the kingdom of Christ to Protestantism a result of "exceedingly narrow-mindedness."[80] By 1865, however, Schaff had become an ardent supporter of the Alliance, and in 1869 expressed his hope that the next international meeting of the Alliance could be held in New York.

Two reasons stand out as possible explanations for this abrupt change. First, in 1854 Schaff had visited his colleagues and former teachers in Europe and had found that many of them supported the Alliance. Second, it seems that some of the leaders of the Alliance had moderated their anti-Catholic stance. While some leaders remained staunchly anti-Catholic and saw their involvement in the Alliance as a central part of their fight against Rome — such as Samuel Irenaeus Prime, editor of the influential *New York Observer* — most had shifted their approach from negative criticism against Roman Catholicism to a more positive affirmation of evangelical Protestant unity. To Catholics that shift may have signified little; to Schaff it made all the difference.

Schaff had begun his association with the American branch as early as 1857 when he was asked to prepare a report on Christianity in America for the Berlin meeting of that year. Although he was unable to attend the meeting, a colleague presented his report. During the American Civil War, the American branch of the Alliance had ceased its activities, but Schaff helped reorganize the group with a meeting in

79. Ibid., 64.

80. Philip Schaff, "Ein Blick in die kirchlich-religiöse Weltlage," *Der deutsche Kirchenfreund*, 6 (March 1853): 107.

his home in 1865, and it was formally reconstituted in 1867. The Alliance meeting in Amsterdam later that year accepted the invitation of the American branch to hold the next international meeting in New York. Schaff's association with the Alliance would absorb hundreds of hours during the next few years as he worked to make the New York meeting a reality.

In 1869, Schaff again journeyed to Europe, this time as the agent of the American Evangelical Alliance "to secure delegates from the various branches of the Alliance to the General Conference to be held in New York in 1870."[81] This trip began what would be four and one-half years of strenuous effort by Schaff to organize the conference. He began meeting regularly with the Executive Committee of the American Alliance and in early 1870 began to see that his involvement was growing beyond his initial expectations. "Mailed pamphlets and many letters to Europe," he growled, "in behalf of the Ev. Alliance, which takes too much of my precious time and interferes seriously with my comfort."[82] Later that year, after months of preparation and indefatigable work to insure international attendance at the meeting already postponed from 1869, Schaff was deeply disappointed when forced by the Franco-Prussian War to postpone the meeting indefinitely. "The General Conference is dead and buried," he lamented in his diary. "A very sore disappointment. So much precious time, strength and care apparently wasted." He took heart, however, and noted in his diary the pending defeat of Napoleon III and "perhaps also the temporal power of the pope. God is dealing harder blows now to Rome than the Gen[eral] Conf[erence] of the Alliance [could]."[83]

Alliance leaders rescheduled the meeting for 1873 and Schaff continued his heroic efforts on behalf of this "feast of Christian union." In all, he had crossed the Atlantic four times on Alliance business. The

81. Letter of Philip Schaff to "Rev. S. Irenaeus Prime, D.D., Cor[responding] Secretary Evang[elical] Alliance," 13 April 1869, Philip Schaff Papers, ERHS. Schaff might still have been uneasy about the exclusively Protestant character of the Alliance. In this letter he speaks of the "proposed oecumenical Conference" but between the lines later inserted "Protestant" between "proposed" and "oecumenical."

82. Diary entry for 14 January 1870, Box IV, Philip Schaff Manuscript Collection, UTS.

83. Diary entry for 8 August 1870, Box IV, Philip Schaff Manuscript Collection, UTS.

final time was in the summer preceding the opening of the conference in an effort to change the minds of a number of delegates who had cancelled their plans to attend. Schaff prevailed upon some to change their minds, arranged substitutes for others, and secured greetings from others — including the archbishop of Canterbury and Emperor William IV of Germany. One triumph of his visit illustrates the effort of the Alliance to provide a unified front against revivified Catholicism and to address some of the decrees of the Vatican Council. Schaff was delighted to obtain the promises of a letter of salutation from the third Old Catholic Congress to be held in September and attendance of three Old Catholic delegates to the New York Conference. The letter, he recalled, "proved to be one of the most interesting documents brought before the General Conference."[84] He was disappointed that the famed preacher Charles Haddon Spurgeon rejected his invitation, in part because he felt snubbed by the English Alliance.[85]

Upon his return to the United States on September 25, Schaff found that arrangements for the conference had "assumed unexpected proportions," including the early arrival of some of the European delegates he had recently "stirred up." In the midst of the flurry of activities prior to the start of the conference, he entertained around 150 delegates and American friends at his home. In the days before the beginning of the meetings, Schaff reflected, "now begins the most busy and perhaps the most important week of my life, where I must be literally *servus servorium Dei* and a universal pontifex, i.e., bridge maker between a variety of conflicting national, sectional, sectarian, and professional interests."[86] The conference itself was an enormous success, according to Schaff, surpassing his greatest expectations.

> It was a feast of Christian union and a universal encouragement of faith and hope and Christian work. No serious discord occurred, even during the debate on exciting and delicate subjects such as Church

84. Schaff, "Autobiographical Reminiscences," 40, 42.

85. Diary entry for 25 August 1872, Box IV, Philip Schaff Manuscript Collection, UTS.

86. See diary entries 28 September 1873 and 2-12 October 1873; quoted in Klaus Penzel, ed., *Philip Schaff: Historian and Ambassador of the Universal Church* (Macon, Ga.: Mercer University Press, 1991), 217-18. See also Schaff, "Autobiographical Reminiscences," 41-42.

> and State. There were many explosive elements and antagonistic interests in the meeting, national jealousies between the French and the German, sectional prejudices between North and South, not to speak of the denominational, sectarian and personal rivalries; but they were all subdued by a higher power and made subservient to the general harmony.[87]

The results of the meetings caused Schaff to reflect on the future when "all disharmonies of human creeds will be dissolved into the harmony of divine truth and love." During the weeks that followed, reports reached him daily of follow-up meetings of thanksgiving which inspired thousands who had been unable to attend the conference itself. Americans could be proud of their nation and its unique form of Christianity.

> There never was a better investment of American hospitality and generosity, and one of the incidental happy effects is the better appreciation of American character and institutions by representative men from abroad. The hospitality they received surpasses every thing they experienced before, and the working of our voluntary principle made a deep and lasting impression upon the mind even of those who were brought up in the traditions of the union of Church and State.[88]

In his diary, he concluded, "all my labors of four years abundantly rewarded."[89]

While union of individual Christians and unity among Christian institutions was desirable, Schaff believed that there must also be unity of belief. He was certainly not so naive as to expect complete unity in doctrine among all Christian communions, but he did believe that there was a common Christian core shared by all who were truly Christian, and which all should affirm as a basis of unity. Schaff believed that unity should be based on common devotion to Christ. On a religious rather than a theological level, all Christians were devoted to Christ. He

87. Schaff, "Autobiographical Reminiscences," 42-43.

88. Ibid., 43.

89. Diary entry for 11 October 1873, Box IV, Philip Schaff Manuscript Collection, UTS.

encouraged Christians to "remember that there is an important distinction between theological and religious differences."[90] True to his pietistic heritage, Schaff valued religious commitment more than technical theological expression. Nonetheless, theology was crucial and provided one foundation for piety.

Schaff believed the basis for theological understanding of the person of Christ was found in the confession of Peter at Cæsarea Philippi, a version of which was recorded in each of the synoptic Gospels. This confession, that Jesus was "the Christ, the Son of the living God," furnished "the standard and rule of every creed." All other statements of faith must be judged by their loyalty to this affirmation. In Schaff's mind, there was no doubt of Peter's meaning.

> Christ, the God-Man, the Lord and Saviour, is the beginning, the middle, and the end of our Christian faith and spiritual life. Every other article must cluster around this Christological centre. The creed of the reunited Church of the future will be but an expansion of the confession with which it started.[91]

Schaff worked with a committee that attempted to develop a "consensus creed" for all Reformed churches, and prepared an address entitled "The Consensus of the Reformed Confessions" for the First General Presbyterian Council that met in 1877 in Edinburgh. He argued that the Reformed confessions were "variations of one theme" and that differences were products of different cultures and needs of specific times. Leaders should prepare a confession that would testify to "the living faith of the Church, and a bond of union among the different branches of the Reformed family." It would be an encompassing confession that would not interfere with particular confessions of various Reformed groups, but would unite them by affirming their common beliefs. An ecumenical Reformed confession would not set aside old creeds, but would affirm the essentials of Reformation faith and translate those ideas into the theology of the nineteenth century, while adding a

90. Philip Schaff, "Theology of Our Age and Country," in *Christ and Christianity*, 18.

91. Philip Schaff, "Creeds and Confessions of Faith," in *Christ and Christianity*, 136. See Matt. 16:16; Mark 8:29; Luke 9:20.

protest against the modern problems of infidelity and rationalism. As he put it elsewhere, "We want a wall to keep off the wolves, but not a fence to divide the sheep; we want a declaration of union, not a platform of disunion."[92]

That venture was doomed to failure, however, and the council decided in 1884 that no further action by the committee would be of value. Undaunted, Schaff turned his attention to a movement underway in the Presbyterian Church for revision of the Westminster Confession of Faith. "Revision is in the air," he wrote. His concern that religious statements be relevant to modern people, expressed a few years before in his tireless efforts toward Bible revision, was now directed toward revision of the Westminster Confession. The principle of revision was sound, he believed, and in harmony with his general conception of development within Christianity. In language that reveals just how "American" Schaff's concept of development had become, he exulted:

> We live in an age of research, discovery, and progress, and whosoever refuses to go ahead must be content to be left behind and to be outgrown. Whatever lives, moves; and whatever ceases to move, ceases to live. It is impossible for individual Christians or churches to be stationary; they must either go forward, or go backward.[93]

Creed revision had gone on throughout the history of the church, Schaff maintained, and was a natural part of organic development. Sections of the Westminster Confession had addressed issues that were vital at the time that it was written, but which were no longer pertinent. In addition, Schaff boldly insisted that some culturally influenced aspects of the confession were blatantly anti-Christian. For example, the articles on church and state cried out for revision to reflect the more truly Christian system of freedom of religion. The confession overemphasized divine sovereignty to the neglect of human responsibility, which modern Christians valued. The idea of damnation of

92. Philip Schaff, "Consensus of the Reformed Confessions," in *Christ and Christianity,* 181.

93. Philip Schaff, *Creed Revision in the Presbyterian Churches* (New York: Scribner's, 1890), 1.

infants was repugnant to modern Christian sensibilities. Finally, the anti-Catholic clauses of the confession amounted to "a colossal slander on the oldest and largest Church of Christendom." Schaff expressed such ideas with a view toward "theological progress and in the interest of truth."[94]

As he completed an article for the 1890 *Presbyterian Review* in which he stated some of these and other equally controversial ideas about creed revision, Schaff noted — perhaps remembering events of nearly a half century earlier — the article "is frank and may provoke opposition." The situation was different now for this elder statesman of the church and he quipped, "I have cleared my conscience and am too old to be tried for heresy."[95]

Though unsuccessful in this venture, Schaff remained committed to theological mediation, both on the international scene and within denominations.

Evangelical-Catholic Historiography

The subdivision of theology with which Schaff dealt most consistently throughout his life was church history.[96] A growing interest in historical studies characterized many nineteenth-century German academics, and Schaff's mentors, particularly F. C. Baur and Johann Augustus Neander, both giants in German historiography, led the movement. The Mercersburg theologians identified the "church question" as the most important issue facing the nineteenth-century church, and it was Schaff's particular expertise to provide the historical foundation for their work. According to Schaff, "Church history is the field on which are to be decided the weightiest denominational controversies, the most momentous theological and religious questions."[97] Klaus Penzel has noted that "to Schaff, the Church was primarily an historical reality and not a dogmatic

94. Ibid., 34.

95. Quoted in D. Schaff, *Life*, 423.

96. For an extensive discussion of Schaff's placement of the discipline of church history in the larger scheme of theology, see Philip Schaff, *Theological Propædeutic: A General Introduction to the Study of Theology* (New York: Scribner's, 1894), 234-306.

97. Schaff, *History of the Apostolic Church*, 94.

abstraction." In order to know what the church should be, one must know what it has been. In fact, Schaff's major contribution during the Mercersburg period was to develop the "organic interrelationship which he tried to establish between the concept of the Church and Church history."[98] As Schaff himself put it,

> Church and History . . . are so closely united, that respect and love towards the first, may be said to be essentially the same with a proper sense of what is comprised in the other. . . . Interest in the Church and a true reverential regard for History, every where and at all times go hand and hand together.[99]

Schaff's general philosophy of history gave him a cosmic framework in which to place the specific developments of American national and religious life. The ruling metaphor of that philosophy was organic growth and development, and while the American context fed this conception of progress in history, its roots go much deeper. Schaff expressed appreciation for the philosophic system of Johann Gottfried Herder, who rose above the rationalistic historiography that prevailed in his day to an "apprehension of [history] as *living spirit,* a process of *organic development.*" Herder correctly saw in the development "a constant *progress towards the better.*"[100] Schaff also appreciated Herder's emphasis on order and meaning in history, seen through organic progression. According to Herder, "time [is] full of apparent disorder; and yet man is obviously so created to seek order, to survey a spot of time so that the future may build upon the past."[101] Such ideas guided Schaff's understanding and his interpretation of events for his entire career. As he put it himself, "*organic development* . . . forms the key to the understanding of history."[102]

The entire history of the world, and especially the history of the Christian church, could be understood rightly only from such a perspec-

98. Penzel, "Church History and the Ecumenical Quest," 146-48.

99. Schaff, *What is Church History?,* 25-26 [9-10].

100. Ibid., 89 [73]. Italics his.

101. Herder is quoted in Bernard M. G. Reardon, *Religion in the Age of Romanticism* (Cambridge: Cambridge University Press, 1985), 11, 24-25.

102. Schaff, *What is Church History?,* 96 [80]. Italics his.

tive, according to Schaff. The rationalists were correct, he noted, in their recognition of the "life and doctrine of the church as something moveable and flowing," yet he took exception to their assertion that such movement was guided only by "the lawless play of caprice." On the contrary, the Organizer of development was the Spirit. Schaff sounded a Hegelian theme as he spoke of the "higher spirit which urges forward the wheel of history, turns even the passions and errors of men to its own service." He was not entirely satisfied with Hegel's scheme either, however, and left no uncertainty about the identity of the guiding Spirit. The "glorious end" toward which all history moved had been "established for it in the eternal counsel of God."[103] If one expected to understand rightly the history of the Christian church, the complementary principles of providential purpose and organic development must guide the investigation.

One reason that Schaff's ideas did not capture the imagination of more American Protestants was the reaction of many to Charles Darwin's controversial ideas. As Andrew D. White put it in 1895, "Darwin's *Origin of Species* had come into the theological world like a plough into an ant-hill. Everywhere those thus rudely awakened from their old comfort and repose had swarmed forth angry and confused."[104] While Christian apologists who worked with less dynamic models of the history of the church faced acute challenges when Darwin's ideas began to be taken seriously, for Schaff Darwin merely echoed what had been a proper understanding of growth within Christianity for centuries. "Secular history," Schaff wrote in 1892, "is the progressive development of the idea of humanity, with its 'struggle for existence and survival of the fittest.'" Evolutionary development was a given for Schaff. To be sure, the ideas of Darwin needed modification to fit a truly Christian position, but Schaff seemed puzzled and surprised by the heat of the controversy over evolutionary concepts. Evolution (which he equated with "development") in biology was no more remarkable, or threatening, than ideas of development in other areas.

103. Schaff, *What is Church History?*, 98-99 [82-83]. On Schaff's qualified acceptance of Hegelian ideas see pp. 40, 91-93; [24, 75-77]. See also Penzel, "Church History and the Ecumenical Quest," 156, 196-98, 219, and Penzel, ed., *Philip Schaff*, 123-50.

104. Andrew D. White, A *History of the Warfare of Science with Theology in Christendom* (New York: George Braziller, 1955, orig. 1895), 1:70.

> The modern scientific theory of evolution in nature corresponds to the theory of development in history, which was previously discovered by historians and philosophers (like Hegel). But evolution in nature presupposes a creative beginning and God's continued omnipresence and immanence. In the same way, development in history implies a supreme intelligence which endowed man with reason and will, set history in motion and directs it by an omnipotent will.[105]

In Christian history, the theory of historical development corresponds to yet preceded the ideas of Darwin; such ideas were to be found in Augustine and the New Testament. In fact, Christ himself set down the guiding principles of organic development in his parables.

> The law of progress for his kingdom is laid down by our Saviour in the twin parables of the mustard seed and the leaven (Matt. 13:31, 32): the one illustrates chiefly the external growth; the other, the internal mission of the Church in pervading, transforming and sanctifying humanity.[106]

It is important to note that Schaff wrote these lines during the 1890s near the end of his life, before the goal-oriented evolutionary ideas of the French naturalist Jean Baptiste Lamarck lost out to more consistently Darwinian ideas. Schaff was part of a growing minority in America for whom Lamarckian ideas of development were compatible with the Christian faith. Even Darwin's ideas of natural selection and struggle for survival need not be rejected as they had been by some conservatives like Princeton's Charles Hodge. Hodge answered the question posed in the title of his book of 1874, *What Is Darwinism?*, with the unequivocal "it is atheism." In contrast to Hodge's belief that natural selection, of necessity, implied atheistic randomness, Schaff insisted, along with theologians such as Augustus H. Strong, President of Rochester Theological Seminary, and James McCosh, President of

105. Schaff, *Theological Propædeutic*, 240-41.

106. Ibid., 240. A more complete discussion of these metaphors is found in chapter 7. See also Kathryn L. Johnson, "The Mustard Seed and the Leaven: Philip Schaff's Confident View of Christian History," *Historical Magazine of the Protestant Episcopal Church* 50 (June 1981): 117-70.

Princeton University, that evolution could well have been God's method of development.[107] Yet Schaff was determined not to compromise essential Christian doctrines and insisted that limits to evolutionary theory must be recognized.

The most important limit that Schaff established for the progress of the Christian church was that development must be only *in* Christ and never *beyond* Christ, or *beyond* Christianity. The limit Schaff established may be generally identified with the traditional understandings of the church's ecumenical creeds. That Christ was both fully God and fully human and that he rose bodily from the dead, for example, were teachings this historian believed essential to the Christian faith, and any development that went beyond the substance of those assertions had to be in error.[108]

Schaff cautioned those in contemporary cultures against what has been called "chronological snobbery," and insisted that while modern principles of historical understanding and historical perspective are superior, individuals might even be worse than those of previous ages. It is the ideas of later times that give evidence of the progressive development of history. Institutions and other externals may give evidence of development; indeed, they are necessary outcomes of the unfolding ideas, but it is the ideas themselves (which are but aspects of the Idea) that "rule in the last instance the History of the world."[109]

Schaff also drew upon Hegel's pattern of development through conflict. He argued that "every stage of development has its own corresponding *disease,*" and as development becomes more and more advanced, the disease becomes more and more threatening. For example, the rationalism that threatened the nineteenth century was far more dangerous to the overall well-being of the church than the tyranny of medieval popes had been.[110] Once again, however, Schaff set a precise

107. See Frederick Gregory, "The Impact of Darwinian Evolution on Protestant Theology in the Nineteenth Century," in *God and Nature: Historical Essays on the Encounter between Christianity and Science,* ed. David C. Lindberg and Ronald L. Numbers (Berkeley: University of California Press, 1986), 369-90.

108. Schaff did work toward revision of such standards as the Westminster Confession, and even allowed that changes in the language of the Chalcedonian Definition might be beneficial. Yet doubt of the central affirmations of the latter he deemed unacceptable.

109. Schaff, *What is Church History?,* 29 [13].

110. Ibid., 114-15 [98-99].

limit to the scope of the dialectic of history. All conflicts in history could be resolved in the Hegelian pattern except the absolute antithesis between the divine life-principle of Christianity and the death-principle of sin. In order for that conflict finally to be resolved, the pattern of thesis-antithesis-synthesis had to be overruled, since no synthesis of the two could ever emerge. Instead, a force outside the historical process was necessary to bring about complete victory of the former over the latter. This type of appeal beyond the scope of history for solutions to historical problems would soon be rejected by scientific historians, but for Schaff there was no difficulty. His theological understanding of the historical process allowed him to view providential and natural causes as equally valid. The incarnation had uniquely joined the temporal and the eternal in a fashion that was ultimately a mystery, to be sure, but in a way that revealed specific answers to the ultimate questions of life.

What then is to be the exact relationship between these two guiding models for historical change, the model of organic development and the Hegelian model of change through conflict? According to James Hastings Nichols, there was a contradiction in Schaff's thought between the "ideas of development through logical contraries and the continuity of type essential to biological growth." The solution to this dilemma in his thought is that he was not always a consistent Hegelian. As Nichols points out, the antitheses that Schaff fit into the pattern, particularly those within the history of the church, were seldom logical contraries, but usually differences of emphasis. Normally the "synthesis" between them was no more than "the path of moderation, or the golden mean." Schaff used Hegel, then, as an overarching pattern for the interaction of ideas in history, but the conflict between them was rarely as severe as Hegel's absolute antitheses implied, and in the end it was the model of organic growth that ruled in Schaff's mind.[111]

A final characteristic that helps illuminate Schaff's explanatory

111. Nichols, *Romanticism in American Theology*, 115-17. See also David W. Lotz, "Philip Schaff and the Idea of Church History," in *A Century of Church History: The Legacy of Philip Schaff*, ed. Henry W. Bowden (Carbondale, Ill.: Southern Illinois University Press, 1988), 1-35; and Klaus Penzel, "Church History in Context: The Case of Philip Schaff," in *Our Common History as Christians: Essays in Honor of Albert C. Outler*, ed. John Deschner et al. (New York: Oxford University Press, 1975), 217-60.

model for historical development was his belief that great persons provide leadership for epochs of change. "Reformatory movements," he said, "are characterized by having at their head *great religious personalities*. . . . History proceeds aristocratically. . . . The spirit of the age . . . becomes flesh." Figures such as Paul, Augustine, and Luther were such leaders. Most important, however, was Jesus Christ, who became the key of all history and life.[112] Further, following the ascension and Pentecost, the life of Christ has been transferred from his individual person to the church, which is correctly called his "body." As the church continues to manifest the life of Christ in the world, his influence will gradually infuse *every* facet of society until ultimately the life of Christ will triumph over all.

It was this understanding of the place of Christ in world history that helped Schaff understand the relationship between sacred and secular history. He defined the "historical" as that "which has exercised a determining influence on the progress of humanity." Thus all nations or individuals are not technically "historical," but only those who "have made themselves felt in a living way upon the actual development, inward and outward, of the world's life as a whole."[113] Given this standard of value and definition of "history," Schaff came very near to collapsing all history into sacred history, and insisting that only as secular history was related to the history of redemption in Christ was it of any real value. For Schaff, Christ was the center of history.

> Christianity forms the turning point of the world's history; and Christ, the true pole star of the whole, is the center also around which it revolves; the key . . . which alone can unlock the sense of all that has taken place before his advent or since. . . . All history before him must be viewed as a preparation for his presence. . . . All history since Christ, finds its central movement in the development of the divine principle of life, which he has introduced into human nature, and which is destined gradually to take up into its own element, as revealed in his person. *In this view it becomes Church History.*[114]

112. Schaff, *What is Church History?*, 120-21 [104-5]; Penzel, "Church History and the Ecumenical Quest," 164.

113. Schaff, *What is Church History?*, 54-55 [38-39].

114. Ibid., 56 [40]. Emphasis mine. Schaff also distinguished between the sacred history recorded in the New and Old Testaments and a broader definition of sacred

"Secular history," Schaff maintained, "is but a John the Baptist pointing to Him who was before him, and decreasing that Christ may increase."[115]

While Schaff's scheme clearly subordinated secular history to sacred history, he sometimes followed the Augustinian pattern of contrasting the realms of sacred and secular history in conflict. Their relationship should be like the relationships of nature and grace, or reason and revelation. That is, ideally there should be no opposition between them. Due to human sin, however, the secular "hates and persecutes the church." In secular or profane history, humans take the lead and God is related to them as Creator, Preserver, and Ruler. In sacred history, on the other hand, God takes the lead as Savior and Sanctifier. The two forces, the divine and the human, are sometimes at odds, but the final victory is with the sacred, and it continues to exert "a regenerating and sanctifying influence on the secular. . . . It is like the leaven, which is gradually to leaven the whole lump (Matt. 13:33)."[116] Without this leavening, secular history would be meaningless, all would indeed be chaos. Without Christ, Schaff insisted,

> history is a dreary waste, a labyrinth of facts without meaning, connection, and aim: with him, it is a beautiful, harmonious revelation of God, the unfolding of a plan of infinite wisdom and love; all ancient history converges to his coming, all modern history receives from him its higher life and inspiration. He is the glory of the past, the life of the present, the hope of the future.[117]

Schaff borrowed from his teacher Friedrich Schelling a conception of the ages and periods of church history.[118] While he worked with the traditional divisions of church history into ancient, medieval, and reformation/modern ages, Schaff illustrated the organic model by relating

---

history which also included the history of the Christian church. It is the latter definition that will be used here.

115. Schaff, *Theology for Our Age and Country,* 10.

116. Schaff, *History of the Apostolic Church,* 2-3. The "General Introduction" is reprinted in Yrigoyen and Bricker, eds., *Reformed and Catholic,* 157-315. See pp. 158-59.

117. Schaff, *The Person of Christ,* 143.

118. Schaff, *History of the Apostolic Church,* 36-46.

periods in church history to the lives of prominent apostles, and using events of the apostolic church (30-100 A.D.) as a pattern for all subsequent development in the church. Earlier Schelling had argued that the church had developed from a Petrine type that emphasized objectivity and authority to a Pauline model that stressed freedom and subjectivity. The final and highest development was the developing Johannine age of "evangelical catholicism" in which the best elements of all that had gone before would be incorporated.[119] According to this pattern, then, the era in which Catholicism dominated was the Petrine era, the Pauline period encompassed Protestant dominance, and the church of the future, the evangelical-catholic church, would correspond to the apostle of love, John.[120]

Schaff based his concept of the nature of development on his understanding of Hegel's multiple definitions of the word *aufheben*. According to Schaff, the term denoted a threefold action. First, each new stage in history negates the former stage "by raising its inmost being to a more adequate form of existence." But only the outward is annihilated; the substance remains. As the seed must die to make way for the plant and the child must disappear for the youth to emerge, so the outward form of epochs in history must be destroyed. The second aspect of the definition is "to preserve." Even though in historical development the outward form of past ages is destroyed, that which is highest, most true, and best is continued into the next stage. What was true in the Old Testament the New Testament preserved and carried on. Finally, the term refers to the elevation to a higher state of what is carried forward. The truths of the Old Testament are not merely preserved and restated, but the coming of Christ revealed their deeper meaning.[121]

Given this understanding of the importance of history, it is easy to imagine Schaff's frustration with the thoroughly antihistorical character of much of American Christianity. Even American theological

119. See George H. Shriver, *Philip Schaff: Christian Scholar and Ecumenical Prophet* (Macon, Ga.: Mercer University Press, 1987), 9; and Klaus Penzel, "An Ecumenical Vision of Church History: F. W. J. Schelling," *Perkins Journal* (Spring 1964): 5ff.

120. For more on Schaff's conception of the significance of the apostolic era, see Lotz, "Philip Schaff and Church History," 15-18.

121. Schaff, *History of the Apostolic Church*, 91; Schaff, *What is Church History?*, 100-103, 108 [84-87, 92]; Lotz, "Philip Schaff and Church History," 17.

seminaries, where some lip service was paid to historical studies, were wholly deficient in their actual course offerings. For example, Yale and Harvard did not establish positions in church history among their theological faculties until the later years of the nineteenth century. Andover and Princeton gave the subject somewhat more attention, but for decades allowed instructors to devote only part of their time to it, and even Union Seminary, noted for its progressive character, did not establish a chair of church history until 1850.[122] Indeed, Schaff argued that a prime cause of the divisiveness within American Christianity was the appalling lack of historical consciousness among American Christians.

Once again, the solution to the problem was to be found in a deeper appreciation of the historical methods and studies produced in Germany. The work of Neander, for example, was characterized by both rigorous science and Christian piety, and that of other German scholars was notable for catholicity and impartiality. When Schaff spoke of the necessity for church historians to be "scientific" in their vocation, it was Neander's definition of that term that he had in mind. That is, the historian should be rigorously accurate in dealing with primary sources and should not shrink from relating the story from the sources, no matter how threatening it might be to historical "sacred cows." The historian must also utilize the findings of all related branches of scholarship and "work up the results of these discoveries and researches into a connected whole."[123] Schaff was convinced that such academic rigor could only complement his theological understanding of the nature of the church since God is author of all truth.

That Schaff's theological foundation was also a form of historical bias is clearer to us than it was to him. Nonetheless, we must remember that his work was done prior to widespread acceptance of the vast changes about the understanding of "scientific" history within the historical profession. Henry Warner Bowden speaks of turn-of-the-century proponents of such attitudes as characterized by "three values: an icono-

122. See Henry Warner Bowden, *Church History in the Age of Science: Historiographical Patterns in the United States, 1876-1918* (Chapel Hill: The University of North Carolina Press, 1971), 35-40. Near the end of his life, Schaff urged that seminaries establish chairs in the area of American church history. See D. Schaff, *Life*, 465.

123. Schaff, *Theological Propædeutic*, 19.

clastic attitude, an emphasis on objective empiricism, and a naturalistic bias." While Schaff believed he emphasized the second of these, and could at times reveal an iconoclastic attitude, it was the naturalistic bias of late-nineteenth- and early-twentieth-century "scientific" history that he could never have accepted. Such a denial of the theological basis for history, particularly church history, in Schaff's opinion smacked of the "awful rationalistic apostacy [sic] from the faith of the fathers" of John Solomon Semler in Germany or the "free vent to the sceptical and infidel spirit of the so-called philosophic age" displayed by Edward Gibbon in England. In opposition to such versions of so-called "scientific history," Schaff worked diligently to create a deeper sense of theologically based "scientific" history among his students during his half-century of teaching and writing, and left an enduring legacy of such concerns through the American Society of Church History, which he founded in 1888.[124]

During the 1880s, Schaff had once again become alarmed by the "negative and destructive criticism" that continued to grow in America.[125] His way to combat such tendencies was to help develop opposition on the highest intellectual level. Schaff created the American Society of Church History to foster such intellectual power in American theology, and at the same time to maintain a correct understanding of church history as a theological discipline. Concerning the latter emphasis, he was conspicuously out of step with the emerging methodological understanding of historians in the last decade of the nineteenth century. His belief that church history was a particularly *theological* discipline and not a subspecies of general history became a point of contention both within the ASCH and between leaders of the ASCH and the American Historical Association. Finally, in 1896, just three years after Schaff's death, lacking his personal presence to lend credibility to the "theological" view of church history, the "modern" view prevailed and the ASCH was dissolved as a separate organization, its membership becoming a section of the American Historical Association.[126] Schaff would have

124. Schaff, *History of the Apostolic Church,* 83.

125. D. Schaff, *Life,* 443. See Bowden, *Church History,* 58-68, 239-45.

126. Bowden, *Church History,* 67. Earlier, Schaff had criticized his mentor Neander for the latter's tendency to yield too much to modern criticism. For example, Neander's work lacked proper emphasis on the "churchly" aspect of church history. That is, he failed to maintain the "strictly historical character of certain sections of the

been deeply disturbed by this development. The study of church history was becoming more and more a purely scientific discipline and the question of belief was deemed at best irrelevant to quality historical study of the church. When the ASCH was reestablished in 1906, it was without the methodological focus that had been one of the ruling themes in Schaff's original vision.[127]

Schaff described five periods of Protestant church history writing: the "*orthodox polemical,* the *unchurchly-pietistic,* the *pragmatic-supernaturalistic,* the *negative-rationalistic,* and the *evangelical-catholic.*"[128] While late-nineteenth-century "scientific" history usually avoided the overtly negative character of the "*negative-rationalistic*" period, Schaff still probably would have rejected then current trends as taking a step backward in historiographical development. He believed that rationalistic and negative methods like those employed by members of the Tübingen school had become outmoded. The "evangelical-catholic" period of church historiography was characterized by "a new theology," of which the study of church history was a part, and, most importantly, it was "pervaded by the life of faith."[129] The modern rejection of faith as a valid ingredient in historical work would have seemed perverse to Schaff. Yet it is impossible to conclude that he would have been totally disappointed with the history of the ASCH. With his eternal optimism, he most surely would have found a way to appreciate the advance of scholarly work on church history, and to see the ebbs and flows in the discipline as part of the larger scheme of the advance of the kingdom of God.

Rationalism was a source of danger in America, but Schaff had no fears regarding the ultimate outcome of the struggle. The political situation in America, which was so advantageous to the church in other areas, was beneficial in this as well. "Rationalism," Schaff promised,

---

Gospel history, and the genuineness of particular books of the sacred canon" (I Timothy II Peter, and Revelation). He was also lacking in his "comparative disregard for the *objective* and *realistic* character of Christianity and the church, and his disposition, throughout his writings, to resolve the whole mystery into something purely inward and ideal." Schaff, *History of the Apostolic Church,* 101.

127. Bowden, *Church History,* 239.

128. Schaff, *History of the Apostolic Church,* 63. Italics his.

129. Ibid., 86-87. See also Penzel, "Church History and the Ecumenical Quest," 347.

"will soon starve to death without governmental support." The reason was simple. In the free marketplace of ideas which characterized America, people expected return on the investment of their time and money. The same held true of their expectations of their church. People go to church for spiritual nourishment, he argued, and since sustenance is entirely lacking among those who hold to rationalistic ideas, the free market will insure their demise. Schaff concluded that shoppers for religion "will not listen for any length of time to preachers who take from them their only comfort in life and death."[130]

Schaff made some significant changes in his views as his exposure to the distinctive American situation increased. His appreciation for American zeal in religion allowed him to recognize the value of the breadth and practicality of American education in contrast to the characteristically German emphasis on depth and theory. He expressed amazement that American education had progressed as much as it had, given the obstacles it faced. In addition, he developed progressive views, well in advance of many Protestant and Catholic peers, in his concern that the rights of no group be violated in the attempt to maintain a religious foundation for public education.

In contrast to these modifications of earlier ideas, however, Schaff remained true to his fundamental vision of united evangelical-catholic Christianity in his concern to improve all levels of education in America. He was convinced that the intellectual challenges the church in America faced could only be met by intellectual excellence among American Christians. Therefore, he wrote, edited, and promoted various endeavors that he believed would benefit American Christianity both intellectually and ecumenically. His devotion to education was lifelong and his influence upon theological disciplines in America, especially church history, was profound. His conviction that public education must be founded on religious faith was also enduring. To that end, he proposed various alternative models for public religious education which would both safeguard the religious freedom of students and provide them with the religious foundation he believed necessary for proper citizenship in a democracy. A key to fighting battles against infidelity in America was the union of the best characteristics of German and American scholarship. To that end Schaff worked through publications

130. D. Schaff, *Life*, 11.

and ecumenical agencies to promote the sharing of ideas and to encourage the development of a truly international theology.

Finally, Schaff remained firm in his belief that the study of church history could be both scientific and theologically based. He worked tirelessly to infuse American Christianity with superior German principles of historical scholarship. The legacy of the American Society of Church History is a lasting tribute to his vision of a church united, believing, and intellectually sound.

The intellectual battle was crucial and it could be won if American Christians would only take seriously enough the threat and the German remedy. Yet there were aspects of the American experiment for which there were no European parallels. One such aspect was the separation of civil and religious authorities. To address that situation, Schaff would have to utilize creatively both his German training and his experience in America.

CHAPTER 4

Church and State

The Voluntary System

The month of June 1844 saw one of the few American examples of bloodshed in religious conflict. A mob stormed the Carthage, Illinois, jail and murdered Joseph Smith, founder of a new and increasingly powerful — and for some threatening — religious movement, the Church of Jesus Christ of Latter-day Saints. Smith's death as the martyr of a movement with theocratic aspirations foreshadowed a legacy of conflict between the Mormons and the government of the United States which would regularly test the new experiment of separation of church and state.

Less remembered was the quiet death of Abner Kneeland at age seventy, also in 1844. Kneeland, preacher of infidelity and former editor of the scandalous *Boston Investigator* (with its "cheerful assault on the churches and on Calvinist theology"), was the last person to be prosecuted and convicted by the state of Massachusetts of the crime of blasphemy. While Kneeland lost his case and served sixty days after over four years of legal process, the very conception of the relationship between church and state that had led to his conviction had, according to Arthur M. Schlesinger, Jr., "at the same time condemned itself to extinction."[1]

1. Arthur M. Schlesinger, Jr., *The Age of Jackson* (Boston: Little, Brown, 1945), 359.

The voluntary system in American religion, patented so recently, made such a strong impression on Philip Schaff when he arrived in 1844 that he had to come to terms with it. He echoed Robert Baird's assertion that the heart of the matter lay in the Constitutional separation of church and state in America.[2] How could he harmonize his vision of Christian union with a situation that by its very nature promoted diversity, even fragmentation? In this as in other areas it was necessary for Schaff to modify his understanding of the processes by which Christian union would come about, yet he was determined to maintain his firm conviction that unity was the ideal state and ultimate goal of Christianity. Americans had just begun to sort out the meaning of their situation, and Schaff's contributions played a significant role in clarifying the issues and gaining understanding.

According to Schaff, the "most characteristic feature of American Christianity" was "the *complete separation of Church and State* and the *absolute freedom of religion*" that he found there. This feature of American Christianity announced the beginning of a "new chapter in church history."[3] His Swiss background was helpful initially in giving Schaff a model with which to compare the American situation. In fact, Schaff referred to America as "in many respects . . . an extended Switzerland." He praised the "intelligence, education, love of freedom, and good morals" of the Swiss people, and believed that his youth in Switzerland allowed him to adapt more easily to the American situation than those immigrants from Germany who tended to the political extremes of either a strong centralized government or an excess of democracy.[4]

Nonetheless, the religious situation was more advanced in America than Switzerland because of the legal separation of church and state. Protestantism in Switzerland, along with that in Germany and England, had made a serious error in binding itself so closely to secular power.

2. Robert Baird, *Religion in the United States of America* (Glasgow: Blackie and Son, 1844; reprint ed., New York: Arno Press and the New York Times, 1969), chaps. 25-34.

3. Philip Schaff, "Christianity in America," *Mercersburg Review* 9 (October 1857): 498; reprinted in *Reformed and Catholic: Selected Historical and Theological Writings of Philip Schaff*, ed. Charles Yrigoyen, Jr. and George M. Bricker (Pittsburgh: The Pickwick Press, 1979), 352. Italics his.

4. David Schaff, *The Life of Philip Schaff: In Part Autobiographical* (New York: Charles Scribner's Sons, 1897), 4-6.

Schaff favored a model of voluntary "restraint of individual freedom, regard for law and custom, self-government and discipline," and believed that America provided the best opportunity for the development of such a system.[5] Of course, he admitted, there was always the danger that numbers of people would use their freedom to separate themselves completely from the church, while in Europe similar people would at least be kept within the pale of the church's influence. Yet even with its faults, the American system was superior because of the zeal of American Christians. "Beyond a question, the Americans are a people thoroughly in earnest, full of enterprise, energy and tireless industry. Yes, a people more capable than any European nation of spreading Christianity in spite of the separation of church and state." In fact, by separating civil and religious authorities, Americans had avoided one of the "most fruitful sources of evil in Europe."[6]

Schaff was becoming increasingly "democratized," yet the influences of the German aristocratic pattern still helped shape his ideas. His early view of the separation of church and state in America accorded that relationship no more than provisional and temporary status.[7] Schaff was initially a political moderate and spoke of mid-century European political revolutions with contempt. He feared the social chaos that would result if anarchists were to attain power in America. Later Schaff could speak with deep regret of the struggles — known as *Kulturkampf* — between civil and religious authorities in Germany. During the mid-1800s, Prussia had moved toward true religious liberty, but the situation was abused by over-aggressive Roman Catholics who viewed the free-

5. Ibid., 6. Schaff may have been influenced to respect American "separation of Church and State, of politics and religion[!], the voluntary principle and unchecked growth of religious life" by his teacher Neander. It is curious that Schaff mentions this in retrospect while at the time of his arrival in America he seemed to have little regard for the system at all. See Philip Schaff, *Germany: Its Universities, Theology and Religion* (Philadelphia: Lindsay and Blakiston, 1857), 272.

6. D. Schaff, *Life,* 141, 240. Schaff mentioned two prime sources of evil, union of church and state and the "awful desecration of the Lord's day."

7. See James Hastings Nichols, *Romanticism in American Theology: Nevin and Schaff at Mercersburg* (Chicago: The University of Chicago Press, 1961), 133. In part because of his focus on Schaff's Mercersburg period, Nichols fails to describe the development of Schaff's ideas in terms of his growing respect for the American system and the ideal of church-state separation.

dom of some religious institutions from state control as an opportunity for dominance. In response, the government felt compelled to impose restrictions. The Vatican increased tensions with the papal *Syllabus of Errors* in 1864 and the dogma of papal infallibility in 1870. But the problem was not merely one of Roman Catholic aggression. Many Protestants had supported the infamous "May Laws" because of prohibitions against Catholicism contained therein, but were themselves losers in the long run, since the legislation also proclaimed the absolute authority of the state over all religious authorities. According to Schaff, such political involvement in ecclesiastical matters could never be beneficial to either side. The upshot of the whole situation was what he called the "unnatural alliance of religion with political conservatism, and of liberalism with infidelity."[8]

Schaff was certainly no political revolutionary, but quite early in his career he developed a theological justification of democracy which virtually identified it with Protestant Christianity, and, one might add, which scandalized many of his aristocratic European colleagues. After little more than a decade in America (in 1857), he wrote that "self-government is Protestantism itself, viewed as a social and political principle, or the general kingship as an emanation of the general priesthood of true Christians."[9] As Christ was prophet, priest, and king, so were his followers as members of his body, the church. Luther had insisted on the priesthood of all Christians; Schaff applied the principle to the political realm and insisted that "as a king [the Christian] has a share in the government of the people by the people and for the people."[10] The keystone of the political kingship of Christians was their freedom

8. Philip Schaff, *Church and State in the United States, or the American Idea of Religious Liberty and Its Practical Effects with Official Documents* (New York: Scribner's, 1888), 99. See E. E. Y. Hales, *The Catholic Church in the Modern World: A Survey from the French Revolution to the Present* (Garden City, N.Y.: Doubleday, 1958).

9. Schaff, "Christianity in America," 375. Schaff was influenced by the Hegelian idea that significance in history was based on contribution to the development of the *Geist*. Schaff substituted the church for Hegel's state as the central institutional focus of the developing Spirit, but he also maintained the significance of national characteristics.

10. Philip Schaff, "The Principles of the Reformation," in *Christ and Christianity: Studies on Christology, Creeds and Confessions, Protestantism and Romanism, Reformation Principles, Sunday Observance, Religious Freedom, and Christian Union* (New York: Scribner's, 1885), 133.

of choice in religious matters apart from any interference by the state. Yet the question remained of limitations on democratic freedom. As he explored the American religious and political landscape, Schaff discovered territories that required boundaries.

Mormons and Catholics

Schaff first directly commented on church-state separation in America in *The Principle of Protestantism.* This expanded version of his inaugural address as professor of church history at Mercersburg contained a series of "Theses for the Time" which summarized the arguments of the treatise. In the theses that discussed the "present state of the church," Schaff lamented the growing separation since the time of the Reformation between the "secular interests — science, art, government, and social life," and the church. Such a separation had resulted in a "false position," according to Schaff, since "the idea of the kingdom of God requires that all divinely constituted forms and spheres of life should be brought to serve him in the most intimate alliance with religion, that God may be all in all."[11] Schaff later identified "an abstract separation of religion from the divinely established order of the world in other spheres" as one of the six parts of the "great defect" of the orthodox Protestantism of his day, and, although he did not specify, he obviously had the Protestantism of America foremost in his mind.[12]

After having spent a few years in America, Schaff began to appre-

11. Philip Schaff, *The Principle of Protestantism,* trans. John W. Nevin (Chambersburg, Penn.: Publication Office of the German Reformed Church, 1845; reprint ed., Philadelphia: United Church Press, 1964), 227. Schaff's was a model of "Christ transforming culture." See H. Richard Niebuhr, *Christ and Culture* (New York: Harper & Row, 1951); Mark A. Noll, *One Nation Under God: Christian Faith and Political Action in America* (New York: Harper & Row, 1988), esp. pp. 14-31.

12. Schaff, *Principle of Protestantism,* 227-28. The six parts of the "want of an adequate conception of the nature of the church and of its relation to the individual Christian on the one hand, and the general life of man on the other," include indifference toward sectarian division in the church, lack of respect for history, undervaluation of the sacraments, overemphasis on preaching to the neglect of liturgy, lack of understanding of the leaven-like nature of the gospel as it pervades *all* spheres of life, and a lack of understanding of development in Christianity.

ciate more fully the benefits of the system of separation, and in 1848-49 he expressed his maturing ideas in a series designed to serve as an "Introduction to the Church History of the United States."[13] According to Schaff, the American pattern of separation was an unqualified benefit to the church. "The State," he insisted, "lays not the smallest hindrances in the way of the purely religious operations of the Church, but affords her the protection of its laws, and, despite its deistic theory, nevertheless professes adherence to Christianity, and that too to Protestantism."[14]

At this point in his career Schaff still believed that this "state of separation" was not "the normal and ideal" relationship between civil and religious authorities, but it was a transition step in God's plan, and was "infinitely preferable to the slavish dependence upon the State" that prevailed in Europe. In fact, Europe itself was moving in the direction of freedom, and in regard to separation of church and state, he insisted — to the delight of his American readers and to the consternation of any Europeans who might be listening — this was one of "many things that the mother might then learn of the daughter."[15]

By the time of his lectures in Germany on American religion and society in 1854, Schaff had become a firm believer in separation of church and state and attempted to explain the theoretical foundations of the American system to his audiences. Schaff carefully steered a middle course between objective representation of the merits of the American situation (and his own approval of that situation) and the frequently hostile attitudes of his audiences toward separation of civil and religious authorities. Schaff undoubtedly desired to give evidence of the success of his "mission" to America, and must have been acutely aware that what he was about to say would sound like surrender to ecclesiastical anarchy. Nonetheless, with a boldness reminiscent of his inaugural address, he forged ahead. After a brief discussion of the benefits that accrued for America because of its distinctive Protestant foundations in contrast to the Roman Catholic heritage of the old world, he plunged into a dis-

13. Schaff had alluded to church-state separation in his ordination sermon of 1844, but spent no time discussing the theoretical grounds for the division and only pointed out the lamentable results of the situation. Philip Schaff, "Introduction to the Church History of the United States," *German Reformed Messenger* 14 (Dec. 20, 1848–Feb. 21, 1849): 2754, 2760, 2768, 2776, 2784, 2788, 2792.

14. Ibid., 2792.

15. Ibid.

cussion of the benefits of church-state separation.[16] According to Schaff, America had proved, once and for all, that the church could survive, even thrive, when separated from the patronage of the state. Civil leaders had no inherent power within the American churches, and, in fact, were forbidden to exercise influence within them on the basis of their political offices. They could, however, be members of particular denominational bodies just like ordinary citizens and exercise whatever influence they might have through proper church channels.

To the surprise of his European hearers, Schaff alleged that the situation of the church in America was actually one of great advantage. It was protected by the state authority, yet was accorded freedom to manage its own affairs with an independence not enjoyed in Europe by either the established churches or tolerated dissenting bodies. Had their former student capitulated to the religious anarchy of the new world? Had he abandoned the common dream of Christian unity? By no means. While Schaff admitted, to the relief of his audience, that he could not "vindicate this separation of church and state as the perfect and final relation between the two" — since he insisted that the church should permeate all aspects of society like leaven — yet the system worked impressively in America and religion flourished. In addition, the government respected equally the rights of *all* persons and groups within the state. In contrast to situations in other countries in which either one or the other of the authorities absorbed its counterpart, the American situation was distinctive. Neither authority annihilated the other and their relationship was one of "an amicable separation of the two in their spheres of outward operation; and thus equally the church's declaration of independence towards the state, and an emancipation of the state from the bondage to a particular confession."[17]

Schaff came to believe that despite separation, or perhaps even because of it, America was "still Christian" and Christianity exercised "even greater power over the mind[s]" of Americans since it expressed

16. Philip Schaff, *America: A Sketch of Its Political, Social and Religious Character*, ed. Perry Miller (Cambridge: Harvard University Press, 1961), 72. The benefits included the presence from early times of religious toleration and freedom of conscience as part of the foundations of American civilization. Where the Roman Catholic Church was present, it had the status of just another of the many religious communions.

17. Ibid., 76.

free choice based on personal conviction. Americans manifested their Christian faith through "strict observance of the Sabbath, the countless churches and religious schools, the zealous support of Bible and Tract societies, of domestic and foreign missions, the numerous revivals, the general attendance on divine worship, and the custom of family devotion," all of which demonstrated the greater outward effect, at least, of American Christianity than that of much of Europe.[18] The "busyness" of American Christians did not reveal merely chaos, but rather unparalleled vitality. The American churches eventually would overcome even the sin of disunion if workers were diligent and sensitive to God's own method and timetable.

One aspect of the situation that Europeans generally failed to recognize was the refusal of the Americans consistently to maintain strict separation between church and state. As examples of official "transgressions" of separation Schaff cited the appointment of chaplains for the military, the opening of sessions of Congress with prayer, and worship services held in the Senate chamber on Sundays. In addition, he noted legislation in various states prohibiting "blasphemy, atheism, Sabbath-breaking, polygamy, and other gross violations of general Christian morality."[19] The reason for this continuing interaction between the two spheres was, according to Schaff, the "influence of Christianity on the popular mind." Yet, Schaff predicted, the two authorities might well "come into collision" in the future, in ways more fundamentally antagonistic than they had in the past.

As a specific example of the confrontation between religion and government, Schaff cited the limit the American people had placed on religious freedom when faced with the offenses to "religious and moral sense" of Mormon polygamy. That example was particularly appropriate because Utah, where the Mormons attempted to set up their theocracy, was a territory under direct federal control. In contrast, legal experts debated whether or not the Bill of Rights as the First Amendment to the federal Constitution was applicable to the states. Thus, First Amendment freedoms could only be directly applied or tested in federal territories. Indeed, it would be some fifty years before legislators changed that pattern.

18. Ibid.
19. Ibid., 77.

Founded in 1830 by Joseph Smith, The Church of Jesus Christ of Latter-day Saints eventually represented "the nearest approach to a theocracy on a large scale which this country has known since early Puritan days."[20] Following a rather inauspicious beginning, the Mormons began to attract adherents and the attention of their neighbors. Opponents severely persecuted them for their strange and unorthodox beliefs and practices, and they migrated westward in hopes of finding their own space. They were driven from New York, then Ohio, and also from Missouri, when the governor of that state responded to appeals from anti-Mormons and issued what came to be known as the "Boggs Exterminating Order." The governor ordered that "the Mormons must be treated as enemies and must be exterminated, or driven from the state if necessary, for the public good. Their outrages are beyond all human description."[21] As a result, a battle broke out in which a mob killed nineteen Mormons and Smith decided to move his followers across the Mississippi River to Illinois.

In 1839, the Mormons founded the city of Nauvoo, and due to the wording of the charter granted by the Illinois state legislature, the city became, according to Anson Phelps Stokes, "in effect an independent, self-governing theocracy under their 'Prophet.'" Smith petitioned Congress to make Nauvoo, by then one of the largest towns in the middle West, a separate territory, and made no secret of his designs for both the city and, eventually, the nation. Smith astounded patriots of every religious tradition by boasting in 1843, "I will raise up a government in these United States which will overturn the present government, and I will raise up a new religion that will overturn every other form of religion in this country."[22] Since Smith controlled the local militia, the Nauvoo Legion, numbering several thousand members with access to the state armory, it seemed clear to many that he could make good his threats. In 1844 Smith announced his candidacy for president of the United States, and when a local newspaper sharply criticized him, the situation came to a head. Smith devised plans for the Nauvoo Legion to seize the newspaper office, and in response the governor called out

20. Anson Phelps Stokes, *Church and State in the United States* (New York: Harper and Brothers, 1950), 2:42.

21. Quoted in Stokes, *Church and State,* 2:43.

22. Stokes, *Church and State,* 2:44. Smith is quoted in ibid., 2:45.

the state militia to force the Legion into surrender. The authorities arrested the prophet and his brother for treason and jailed them in nearby Carthage. The situation had reached such intensity, however, that a mob stormed the jail and murdered both prisoners.

Even greater conflict between Mormon religious authorities and the United States government was to come, however. In 1846-47, Smith's successor, Brigham Young, led the Mormons away from Nauvoo to the Salt Lake Valley, once again intending to set up a Mormon theocracy. In fact, from 1850 to 1854, Young served as both president of the church and as territorial governor of Utah on appointment by the president of the United States. Tensions increased in 1852 when Young officially pronounced the practice of "plural marriage" a doctrine of the Mormon Church. The expansion of the United States into the West according to the dreams of Americans of a continental nation inevitably brought a final confrontation between Mormon theocratic aspirations and those of the American nation. In 1857 the federal government of the United States established its formal hegemony over the Utah territory. Later in that same year word that Latter-day Saints and Indians had massacred a group of pioneers crossing the Utah territory inflamed American passions against the Mormons.

By 1862, the federal government had been persuaded to stamp out the evil of polygamy and passed the Morrill Act, which forbade the practice of polygamy in American territories. Mormons challenged the act, but in 1878 the Supreme Court of the United States ruled in *Reynolds v. U.S.* that legislation such as the Morrill Act was not contrary to the religious freedom guarantees of the Constitution. The U.S. government passed progressively stricter laws against polygamy until in 1890 the president of the Church, Wilford Woodruff, declared that the Latter-day Saints no longer sanctioned plural marriage. Thus one of the most violent confrontations between civil and religious authorities in the United States had finally come to an end. The Union admitted Utah to statehood in 1896, and ended the saga of Mormon aspirations to theocracy.

Throughout the nineteenth century, Mormons remained a small minority whose theocratic designs had little chance of success in America. In contrast, another group that would be deeply involved in issues concerning the relationship of church and state had become, by 1850, the largest single denomination in America.[23] The rapid growth and influence of the Roman Catholic Church caused numerous conflicts with the "great Protestant majority."[24] Already there had been what Schaff called "slight skirmishes" in Philadelphia and Charlestown, Massachusetts, where mobs rioted and burned in response to what they perceived as Catholic immoralities and attacks on the Bible. The key church-state issues involved were based on Catholic objections to the Protestant character of religious instruction in public schools (including enforced reading of Protestant versions of the Bible), the question of using public funds to support sectarian schools, and the issue of trustee ownership of church property.

Various legislatures during the mid-nineteenth century wrestled with the issue of religious instruction in the increasingly popular public schools. A common consensus emerged that religious instruction was essential, and most agreed that it should be Protestant in substance, though not sectarian. Problems arose, however, when Catholics refused to accept the "common Christianity" that undergirded nondenominational Protestant instruction, and labeled Protestantism and the Protestant King James Version of the Bible as "sectarian." Schaff found Catholic motives for their opposition to the Protestant flavor of the public schools more understandable than most of his Protestant peers did. Rather than citing a popish conspiracy to take over the minds of American children or Romanist hatred of the Bible, the advocate of church harmony and unity admitted that Catholics were merely being consistent in trying to avoid the Protestant influence that would break the hold of the Catholic Church on its young people.[25] He favored religious instruction in the public schools, but advocated a "released time" program during which students could receive religious instruction from a teacher who represented the denomination of their choice.

The results of legislative battles over the Protestant character of public education were mixed. The dominant court decision was that of the Supreme Court of Maine in 1854 which decided that "if the majority

23. Edwin Scott Gaustad, *Historical Atlas of Religion in America* (New York: Harper & Row, 1962), 108.

24. Schaff, *America*, 76-77.

25. Philip Schaff, "Progress of Christianity in the United States of America," *The Princeton Review* 55 (September 1879), 227; Schaff, *America*, 197.

of the people in any state showed through constitutional legislation their wish to continue to allow the Bible to be read without comment at the opening exercises of public schools, methods would be found to carry out their wish in spite of opposition by minority groups." According to Stokes, this decision generally guided rulings of state courts until its reversal in 1890.[26]

Catholics regularly demanded a share of public money for their schools equal to that received by "Protestant" public institutions. In addition, they chafed under taxation to support public schools regardless of whether their children attended them or went to private Catholic schools. Although state and local authorities fashioned various compromises that allowed limited governmental support for parochial schools, the majority of Americans so vehemently opposed such cooperation that accommodations remained local and uncommon.

According to Roman Catholic canon law, Americans must get rid of the "false notion . . . that the parishioners are the owners of the parish church. Such an idea may suit a Protestant community, but does not agree with the fundamental principles of the Catholic Church." Despite the antidemocratic tone of such a pronouncement, Catholic authorities deemed it necessary since at stake was no less than the issue of the full prerogatives of the hierarchy. For example, a number of congregations who had gained lay trustee control over property also believed it their right to choose and dismiss priests, a presumption most American bishops furiously denounced. Church authorities eventually quashed such blatant insubordination, but it took "two generations of tact and trial and error" and numerous court battles before clergy and laity reached a compromise settlement.[27]

"Christian" America

Speaking to a German audience in 1865, Schaff was somewhat less harsh than previously in his strictures against established religion, insisting that he did not wish to undervalue the "great blessing of Christian

26. Stokes, *Church and State,* 1:832.

27. Anson Phelps Stokes and Leo Pfeffer, *Church and State in the United States,* rev. ed. (New York: Harper & Row, 1964), 221-25, 542-46.

government."[28] Even less would he support separation of church and state on grounds of state hostility against the church, as was the case in the French Revolution. Anglo-American freedom was of a different sort than that of the German radicals. It was "freedom *in* law rather than a freedom *from* law."[29] The self-government of the American system required respect for the rights of others and restraint of personal rights under moral considerations. Most important among these voluntary self-restraints were those that resulted from religious beliefs. According to Schaff, the many who joined churches in America did so because of personal conviction, not because of governmental compulsion, and such belief was infinitely stronger than coerced conformity.

In America, where Christians most fully actualized the ideas of the universal priesthood and kingship of all believers, the various denominations would be forced to come into contact and coexist. This acquaintance would, according to Schaff, "remove many prejudices, and foster a spirit of large-hearted Christian liberality and charity." The result of the "noble rivalry" was that in America, Schaff believed, there were more sincere and zealous Christians who put forth "more individual effort and self-sacrifice for religious purposes, proportionally, than in any other country in the world, Scotland alone perhaps excepted."[30] Again, the most important reason for this devotion was that true religion could never be coerced, but must always be the result of voluntary decision. In the American situation of complete religious liberty, Schaff insisted that, for the most part, the people who had made the decision to become or remain Christians had done so because they sincerely wanted to, not because of any kind of compulsion.

In America, Schaff learned, it was possible to distinguish between two types of religious people. He noted the "momentous division" between a "church of believers" and a mere "congregation of hearers." In contrast to the latter, which was formed through Christian descent and baptism, the former included only those who had "living faith in Christ,"

28. Philip Schaff, *Der Bürgerkrieg und das christliche Leben in Nord-Amerika* (Berlin: Berlag von Wiegandt und Grieben, 1866), 34. An English translation by C. C. Starbuck was published in the *Christian Intelligencer* 37 (March 29, 1866): 1. Both references will be given; the *Christian Intelligencer* will be noted as *CI*.

29. Ibid.

30. Philip Schaff, *The Theology for Our Age and Country* (New York: Rogers and Sherwood, 1872), 15; Schaff, *America*, 98.

and who made "public profession of Christ." Americans did not of necessity become full members of their chosen denomination (that is, become "believers" instead of "hearers"). Attaching oneself to a church in at least a nominal way was "necessary for respectability," though such persons were not allowed to partake of the Lord's Supper. If people did choose to become full members, they submitted themselves to the discipline of the church, even to the point of suspension or excommunication for particularly serious offenses. The system of European state churches, on the other hand, was guilty of the "crying abuse" of "indiscriminate confirmation" of all who went through the educational process regardless of whether or not they had actually felt "the power of religion in their hearts."[31]

Along with the prevalence of churches filled with zealous believers, America could also boast less danger of unbelief among pastors and teachers. In the state-church system, there could be no true defense against infidelity because it was shielded under the canopy of the state churches. Separation of the churches from state support exposed unbelief to the light of day, and forced its ideas to compete on equal terms with alternative systems. Schaff regularly asserted his belief that in the free marketplace of ideas, unbelief could never stand a chance against true Christianity, which gave people something solid on which to stand. In America unbelievers were found in taverns and theaters, not in the churches. Schaff shared with his cultured European hearers an American colloquialism which illustrated the greater danger of well-camouflaged enemies: the "serpent" of skepticism, he observed, "is more dangerous in the grass than out of the grass."[32]

Schaff again acknowledged the mutual advantages for both church and state within a situation of separation. Both spheres have their work to do, and it is best done without interference from the other. As much as this sounds like the Jeffersonian language of a "wall of separation" between civil and religious authorities, Schaff by no means intended to erect an impenetrable barrier. He noted constitutional and practical instances in which strict separation was not observed. The military and Congress appointed chaplains, Christian oaths were used to assure veracity, and the foundations of English traditional common law recog-

31. Schaff, *Bürgerkrieg,* 43; *CI* 37 (April 12, 1866): 1.
32. Schaff, *Bürgerkrieg,* 35; *CI* 37 (March 29, 1866): 1.

nized Christianity as the religion of the land. The difference between America and European nations was that the American government favored no particular sect over another — all were equal in the eyes of the law — but the overwhelming majority of the populace recognized a form of common Christianity as the religion of the land. Those who claimed that the American Constitution was atheistic were totally mistaken. Lack of specific references to Christianity or the existence of God did not mean, in Schaff's opinion, that the Constitution failed to recognize the Christian character of America. The relation between church and state in America, he thought, was a thoroughly natural one and was quite favorable to religion and useful to all churches and confessions. As before, Schaff insisted that separation of church and state was not the ideal situation for all times and places, but it was the best possible condition for America at that time, and any attempt to alter the situation and establish one denomination as the solely favored church could only take place through an illegal act in violation of the legitimate rights of all other religious parties.[33]

In an address at the 1879 meeting of the Evangelical Alliance in Basel, Schaff stated that the American people regarded religious freedom that resulted from the separation of church and state as "one of the fundamental and inalienable rights of man, more sacred than civil freedom or the freedom of thought and speech."[34] Despite particular drawbacks to the system of separation such as economic hardship among young pastors and poverty of some congregations, there were more "able, energetic, and devoted clergy" in America than anywhere else on earth. Again Schaff opined that problems in the system were not nearly as severe as they might be in other circumstances because in America at least "the separation of Church and State is not and cannot be absolute." Separation of church and state did not entail a "separation of the nation from religion." The state held no official religious creed and favored no particular denomination, but, Schaff maintained, "the American people are nevertheless in fact a Christian nation."[35]

33. Ibid., 38.

34. Philip Schaff, "Religion in the United States of America," in *The Religious Condition of Christendom: Described in a Series of Papers Presented to the Seventh General Conference of the Evangelical Alliance, Held in Basle, 1879,* ed. J. Murray Mitchell (London: Hodder and Stoughton, 1880), 85.

35. Ibid., 86.

America was Christian, according to Schaff, because of the profusion of Christian institutions (Sunday schools, colleges and seminaries, and voluntary societies), the prevalence of Christian practices (Bible reading, church attendance, giving to Christian causes, and works of Christian charity), respect for clergy, and the Christian consciousness of national leaders evidenced by national days of thanksgiving and prayer. Christianity was part of the common law of the land, and most importantly for Schaff's understanding, it was "deeply rooted in national habits, which are even stronger than laws."[36] Nonetheless, the actions of various groups within American society threatened to erode these habits, and Schaff sensed that conflict between civil and religious authorities could hardly be avoided. As always, however, he was able to view conflict as the crucible out of which a refined and strengthened relationship would emerge which would benefit both authorities.

Church and State in the United States

Schaff's most fully developed discussion of the relationship between church and state in America appeared on the occasion of the centennial of the Constitution. He focused on "that part of the Constitution which protects us against the despotism of a state church, and guarantees to us the free exercise and enjoyment of religion, as an inherent, inviolable, and inalienable right of every man." His study was, as he put it, the first analysis of the First Amendment "from the stand-point of a church historian and theologian."[37] The frequency with which the topic of church and state is debated today obscures the novelty of Schaff's effort. Today's debate is based on numerous precedents, many of which have been set in the last few decades. At the time of the centennial of the Constitution, there had been very few attempts to analyze the relationship between civil and religious authorities in America. Schaff explored

36. Ibid., 87. In support of these ideas Schaff received a statement from Judge Theodore W. Dwight, President of Columbia University Law School in New York, which cited court decisions in New York, Pennsylvania, and Massachusetts which affirmed that "Christianity is a part of the common law of the State." Three specific areas were noted in which church and state are in close contact and harmony: marriage, observance of Sunday as a Sabbath day of rest, and the educational system.

37. Schaff, *Church and State*, 5.

virgin territory and his work must be seen as an extraordinarily astute piece of map making that set up signposts for later explorers. There were only nine United States Supreme Court decisions on church and state matters prior to the twentieth century, and four of those came in the last decade of the nineteenth century. State courts had ruled in only a relatively few cases as well. According to John F. Wilson, Schaff was peerless in his "concise characterization and judicious assessment" of religious life in the United States, but even more remarkable was the consistency of his essential views on the relationship between church and state in America. Within just a few years of his immigration to America, Schaff had come to see the heart of the relationship, and his half century of experience only strengthened and confirmed those views. According to Wilson, "no comprehensive analysis subsequent to Schaff's monograph can rival it in range and depth."[38]

The distinctive thing about American Christianity, Schaff insisted, was not that it was expressed through so many different sects and denominations — which was usually the caricature it received from non-Americans — but that it was a "FREE CHURCH IN A FREE STATE, or a SELF-SUPPORTING AND SELF-GOVERNING CHRISTIANITY IN INDEPENDENT BUT FRIENDLY RELATION TO THE CIVIL GOVERNMENT." This situation heralded "a new chapter in the history of Christianity," and the most important contribution of American Christianity to the development of the faith.[39] Schaff reasserted his belief that religion was inherently a voluntary matter and that the American Constitution jealously guarded that liberty of choice. Such liberty, he insisted, was "impossible on the basis of a union of church and state," where one of the authorities would inevitably control the other. What was needed was "friendly" separation.

> The church, as such, has nothing to do with the state except to obey its laws and to strengthen its moral foundations; the state has nothing to do with the church except to protect her in her property and

38. John F. Wilson, "Civil Authority and Religious Freedom in America: Philip Schaff on the United States as a Christian Nation," in *A Century of Church History: The Legacy of Philip Schaff,* ed. Henry W. Bowden (Carbondale, Ill.: Southern Illinois University Press, 1988), 152.

39. Schaff, *Church and State,* 9. Emphasis his.

liberty; and the state must be equally just to all forms of belief and unbelief which do not endanger the public safety.[40]

Schaff used the analogy of the human soul and body to illustrate the ideal relationship between church and state. Both are equally necessary, they are inseparable, and yet they are distinguishable in essence and function. As the state cares for the person's "secular interests" and "temporal welfare," so the church addresses "religious interests" and "eternal welfare." They complement one another, but operate with different standards. "The church is the reign of love; the state is the reign of justice. The former is governed by the gospel, the latter by the law. The church exhorts, and uses moral suasion; the state commands, and enforces obedience." Schaff based his theory of church-state separation on the New Testament and insisted that from the time of Jesus to that of Constantine, civil and religious authorities were separate and functioned properly within their ordained spheres. With the coming of the imperial church, however, this balance was upset and Schaff could only lament the sad results of the situation. "Secular power," he insisted, "has proved a satanic gift to the church, and ecclesiastical power has proved an engine of tyranny in the hands of the state."[41]

With his organic view of history, Schaff had no desire to degrade the European heritage of American religion, and he was quick to identify positive results of the church-state relationship in every epoch of the history of Christianity. The Roman persecution of Christians had led to the conversion of the Empire; the medieval world needed a church which could exercise temporal as well as spiritual power in order to civilize and evangelize the peoples of Europe. Eastern Orthodox caesaropapism also had its time and place, but would be totally out of step with the pluralistic character of modern America. Finally, modern

40. Ibid., 10.

41. Ibid., 10, 12. In his *History of the Christian Church,* 5th rev. ed. (Grand Rapids, Mich.: Eerdmans, 1950), 3:5, 12, Schaff was more ambivalent about the initial union of church and state under the Roman emperor Constantine. "The union of church and state," he said, "extends its influence, now healthful, now baneful, into every department of our history." In general, however, "Constantine stands . . . as the type of an undiscriminating and harmful conjunction of Christianity with politics, of the holy symbol of peace with the horrors of war, of the spiritual interests of the kingdom of heaven with the earthly interests of the state."

European situations of religious *toleration* were not to be rejected out of hand, even though they were qualitatively different than the situation of religious *liberty* that existed in America. Perhaps, Schaff suggested, Europeans were not ready for religious liberty yet, but neither should they cast aspersions on the American situation. Far from being a regrettable situation because its freedom allowed the profusion of sects — the attitude of most Europeans of Schaff's day — the American situation of freedom of religion was "one of the greatest gifts of God to man."[42]

Schaff was careful to distinguish American religious liberty from the false and negative liberty of "infidels and anarchists," which brought disaster in the French Revolution. There were those who desired to create such a situation in America, Schaff believed, but the American system had safeguards which limited even religious liberty within the bounds of the order and safety of society. America boasted "freedom *in* religion, not freedom *from* religion," said Schaff. He further insisted that if infidels ever removed religion from the free American situation, only ruin could result. Democratic government balanced on the edge of a precipice, and only the steadying force of Christian virtue could keep it from plunging to destruction. Schaff sensed the danger that this force might decay and, he claimed, the threat increased every year. The alternatives were clear:

> Destroy our churches, close our Sunday-schools, abolish the Lord's Day, and our republic would become an empty shell, and our people would tend to heathenism and barbarism. Christianity is the most powerful factor in our society and the pillar of our institutions. . . . Christianity is the only possible religion for the American people, and with Christianity are bound up all our hopes for the future.[43]

Legally, the Constitution established and regulated this situation in both negative and positive ways. Article VI prohibited religious tests

42. Schaff, *Church and State,* 15.

43. Ibid., 16. Tocqueville expressed a similar idea in his *Democracy in America,* trans. George Lawrence, ed. J. P. Mayer (Garden City, N.Y.: Doubleday, 1969), 444-45. "I doubt whether man can support complete religious independence and entire political liberty at the same time. I am led to think that if he has no faith he must obey, and if he is free he must believe."

as qualification for political office, while the First Amendment insured protection of religious rights. For the first time in history, noted Schaff, a government had voluntarily deprived itself of legislative control over religion. In fact, however, Congress had merely recognized what already had become an established condition due to the plurality of religious groups in America. Technically, then, the Constitution and its amendments did not institute freedom of religion in a pluralistic society. More accurately, they recognized an already existing pluralism and legislated in favor of equal protection for every member group of the religious community. Providence had "predestined" America to such a comingling of creeds, and credit was due to the nation's founders who in their wisdom discerned "providential destiny, and adapted the Constitution to it."[44]

Connecting Links

While Schaff clarified many of the issues that have characterized the church-state debate in America, later interpreters abandoned certain of his assumptions about the relationship between church and state. His conception of progress in history, for example, though not at all uncommon when he wrote, has been strongly questioned by those who have experienced the wars of the twentieth century and the threat of nuclear destruction. Even more important for present purposes, however, is the changed conception of religious pluralism from the nineteenth century to the present. Though "religion" is not defined in the Constitution, Schaff insisted that it must include "all branches of the Christian Church which then existed in the various States." In addition, he included within religious liberty non-Christian religions that had found a home in America. Not only are obviously "religious" groups protected, but those that espouse various forms of "irreligion and infidelity" must also be given equal status in the eyes of the law as long as their public practices are "consistent with public safety."[45] On the other hand, any

44. Schaff, *Church and State*, 24. See Sidney Mead, *The Lively Experiment: The Shaping of Christianity in America* (New York: Harper & Row, 1963), 19ff.

45. Schaff, *Church and State*, 35. Schaff was confident that truth would prevail in the free marketplace of ideas. He spoke strongly against religious persecution as being

religion or system of belief that "injures *public morals* and enjoins *criminal practices* is a public nuisance, and must be treated as such."[46] There was cause for hope that such evils might be avoided because, said Schaff, "so far religious liberty in America has moved within the bounds of Christian civilization and public morality, and it is not likely to transgress those bounds."[47]

Religious liberty, though based on religious principles, was a civil right and could therefore be limited by civil legislation based on public opinion. Schaff was no theocrat. But on the other hand, he did not need to be. He had complete confidence that distinctively Christian morality would continue to shape public opinion as he believed it had always done in the United States. There would be a plurality of religious faiths in America, but Schaff had no doubt that the Christian faith would continue to shape public opinion in a way that would reinforce America's Christian character. The Christian church must continue to exert vigorous effort to maintain its dominance, and he believed that it would do so. It would be interesting to know how Schaff might have modified his theories had he foreseen the dramatic changes that were to come in American society. By the end of his life, the nation was beginning to move discernibly away from its moorings in the Christian tradition. Schaff's creativity would have been strenuously tested by the thoroughgoing pluralism of twentieth-century America.

Schaff carefully addressed the charge of political atheism that was sometimes lodged against the American Constitution. If the lack of explicit reference to God in the Constitution was a sin, Schaff asserted, it was one of omission, and not one of deliberate slight. He believed that those who sought to add an explicit reference to God to the Constitution were misguided, though he had originally supported the concept himself. Various Christians had voiced their desire for a so-called "Religious Amendment" since the drafting of the Constitution

---

of "heathen origin." The practice came into the church at the time of its union with the state, and therefore, according to Schaff, it arose out of that union. Religious freedom, on the other hand, was the "inevitable result of a peaceful separation of the two." See Philip Schaff, "Discord and Concord of Christendom, or Denominational Variety and Christian Unity," in *Christ and Christianity*, 276, 284.

46. Schaff, *Church and State*, 35-36. Emphasis his.

47. Ibid., 36.

in 1787. At least five state conventions called to ratify the U.S. Constitution expressed regret that it made no mention of God. The earliest large-scale movement in favor of such an amendment was led by the National Reform Association in the 1860s. One of the major goals of this association was to secure an amendment to the Constitution that would "'declare the nation's allegiance to Jesus Christ . . . its acceptance of the morals of the Christian religion, and to indicate that this is a Christian nation, and place all the Christian laws, institutions, and usages of our government on a undeniable legal basis in the fundamental law of the land.'"[48] According to Schaff, the proposed amendment, sponsored by a group under United States Supreme Court Justice William Strong's leadership, would not only have recognized God and Christ explicitly in the Preamble to the Constitution, but would have established a Christian government, and theoretically forbidden the exercise of non-Christian religions. The closest the attempt came to success was in 1874 when the proposal was carefully considered by Congress, but finally rejected by the Judiciary Committee.

Unlike many of his Christian colleagues from across the Christian spectrum, from Episcopal Bishop Charles P. McIlvaine to the revivalist Charles G. Finney, Schaff came to oppose the movement. It is instructive that his objections to the movement and its amendment did not take the form of insistence on the rights of people to practice all world religions, but rather emphasized the inherent Christian character of the substance of the Constitution. The pluralist argument would have carried little weight with his audience. To say that the Constitution was already Christian, however, was just what they wanted to hear. The document was already "pervaded by the spirit of justice and humanity, which are Christian." In fact, "the First Amendment could not have originated in any pagan or Mohammedan country, but presupposes Christian civilization and culture."[49] It was a particularly Christian virtue, Schaff insisted, to recognize and protect the human right of freedom of religion against undue encroachments of the state. Schaff also cited more common arguments for the Christian character of American institutions, such as the oaths taken by the president and other

48. Quoted from the National Reform Association's Preamble to the Constitution of the in Stokes, *Church and State,* 3:584.

49. Schaff, *Church and State,* 40.

governmental officials, the exemption of Sunday from presidential bill-signing days, and, stretching the point even further, he viewed the phrase "in the year of our Lord" as an assent to the chronology which viewed Jesus as "the turning-point of history."[50] While such arguments might today seem trivial or forced, to many Americans of the nineteenth century, they reflected the Christian consensus of the nation. Perhaps our familiarity with such practices has caused them to lose the significance they had for the people of another day. Schaff, however, maintained his "immigrant's sensitivity" to the institutions and practices of his adopted home, and appreciated their full content.

While Schaff did not attempt to Christianize the founding fathers of America as some Christians have tried to do, he did believe that their recognition of divine providence, belief in God, and belief in future rewards and punishments caused them, if not to affirm the Christian character of the nation, at least not to deny it. Schaff had at one time, however, made a distinction between the leaders who had fashioned the Declaration of Independence and those who produced the Constitution. Thomas Jefferson, for example, who was the primary author of the Declaration of Independence and who had led the struggle for separation of government and religion in Virginia, was a Deist and had an extremely broad view of religious liberty. It was significant, according to Schaff, that Jefferson was in France during the framing of the Constitution, since given his understanding of religious liberty he might have sought to "'comprehend, within the mantle of its protection, the Jew and the Gentile, the Christian and the Mahometan, the Hindoo and infidel of every denomination.'"[51] In contrast, those who shaped the Constitution were "all Christians, at least in name." Their conception of religious liberty "presupposed Christianity as [its] general basis, and it never entered their minds that heathenism, or Mohammedanism, or Judaism, or any other religion would ever take the place of the Christian, or assume any importance in the country sufficient to justify a restriction of that liberty."[52] Schaff had expressed such ideas as early as 1857, and while his concept of religious liberty did broaden to include as legitimate

50. Ibid., 41.

51. Quoted from Jefferson's *Autobiography* in Schaff, "Christianity in America," 356.

52. Ibid., 357.

the protection of nearly all forms of religious belief and unbelief, he was certain that Protestant (better "evangelical catholic") Christianity would remain so dominant in American culture that its system of morals would guide interpretation of the Constitution.

Schaff explained the treaty with Tripoli of 1796, which asserted that "the government of the United States of America, is *not in any sense founded on the Christian religion,*" in a way that reflected his developed views. The treaty was signed by George Washington, who certainly could not have intended to "slight the religion he himself professed." On the contrary, the document was merely intended to affirm the neutral character of the government of the United States toward all religious bodies. And for Schaff, neutrality turned out to be a positive. He cited the words of Jesus, "who is not for me is against me," and "who is not against me is for me," and insisted that it was the latter which best described the proper Christian understanding of the role of the American government. He concluded, "a mere verbal recognition of God and Christ might be construed as an empty patronizing formality. Having the substance, we may dispense with the shadow, which might cast suspicion upon the reality."[53]

As improper as the religious amendment movement was, so much more so was what Schaff called "the infidel program." Headed by the "Liberal League," this movement attempted to deny tax-exempt status to religious property, eliminate government-employed chaplains, remove the Bible from public school use, repeal all Sabbath legislation — in short, effect "the entire secularization of our municipal, State, and national government." Such a program was an impossibility, according to Schaff. The reason was one of morality. "The state cannot be divorced from morals, and morals cannot be divorced from religion. The state is more in need of the moral support of the church than the church is in need of the protection of the state." The logic of the relationship was simple, according to Schaff: (1) Morality — the noblest virtues of which were "unknown before and outside of revelation" — was absolutely necessary for the proper functioning of government. (2) Morality was impossible outside the arena of religious belief and practice. Therefore, (3) the state could not function properly without religion.[54]

At this point in his discussion Schaff introduced a creative dis-

53. Schaff, *Church and State,* 42.
54. Ibid., 43-45.

tinction between separation of "church" and "state," and separation of "the nation" from "religion." Schaff's "quite extraordinary sensitivity to the cultural relationship between nationalism and religion," as John Wilson put it, allowed him to affirm their interdependence, and yet avoid either the theocratic or secularist extremes. Schaff's analysis could even be seen as a basic understanding of the civil religion component of the church-state question in the United States, nearly eighty years before the concept was to gain prominence in discussions of American religion.[55] The Constitutional separation of civil and religious authority did not entail an absolute practical separation between Christian beliefs and the nation. "The nation," Schaff insisted, "is much broader and deeper than the state, and the deepest thing in the nation's heart is its religion." The "nation" he defined as the totality of persons, associations, and institutions that make up a country, whereas the "state" referred only to governmental bodies. According to Schaff, then, the state could be neutral toward religion while the nation was overwhelmingly Christian — precisely the situation in America. Although there were "unbelievers, misbelievers, and hypocrites" within the American nation, they were decidedly in the minority and Schaff could affirm that the "American nation is as religious and as Christian as any nation on earth, and in some respects even more so, for the very reason that the profession and support of religion are left entirely free."[56]

Schaff agreed with the observation of Alexis de Tocqueville that "'there is no country in the whole world in which the Christian religion retains a greater influence over the souls of men than in America,'" and told of his own change to that way of thinking soon after his immigration to America in 1844. Schaff spoke of American Christian practice in similar terms. "Nowhere are churches better attended, the Lord's Day more strictly observed, the Bible more revered and studied, the clerical profession more respected, than in North America." Forty-three years' experience and various visits to Europe had served to confirm this view of American religious vitality in contrast to the religious indifference of many in Europe. The United States Constitution was an inherently yet not overtly Christian document, and the Christian

55. Wilson, "Civil Authority and Religious Freedom," 162. Schaff called the Constitution "the political Bible of the Americans" in "Christianity in America," 355.

56. Schaff, *Church and State,* 54-55.

character of the American nation was proved beyond doubt by the incredible religious activity of the people,[57] by various legal decisions which affirmed Christianity as the foundation of American common law,[58] by the use of religious oaths in swearing-in ceremonies,[59] by the invocation by presidents of divine aid in various circumstances and proclamation of days of prayer, fasting, and thanksgiving,[60] by exemption of church property from taxation,[61] by the practice of appointing chaplains in Congress and by the military, and legislation favorable to the printing and distribution of the Scriptures in America.[62] Schaff believed that separation "has the advantages of the union of church and state without its disadvantages. It secures all the rights of the church without the sacrifice of liberty and independence, which are worth more than endowments."[63] Thus the nation remained deeply infused by the Christian religion while church and state were legally separated.

57. Schaff, *Church and State,* 55-56. Schaff quoted Alexis de Tocqueville from *Democracy in America,* trans. Henry Reeve (New York, 1838), 1:285-86.

58. Schaff approved of the idea of a "general, tolerant Christianity" affirmed by statesmen and lawyers such as Daniel Webster, which was said to be part of the law of the land and allowed civil legislation against blasphemy of Christianity and profanity, and in favor of observance of Sunday as a day of rest. *Church and State,* 57-62.

59. Schaff made the allowance, remarkable for a Protestant of the nineteenth century, that provisions for those of other religious faiths to swear in patterns common to those faiths — such as Jews using the Old Testament, Moslems the Qur'an, or even a Chinaman breaking a china saucer — were quite acceptable. In fact, such tolerance was "simply just; and Christian, because just." *Church and State,* 62.

60. Schaff particularly noted the deeply religious character of the addresses of President Lincoln, called him "the prophet of the deepest religious sentiment of the nation in the darkest hour of its history," and remarked that "he rose to the highest eloquence when under the inspiration of a providential view of history, such as appears in his second inaugural." *Church and State,* 64-65.

61. Schaff noted the justice of such a system, but at the same time insisted that it could be abolished without detriment to the cause of religion in America.

62. Schaff cited exemptions from a 25% duty on memorial presentation volumes of the Revised Version produced in the 1880s, which saved the American Committee for Revision "several thousand dollars." Schaff, *Church and State,* 68.

63. *Church and State,* 78. The concluding forty-two pages of Schaff's treatise on *Church and State in the United States* are composed of "Official Documents and Standard Opinions on Religious Liberty." The documents range from Article VI, Section 3 of the Constitution and Article I of the First Amendment and United States Supreme Court interpretations of those documents, to Congressional acts in regard to the Bible and opinions of judges, legal scholars, and historians on religious liberty in America.

Legal separation could not be absolute, however, and there were three particular areas of cooperation between church and state on religious matters in America that Schaff called "connecting links" between them: marriage, Sunday laws, and the public schools. Since all three "belong to both Church and State," he insisted that they all "must be maintained and regulated by both." Monogamy in marriage, reaffirmed by legislation against Mormon polygamy, was an example in which church and state had cooperated in order to maintain Christian values, according to Schaff. Further cooperation between the two authorities, he hoped, might help assure the "safety and prosperity of the family" by stronger legislation against divorce.[64]

The observance of the "Christian Sabbath" was also an area of cooperation between civil and religious authorities because of the dual character of the day. Civil authorities must uphold Sabbath observance because of its social value as a day of rest. In addition, there could be legal restrictions placed on Sunday activities in order to safeguard its religious function. Schaff cited a New York Supreme Court decision which prohibited "theatrical and dramatic performances" on Sunday, since they fell under the general category of actions "which tend to the destruction of the morals of the people, and disturb the peace and good order of society."[65]

Finally, the public schools were both civil, since supported by state funds, and religious, since they helped shape the morals of American children. Schaff admitted that "the relation of state education to religion is a most important and most difficult problem, which will agitate the country for a long time." Yet he was sure that church and state could cooperate and the goals of each be reached. Moral education could not be abandoned to the state, since it might allow the teaching of rationalism as in some European countries, and parents could not be expected to send their children to "godless" schools. The family and the church, however, could take the initiative in moral education, and the schools could allow voluntary religious education. As a result there would be the opportunity for "every man to become a gentleman, for every woman to become a lady, and for all to become good Christians."[66]

64. *Church and State,* 68-69.
65. Ibid., 71.
66. Ibid., 78.

Each of the three "connecting links" would allow cooperation between church and state, and despite occasional confrontations, Schaff was certain that harmony between the authorities could exist to the benefit of all Americans.

Schaff's approach showed a growing acceptance and approval of the American situation of separation of church and state and gave evidence of his "Americanization." David Schaff's preface to the biography of his father speaks of Philip's "thorough adaptation of himself to American institutions and modes of thought." His defense of the American genius of separated civil and ecclesiastical authorities provides one of the most clear-cut examples of this process. Given the benefits of separation of church and state, it was obvious to Schaff that adaptation to that system was wise and valuable. The goal of the entire church must still be to realize its "oneness," but it must also "adjust to the modern conditions of religious and political freedom."[67] Schaff's grappling with the issue of the relationship of church and state in America is a prime example of the way he harmonized a situation that promoted diversity with his fundamental goal of unity.

Freedom of religion meant not only freedom of the denominations, but also liberty to establish organizations which could supplement the work of the churches. This churchman eventually came to value the work of many voluntary societies. That he became deeply involved in some of them is another example of his growing understanding of and appreciation for American Christianity.

67. Philip Schaff, *The Reunion of Christendom: A Paper Prepared for the Parliament of Religions and the National Conference of the Evangelical Alliance Held in Chicago, September and October, 1893* (New York: Evangelical Alliance Office, 1893), 329.

CHAPTER 5

Shaping Christian America

American Busyness

Philip Schaff understood America as a land of activity and Americans as a people of action. The theory of separation of religious and civil authorities quite naturally bore fruit in the formation of associations joined voluntarily by persons who agreed on a particular course of action. Certain voids were created when state control left ecclesiastical groups on their own; voluntary ecclesiastical organizations helped fill these voids. In *Democracy in America*, Alexis de Tocqueville noted the American tendency to form associations in order to bring about desired social changes. His thesis was that in a democracy all persons have but limited individual influence, in contrast to the strong influence of the leading members of an aristocracy. Therefore, political clout in democracies is "artificially created" through the union of a number of individuals in voluntary associations.[1] Such a pattern, if applied to Christian denominations, can help explain the rise of voluntary organizations for Christian purposes and also helps explain Schaff's involvement in them. Individual Christians or an isolated denomination could exert only limited influence on American society, but when members formed interdenominational bodies they multiplied their influence.

1. Alexis de Tocqueville, *Democracy in America,* ed. J. P. Mayer, trans. George Lawrence (Garden City, N.Y.: Anchor Books, Doubleday, 1969), 513-17. Such groups were deemed so important by Tocqueville that he insisted "nothing, in my view, more deserves attention than the intellectual and moral associations in America."

While he always recognized the practical good performed by such societies, Schaff's theoretical dilemma was that voluntary Christian associations were often no more than additional evidence of the fragmentation of the American church. For some, the associations even took the place of church membership and involvement. The associations had become a fact of life in American Christianity, but how could one whose fundamental vision called for the union of the church accept such institutions, and in fact come to be an ardent supporter of them? How could Schaff harmonize his assertion that the "church question" was the primary issue of the age with his involvement in organizations that could only further cloud American Christians' understanding of the church? Schaff was able to answer these questions by incorporating voluntary Christian associations into his vision as contributors to Christian union.

Perhaps the most illuminating development in America that revealed the church adapting to a situation of religious freedom with characteristically American activism was the emergence of such voluntary associations. Schaff's America was a land of numerous ecclesiastical associations; America's Schaff became more and more involved in such movements. His situation, at first geographically, ethnically, and denominationally isolated, more and more came to reflect his ideals. After he left Mercersburg, Schaff devoted his life increasingly to interdenominational activities as he became more "American" in theory and practice. His attachment to voluntary associations with social reform agendas helps illustrate this development. Three movements with which he was associated that spawned numerous voluntary societies were the temperance crusade, efforts to encourage stricter Sabbath observance, and projects concerned with translation and dissemination of the Bible. Far from being merely the loci of single-issue concerns, Schaff viewed these various crusades as part of the larger mission to permeate American society with Christian influence and to unify the church of Christ.

Before discussing Schaff's role in these associations, however, it is important to understand his developing ideas about the forms of Christianity which helped make those societies so prominent in America.

The Revivalist Style

Since the revival tours of George Whitefield, American Christians had increasingly adopted the revivalist style. Church leaders across the denominational spectrum found that the gospel had to be presented in ways that would attract shoppers in the free marketplace of ideas. While noble rivalry in marketing the gospel was acceptable and even beneficial, Schaff had little regard for those who would practice proselytism, or those who believed that in America toleration of necessity meant indifferentism. The American, Schaff believed, had a paradoxical character. He was "as intolerant as he is tolerant," and, in fact, "in many things he is even decidedly fanatical." One may choose to join whatever denomination one pleases, and the denominations, of necessity, must peacefully coexist, but within each denomination particular beliefs were held with great tenacity, and dissenters were subject to severe discipline — as Schaff had learned through personal experience. Indifference was not a significant problem in Schaff's America, as some like Tocqueville had assumed.[2]

Some engaged in the "noble rivalry," however, were guilty of proselytism. Though Schaff's colleague John Williamson Nevin was more outspoken in his opposition to revivalism which produced much of this proselytism, Schaff also voiced objections to many of the abuses of the revivalistic style. At this point, Schaff again came into direct conflict with the prevailing emphasis in American Protestantism. As the Reverend Calvin Colton put it in the early 1830s, revivals "have become the grand absorbing theme and aim of the American religious world — of all that part of it, which can claim to participate in the more active spirit of the age."[3] Revivals renewed the churches. Denominational memberships exploded numerically as professional revivalists and pastors embued with the revivalist spirit brought thousands into the fold. Lives changed, a

2. See Martin E. Marty, *Religion and Republic: The American Circumstance* (Boston: Beacon Press, 1987), 53-76. Klaus Penzel cites the source of this conception of toleration within strong personal belief as coming from Schleiermacher. Penzel, "Church History and the Ecumenical Quest" (Th.D. diss., Union Theological Seminary, New York, 1962), 211.

3. Calvin Colton, *History and Character of American Revivals of Religion*, 2nd ed. (London, 1832), 59, quoted in Charles C. Cole, Jr., *The Social Ideas of the Northern Evangelists, 1826-1860* (New York: Columbia University Press, 1954), 71.

Protestant empire developed which would usher in the millennium; or so many American Christians thought. According to Schaff, what those in tune with the "more active spirit of the age" failed to see was that these assumed ends did not justify the means through which they supposedly came about. "New measures" revivalism, which Schaff too facilely identified with the style of Methodism, was tainted by "impure motives of proselytism," and was frequently guilty of "the boldest aggressions on other churches, thinking that it alone can really convert." While the new measures might, under proper direction, produce awakened and devout religious life, the fact remained, according to Schaff, that they had led to "most injurious outbreaks of religious fanaticism," and most serious of all, had "nourished a most dangerous distrust of the ordinary means of grace, the calm preaching of the Word, the sacraments, and catechetical instruction."[4] Often, these new measures, these "quack appliances," affected "the nerves far more than the soul."[5]

Not only did new measures revivalism affect the Methodist Church, but it also gained favor within other denominations, including the German Reformed Church. Schaff maintained that such measures could be used appropriately in opposition to "indifferentism and lifeless formalism" which often crept into the churches, but that there must also remain "maintenance of a solid churchly religious life, resting on sound knowledge, wrought through the old yet ever new and effective measures of the Word and the sacraments."[6] The problem in America was that revivalists often sorely neglected "churchly religious life," "sound knowledge," and "the Word and the sacraments" in favor of emotionalism and sensationalism. Renewal would come and society would be transformed — of this Schaff was as sure as any revivalist — but lasting results could only come through historically proven means.

As was characteristic of Schaff, the entire phenomenon could not be dismissed without a legitimate effort to find something good in it. One revivalist whom Schaff found acceptable was D. L. Moody. By the late 1870s the churchman's mind had changed somewhat about mass

4. Philip Schaff, *America: A Sketch of Its Political, Social and Religious Character*, ed. Perry Miller (Cambridge: Harvard University Press, 1961), 138, 143.

5. Philip Schaff, *The Principle of Protestantism*, trans. John W. Nevin (Chambersburg, Penn.: Publication Office of the German Reformed Church, 1845; reprint ed., Philadelphia: United Church Press, 1964), 168.

6. Schaff, *America*, 158-59.

revivals, and he expressed appreciation for the evangelist's work in New York City in 1876. Probably because Moody did not try to form a sect of his own, and because he encouraged those converted or revived at his meetings to remain in or join a local congregation, Schaff insisted that it would be "a sin to act or speak against such a religious revival." He called one meeting "a wonderful phenomenon, altogether exceptional. If only Christ be preached and souls converted." The professors at Union even dismissed classes for two days so that their students might attend Moody's meetings, and "study practical theology at the feet of the fisherman of Galilee." Schaff sat on the platform and "took some part in the exercises" on March 30 and attended the closing service of the revival on April 19. He noted the "immense crowd" and remarked on the close of "the most remarkable revival in America, 10 weeks in all." In the last months of his life, Schaff again expressed a desire to hear Moody, whose revival in Chicago was going on during meetings of the World's Parliament of Religions in 1893.[7]

Schaff's growing appreciation for some aspects of American revivalism was paralleled by his involvement in some of the voluntary associations that the revivals had helped to nurture.

Drying Out the Alcoholic Republic

The interconnectedness of voluntary associations and their memberships is revealed in Schaff's involvement with the closely related Sabbath observance and temperance movements. "The American Sabbath," he lamented, "is in danger of being crucified between two thieves, — Irish whiskey and German beer."[8] Part of the problem, then, was ethnic; Schaff's German countrymen and the Irish who flooded into

7. Philip Schaff, "Diary" (1876), entries from 14 February, 29 March, 30 March, 19 April, The Philip Schaff Manuscript Collection, The Burke Library, Union Theological Seminary, New York.

8. David Schaff, *The Life of Philip Schaff: In Part Autobiographical* (New York: Scribner's, 1897), 226. For more detailed discussions of the "Christian America" theme, see Robert T. Handy, *A Christian America: Protestant Hopes and Historical Realities*, rev. ed. (New York: Oxford, 1984); Martin E. Marty, *Righteous Empire: The Protestant Experience in America* (New York: Dial Press, 1970); Ray A. Billington, *The Protestant Crusade, 1800-1860* (New York: Macmillan, 1938).

America during the latter half of the nineteenth century threatened to upset the "Puritan" custom of Sabbath observance through their riotous behavior, which was fueled by alcohol.

Originally, the American attitude toward liquor was something of a curiosity to Schaff. A letter of 1847 that described aspects of the American character to a friend in Switzerland graphically illustrated the American appetite. "The Americans," Schaff observed, "have a most extraordinary stomach for the digestion of sermons, and indulge in that sort of diet almost to excess." On the other hand, "in the matter of wine and spirituous drinks they are conscientiously abstinent."[9] At that point, however, Schaff failed to see that in the decades prior to his coming to America, alcohol abuse had been a serious social problem. Indeed, many believed it to be a problem worse even than chattel slavery. An historian of the early-national period in the United States was so impressed by the level of alcoholic consumption that he labeled the nation "the Alcoholic Republic." By the 1840s, however, the temperance movement had become extremely popular and that decade had the lowest per capita consumption of alcohol of any decade in American history, with the possible exception of the prohibitionist 1920s. Nonetheless, because of a combination of many factors (for example, American traditions of drinking, excess production of grain, influx of immigrants accustomed to hard liquor, and lack of suitable alternatives to easily produced and cheap whiskey), the dangers of alcohol abuse still threatened Christian America, and Schaff lauded the continuing work of temperance societies.[10]

By the time of his first return trip to Europe in 1854, Schaff had become a firm believer in the temperance cause. While he could praise the "piety and virtue" of the Scottish people, for example, as being superior to most of the world, he thought that they could yet learn much from the Americans in the area of temperance.[11] Schaff had come to believe that "intemperance is one of the greatest evils in America, and the most fruitful source of crime, pauperism, and taxation [!]." Partic-

9. D. Schaff, *Life*, 141.

10. W. J. Rorabaugh, *The Alcoholic Republic: An American Tradition* (New York: Oxford University Press, 1979), 5-21; comparison of alcohol and slavery, 214; popularity of the temperance movement, 202 (by 1834, there were some 7,000 local organizations of the American Temperance Society that boasted 1,250,000 members); statistics concerning consumption, 232; relative cost of whiskey, 82.

11. D. Schaff, *Life*, 173.

ularly afflicted were the "lower classes, both native and foreign." Especially susceptible to the influence of liquor were immigrant Irish and Germans who worked in the most dangerous, physically demanding, and insecure jobs. For such workers, often young single males, taverns served as centers for social life and ethnic identity, as well as places to meet prospective employers.[12]

The nature of the American situation contributed to both the extremity of the evil and to the provision of a cure, according to Schaff. Because of the extraordinary liberty that existed in America, citizens abused liquor with an excess seldom seen elsewhere. In addition, those who profited from liquor trade had created through their greed "a fearful monster" which was able to avoid restrictive legislation through "bribery and corruption," and prey upon the weaknesses of those who had not been prepared for self-control. This "monster," Schaff complained, "devours the hard earnings of the poor, it brings misery and ruin on families, and sends thousands of drunkards reeling with a rotten body and a cheerless soul to a hopeless grave."[13]

The same situation of freedom that allowed the evil to progress, however, also provided the opportunity for a remedy. As a "characteristic proof" of his assertion that American liberty was based on self-control and self-restraint, as opposed to "radicalism and licentiousness," Schaff cited the "really sublime temperance movement," and in particular the "Maine liquor law." This law, passed in 1851, safeguarded personal liberty, he contended, since it did not prohibit consumption of liquor, but served the temperance cause by forbidding "the manufacture and sale of all intoxicating drinks, including even wine and beer, except for medicinal, mechanical, and sacramental purposes." The law originated in the "predominantly Puritanical" state of Maine under the direction of Neal Dow, the "Napoleon of Temperance," but similar legislation was to go into effect in New York, Pennsylvania, and ten other states in 1855.[14] Schaff called the law, which resulted from decades of efforts by temperance crusaders, "one of the greatest

12. Philip Schaff, "Progress of Christianity in the United States of America," *The Princeton Review* 55 (September 1879): 241. See also Ian R. Tyrrell, *Sobering Up: From Temperance to Prohibition in Antebellum America, 1800-1860* (Westport, Conn.: Greenwood Press, 1979), 297-98.

13. Schaff, "Progress of Christianity," 241.

14. Schaff, *America,* 39; Tyrrell, *Sobering Up,* 252-53.

marvels of self-restraining popular legislation," although he had to admit that it was "a dead letter in large cities," due to corrupt city officials whose election depended on the support of law-breakers. The law would deserve even more acclaim had it not become "mixed up with politics, which in its present state seems to spoil whatever it touches, whether men or things."[15]

Mindful of his European audience, Schaff admitted that the Maine law was not ideal, and that such legislation, in Bavaria at least, would "produce a bloody revolution; for '*der schrecklichste der Schrecken, das ist der Bayer ohne Bier*'" (the most horrible terror is the Bavarian without beer). In fact, considered in itself, the law "goes too far . . . is to be ranked with radical legislation," and even "contradicts the letter of the Bible," since Jesus himself drank wine and used it in the Last Supper. On the other hand, Schaff cited the apostle Paul's instructions to the Christians at Corinth concerning abstinence from meat and avoidance of offense to weaker Christians. Schaff approved of the motives of "moderate American temperance men" who argued for temperance legislation on the basis of "present expediency and moral necessity under existing circumstances." While he equivocated concerning judgment about the Maine law itself, he challenged his hearers to "admire the moral energy and self-denial of a free people, which would rather renounce an enjoyment in itself lawful, than see it drive thousands of weak persons to bodily and spiritual ruin."[16] What government among the nations of Europe, Schaff asked, would have the courage to enact such legislation, and what people among them would have the self-denial to submit to it?

Despite prohibitionist victories through the Maine Law and its imitators, the temperance movement suffered a decline in popularity and power. Legal challenges to prohibitionist laws brought rulings adverse to the cause, and enforcement often touched off violent confrontations that alarmed the populace. Public opinion turned against

15. Schaff, *America,* 39. See also the footnote. Schaff, "Progress of Christianity," 242-43. Yankee ingenuity contrived a number of ways to circumvent such legislation. In 1838, for example, a Massachusetts liquor dealer avoided (for a time at least!) that state's law forbidding sale of distilled spirits by painting stripes on his pig and advertising that for six cents a person could view the pig. The viewer was then treated to a "complimentary" glass of whiskey. Rorabaugh, *Alcoholic Republic,* 217.

16. Schaff, *America,* 40. See 1 Cor. 8:1-13.

temperance and prohibition legislation alike, and the mix of politics that Schaff had lamented left little hope for long endurance of the laws. As prohibition became more controversial, politicians warily backed off from supporting it. After 1860, the number of states with intact "Maine Laws" declined rapidly, and by the late 1870s, only Vermont, Maine, and New Hampshire remained dry.

Nonetheless, in 1879 Schaff insisted that, despite the failure of past prohibitionist legislation, the American temperance movement was "among the strongest evidences of the earnest, aggressive, reforming character of American Christianity." The temperance movement will not stop, he prophesied, "until the sale of distilled liquors, such as rum, brandy, gin, and whiskey, as a beverage, is prohibited, and banished from the land."[17] In fact, what Schaff attributed to reforming Christianity was also influenced strongly by economic and social factors. American drinking patterns changed markedly between 1830 and the turn of the century. Although the total per capita amount of alcohol consumed by Americans had risen slightly after the 1840s, the amount of spirits consumed in 1900 was less than one-fourth the amount of 1830. In contrast, consumption of beer had increased more than twelvefold during that same period. There was still much work for temperance advocates, however, especially since many of them were also concerned with Sabbath neglect, a by-product of the drinking habits of many Americans.[18]

New York Sabbath Committee

One of the most characteristic signs of a Christian country, according to Schaff, was the proper observance of Sunday as the Christian Sabbath. He was deeply impressed during his first visit to England by the quiet of the English Sabbath. "On Sunday," he recalled, "the terrible noise and din of the working days have given way to an almost unbroken silence, and only a few people are seen on the streets except at the hours for going to church."

The way to experience an English Sabbath fully was to spend it with a pious family:

17. Schaff, "Progress of Christianity," 243.
18. Tyrrell, *Sobering Up*, 316; Rorabaugh, *Alcoholic Republic*, 232.

> At dinner we had only cold dishes. No cooking is done, that the servants may have rest. As far as possible, all occasions of worldly thinking are withdrawn so that the people may give themselves up uninterruptedly to religious meditation and church attendance. With these things they seek to fill up the entire day. It is truly the Lord's day.

The contrast with Sundays on the continent was all too obvious.[19]

Schaff appreciated the observance of the Sabbath that he found among Americans, and his visit to Europe in 1854 once again reminded him of the contrast between the old world and the new. Tocqueville had noted earlier that "Sunday observance in America is even now one of the things that strike a stranger most," and Schaff's return to Europe gave him the occasion to call European attention to this admirable fact of American Christian life. In Scotland, Schaff remarked that the "Sabbath is one of the most imposing sights, a powerful sermon, the glory of the land and a blessing to the people." The Americans owed a deep debt of gratitude to the Scottish Presbyterians and English Puritans who first placed this "treasure" in the new world. In a letter to his wife, he reported the striking difference between Sabbath observance in London and Paris:

> The most interesting to me in a religious point of view was the life in Paris last Sunday as compared with the previous Sunday spent in London. What a difference between an English and a French Sabbath! There all is quiet, the shops closed, the secular business suspended and most of the people you see in the streets, are with serious and devout faces, either going to, or coming from the house of God.

Parisians, however, had other things on their minds.

> In Paris, the Cafes, Restaurants and places of amusement are open as on week days, the Louvre, the gardens of the Tulieries, the Champ [sic] Elysses, the place of Concorde, the Boulevards are filled with gay visitors and promenaders, on whose faces you read the love of pleasure and the desire for amusement.[20]

19. D. Schaff, *Life,* 84-85; Tocqueville, *Democracy in America,* 714.
20. Letter from Philip Schaff to Mary, Paris, 13 February 1854. Miscellaneous

While in one sense, Sabbath observance served primarily a religious purpose, it also promoted the general well-being of society. After his move to New York City in 1864, Schaff became involved in the work of the New York Sabbath Committee, and served as secretary of that organization for six years. He had won that group's admiration with an address in 1863 to the National Sabbath Convention. Schaff traced the theological background of Sabbath observance and concluded that it was "rooted and grounded in the physical, intellectual, and moral constitution of our [human] nature as it came from the hands of its Creator." In addition, since Sabbath observance was embodied in the moral as opposed to ceremonial or civil law, Schaff insisted that it was obligatory for persons of all times, not just pre-Christian Israelites. The final element of this "threefold basis" of the Sabbath was the redemptive aspect of Christ's resurrection on the first day of the week. Henceforth, Sunday took on the significance of the "day of sacred joy and thanksgiving." Thus, for Schaff, the sacredness of the Lord's Day was based on the triad of "the original *creation,* the Jewish *legislation,* and the Christian *redemption.*"[21]

Having provided this theological foundation for Sabbath observance, Schaff moved to his next object, a distinction between the Anglo-American and the European-Continental theories of the Sabbath. The theory of the Anglo-Americans called for strict observance of the Christian Sabbath as a day of rest, whereas the Europeans, in their desire to avoid legalism, allowed relaxed observance. Schaff defended the Anglo-American model and insisted that it was not legalistic at all, but was based on a unified theory of creation, law, and gospel. Not only was this theory theologically superior, but it revealed numerous practical advantages. One need only look at the two nations that were the "wealthiest and freest on earth," Great Britain and the United States, to see some of the practical results of Sabbath observance. The Lord's day of rest, far from hindering productivity, actually increased it due to its harmony with providentially ordained patterns of human work

---

Correspondence Box, Philip Schaff Papers, Evangelical and Reformed Historical Society, Philip Schaff Library, Lancaster Theological Seminary, Lancaster, Pennsylvania. Hereafter referred to as ERHS.

21. Philip Schaff, *The Anglo-American Sabbath* (New York: American Tract Society, 1863), 1-3. Italics his.

and rest. Moreover, if Anglo-Americans emphasized the fourth commandment in this way, they inevitably placed similar emphasis on other parts of the decalogue resulting in improved moral sense among the people and strengthened family life.[22]

Nonetheless, Schaff and many of his colleagues in the Anglo-American Sabbath observance movement desired to distinguish between the religious character of the day and its civil functions, and to lay greater stress on the latter. In a land where the Constitution legally separated church and state, many advocates of Sabbath observance carefully maintained the legal distinction between them. In fact, a creative interpretation could assert that the separation of church and state made Sabbath laws possible. The government must not coerce religious observances on the Sabbath, yet it was proper and indeed necessary that the Sabbath be "protected" from desecration on moral and patriotic grounds.

> The religious Sabbath cannot, and ought not to be enforced by law; for all worship and true religion must be the free and voluntary homage of the heart. But the civil Sabbath can and ought to be maintained and protected by legislation, and a Christian community has a natural right to look to their government for the protection of their Sabbath as well as for the protection of their persons and property.

For Christians, however, the legal aspects of the Sabbath must take second place to the privilege of observance emphasized in the gospel. Sabbath observance thus becomes "law to all citizens," yet remains "gospel to the believers."[23]

Schaff lived during a time in which the American Christian majority agreed with his assertion that America was a Christian nation. Any person who demanded strict observance of Jefferson's "wall of separation," at least as the phrase is used today, was considered quite radical, and of at best questionable religious commitment. On the other hand, religious leaders who promoted legislation on strictly religious

22. Ibid., 4-12. For example, honor one's parents, do not kill, steal, commit adultery, etc.

23. Ibid., 12.

grounds were not at all uncommon. While acceptance of separation seems natural to twentieth-century Americans whose sensitivity to separation of civil and religious authorities has been developed by two centuries of debate, the situation was far less obvious to those living in the 1870s. Thus, Schaff satisfies neither those who denounce any religious foundation for civil legislation, nor those who would pass coercive legislation in an America that is no longer "Christian" according to Schaff's definition.

The difference between Sabbath practices of continental and Anglo-American Christians had become more and more pronounced during the years since the time of the Reformation, according to Schaff. The work of the English Puritans and Scots like John Knox established Sabbath observance in Great Britain during the Reformation era, and its legacy has continued since. Schaff utilized his conception of the development of doctrine in the Christian church to help defend the more rigorous Sabbath observance of the British, and later their American offspring. He conceded, for example, that the decrees of the Westminster Assembly went beyond "any other symbolical book or confession of faith previously issued in the Christian church." But such evolution represented a legitimate development in understanding of scriptural truth, effecting "real progress in the cause of Christianity and civilization."[24]

Despite the specifically New England and Puritan roots of the American practice of Sabbath observance, Schaff could say that in his time, it had taken on a truly national character. "It is," he insisted, "entrenched in our national habits, embodied in our creeds, and guarded by our civil legislation." Sabbath observance had become an essential

24. Schaff, *Anglo-American Sabbath,* 19. Schaff's theory of the development of Christian doctrine was based on an assumption that the entirety of Christian truth was present in the person of Christ as revealed in Scripture. Near the end of his life, he wrote,

> The true theory of development is that of a constant growth of the Church *in* Christ the head, or a progressive understanding and application of Christianity, until Christ shall be all in all. The end will only be the complete unfolding of the beginning. All other theories of development which teach a progress of humanity *beyond* Christ and *beyond* Christianity are false and pernicious. Christ is the beginning, the middle, and the end of church history.

See Philip Schaff, *Theological Propædeutic* (New York: Scribner's, 1894), 240. Italics his.

part of American Christianity and morality, and an ecumenical movement uniting many Protestant denominations. Schaff described the "trials and triumphs of the American Sabbath," and concluded that the examples of America's greatest leaders and the decisions of its highest courts gave evidence of God's protection of the Sabbath from all who would violate it. Nonetheless, Schaff enjoined his hearers to "eternal vigilance," which "is the price not only of our liberty, but also of our Sabbath." Because of American religious freedom and separation of church and state, national habits and customs played a vital role in maintaining the moral tone of America. Thus, America needed moral disciplines such as Sabbath observance "more than any other nation on earth." Schaff waxed fervent and poetic in the climax of his address. The stakes were incredibly high. "The loss of the Sabbath," he insisted, "with all its conservative, purifying and ennobling influences, I do not hesitate to say, would be a far greater disaster to our people North and South, than a permanent separation of the Union — this cherished idol of every loyal American heart."[25]

Obviously, these were strong words for a people in the midst of civil war, and who perhaps had themselves sacrificed loved ones for the cause. Schaff's remarks are particularly poignant since only a little more than a month earlier Northern forces had won crucial victories at Gettysburg and Vicksburg. Far from being a war-weary prophet, he was confident of Northern victory, but he urged his hearers to recognize the full gravity of the danger that threatened America's spiritual life.

> Take away the Sabbath, and you destroy the most humane and most democratic institution which in every respect was made for man, but more for the man of labour and toil, of poverty and sorrow. Take away the Sabbath, and you destroy a mighty conservative force, and dry up a fountain from which the family, the church, and the state receive constant nourishment and support. Take away the Sabbath, and you shake the moral foundations of our national power and prosperity: our churches will be forsaken, our sunday-schools emptied, our domestic devotions will languish, the fountains of public and private virtue will dry up; a flood of profanity, licentiousness, and vice, will inundate the land.

25. Schaff, *Anglo-American Sabbath,* 24, 31-32.

More than religious institutions would feel the impact, however. In a litany almost incomprehensible to modern Americans, the prophet forewarned,

> labour will lose its reward, liberty be deprived of its pillar, self-government will prove a failure, and our republican institutions end in anarchy and confusion, to give way, in due time, to the most oppressive and degrading military despotism known in the annals of history. Yea, the end of the Sabbath would be for America the beginning of the unlimited reign of the infernal idol-trinity of Mammon, Bacchus, and Venus, and overwhelm us at last in temporal and eternal ruin.

Following this outburst in the mantle of the angry prophet, Schaff returned to his priestly role and reaffirmed his confidence in his God and his country. "If we honour the Lord of the Sabbath, he will honour us, sanctify and overrule our present calamities for our own good, and make us a shining light and example among the nations of the earth."[26] Though such language appears extreme and perhaps even ludicrous to hindsight, one must keep in mind the uncertainties of the youthful nation caught in the grasp of a terrible civil war whose outcome was far from certain in August 1863. Also, the "lively experiment" in religious freedom was less than a century old and those involved were agonizingly unsure of what the results of the experiment might be. On the other hand, a cogent argument could be made that regardless of the exact effect of decline in Sabbath observance, Schaff is remarkably insightful concerning the shift of moral values in America and the conditions that have come to dominate the nation in the twentieth century.

Observance of the Sabbath was, for Schaff, part of the "bright side of American Christianity," and he believed that the churches of Europe could learn much from this pious example.[27] While touring Europe in 1865, he worked diligently to engender the spirit of Sabbath observance among his European audiences. As part of his presentation of the religious situation of the Americans, he highlighted the "cause of Sabbath and Sabbath schools as prominent characteristics of American Christianity which deserve the serious attention of Christians in

26. Ibid.
27. D. Schaff, *Life*, 229.

Europe."[28] He had, he claimed, "found the most earnest and devout men everywhere complaining of the growing evil of Sabbath abuse and ready to coöperate in a reform movement." In fact, the cause received extensive press attention to the point that "the Sabbath question has been more generally and earnestly discussed in German papers during the last few months than I have ever known it to be before."[29]

As a youth Schaff had experienced profound spiritual influences while a student in Stuttgart, which his biographer claims prevented him from being "drawn away by rationalistic teachings" he heard in his later university years. As a token of gratitude to that city and its people, he helped establish the city's first Sunday school during his visit there in 1865. From then on, Schaff was known as the "father of Sunday schools" in Stuttgart. Sunday schools had been established two years before in the cities of Frankfurt and Berlin, and Schaff advocated their spread throughout Germany. He believed the old world could profit greatly from this novel approach, which was a prime example of Anglo-American innovation in religion.

> I am sure there are great blessings in store for Germany from the Sunday school. It is one of the most effective means for developing the lay element and training up a new generation of Christian workers; it will infuse life and vigor into the congregations and make them active, working organizations of practical Christians; it will promote the proper observance of the Lord's day by giving them useful Sabbath work.

28. Ibid., quoting a letter from Philip Schaff to Mr. Norman White of New York. See also Philip Schaff, *Der Bürgerkrieg und das christliche Leben in Nord Amerika* (Berlin: Berlag von Wiegandt und Grieben, 1866), 52-59; *Christian Intelligencer* 37 (May 10, 1866): 1.

29. D. Schaff, *Life*, 229, quoting a letter from Philip Schaff to Rev. James Gilfillan of Scotland. In his presentations on the Civil War and the religious life in America Schaff developed a concept of development within Christianity based on the threefold use of the German word *aufheben*. Concerning the growth of Christian observance of Sunday from the Jewish Sabbath practice, Schaff maintained that the ceremonial form was "*done away*," while the essence of the practice in rest and divine service was "*preserved*," and at the same time "*elevated*" to a higher sphere (i.e., from law and letter to gospel and spirit). For a more detailed discussion of Schaff's use of *aufheben* see chapter 6.

American Christianity was superior in its "energy and efficiency" to that of Europe, and Schaff argued that these qualities supplied the forces to combat "the two most fruitful sources of evil in Europe," the union of church and state and the desecration of the Lord's day.[30]

Other pro-Sabbath leaders viewed Schaff as the ideal emissary to the German population of America to enlist their support in the Sabbath cause. It is a further evidence of his Americanization that he could hold such a position and exclaim with nativist overtones that "the sanctity of the American Sabbath is threatened by infidels and foreigners from the Continent, who would like to turn it into a day of secular amusement, and to substitute the theatre and beer saloon for the church and Sunday-school."[31] As part of his work, Schaff organized mass meetings of German Christians which were conducted in the German language and used to generate enthusiasm for proper Sabbath observance and temperance.[32] Perhaps Schaff had become more "Americanized" than even he realized. These typically "American" gatherings, which were remarkably well adapted to American voluntarism and the marketplace of ideas, tended to take on the characteristics of nineteenth-century revival meetings like those of Finney and others. David Schaff called them "animated and stirring popular gatherings." Schaff worked to extend the reach of the Sabbath committee to other cities throughout the nation, and to organize similar mass meetings of Germans in large cities as far west as St. Louis.

By 1870, Schaff believed that he had completed his part of the work of the Sabbath committee, and he passed that mantle on to others. He was rather surprised to have been such an integral part of that work, but looking back, he saw the hand of God in it all. In his announcement of resignation as secretary of the organization, Schaff concluded that

30. Ibid., 240. See also *Bürgerkrieg,* 59-64; *CI* 37 (May 17, 1866): 1.

31. Schaff, "Progress of Christianity," 226. Schaff's son David spoke of "the vast odds of deep-seated national custom and prejudice" in America — particularly the large German population of New York — against Sabbath observance, which necessitated "courage and vigilant persistence" on the part of the Committee. See also Document 32 of the New York Sabbath Committee, *An Appeal to the Germans in Behalf of the Sunday Clause in the Excise Law of 1866* (New York: John A. Gray and Green, 1867). This document was published on behalf of the committee and names no specific author. The language and arguments of the document, however, point to Schaff.

32. See D. Schaff, *Life,* 226.

"Providence sometimes provides work for us which we never would have chosen ourselves, and the longer I have been connected with the Sabbath Committee, the more I have felt convinced that the hand of God was in the arrangements which led to this connection."[33] Schaff continued to support the Sabbath cause until the end of his life, but other duties demanded his attention in the years to come.

Bible Revision

Schaff was determined that American interests be served and American scholarship contribute to a proposed revision of the English-language Bible. When he heard of plans for Bible revision taking shape in Great Britain, he immediately resolved to make the revision as useful as possible for American as well as English readers. In Schaff's view, American Christianity was so distinctive that a purely British translation could never adequately fit the religious situation of the new world. American Christians had developed variations of language, new customs, and, most importantly, novel forms of Christianity — for example, denominational pluralism, religious freedom (as opposed to mere tolerance), and separation of church and state. In addition, American scholars had developed distinctive interpretations that had to be taken into account for any English translation to be truly representative of the whole English-speaking world.

The position of would-be Bible revisers in America was a delicate one. The King James Version had attained virtually iconic status among many American Christians, and it would be a difficult task indeed, on the one hand, to assure readers that the integrity and language of the King James Version would not be violated, while on the other hand to convince them that their beloved version was so outdated as to demand revision.[34] Schaff believed that more than any other English-speaking

33. Ibid., 230.

34. On the Bible's iconic status in America, see Martin E. Marty, "America's Iconic Book," in *Humanizing America's Iconic Book,* ed. Gene M. Tucker and Douglas A. Knight (Chico, Calif.: Scholars Press, 1982), 1-23. See also Mark A. Noll, "The Image of the United States as a Biblical Nation," in *The Bible in America: Essays in Cultural History,* ed. Nathan O. Hatch and Mark A. Noll (New York: Oxford University Press, 1982), 39-58.

nation, the United States needed a new version of the Bible, and his years of indefatigable labor on the project attest to his determination that American Christians would play a key role in revision.

One of the primary areas in need of updating and a key point of disagreement between the American revisers and the British was the Authorized Version's archaic language. The Americans were characterized by the "progressive spirit of their nationality" and therefore preferred to modernize linguistic forms. Though in most cases the substance of the text remained the same, the American spirit demanded updating. Specific examples of purely linguistic differences between the Americans and British that Schaff mentioned include replacing "be" with "are" in the indicative case, and "which" with "who" when referring to persons. Practical objections by the predominantly low-church and anti-Catholic Americans included rejection of the British use of "Saint" before the names of authors of some biblical books, and disagreement with British retention of confusing names for coinage.[35]

Schaff's direct involvement in the work of biblical revision began when he was called upon to organize an American counterpart to the British committee for revision. In this, as in many other of his life's endeavors, Schaff acted as a mediator and peacemaker, without whom, according to one observer, the task would never have reached completion. From the beginning, the goal of the revisers from both countries was to be denominationally inclusive and avoid sectarian emphases. While in Great Britain that desire took shape with Anglican domination and proportional representation of dissenting groups, in America, pluralism demanded a more equally balanced committee. Probably no better person could have been found to lead such an endeavor than Philip Schaff. According to Dr. Talbot W. Chambers, member of the American Old Testament Committee, "for the American share in the work, the Christian public is indebted to Philip Schaff more than to all other persons together."[36]

Schaff's appointment as chairman of the American committee revealed the committee's confidence in his suitability for the work and

35. Philip Schaff, *A Companion to the Greek New Testament and the English Version* (New York: Scribner's, 1883), 460, 485, 487. See also Philip Schaff, ed., *Anglo-American Bible Revision* (Philadelphia: American Sunday-School Union, 1879).

36. D. Schaff, *Life*, 389.

testified to his facility in the English language. It was indeed "noteworthy that one whose mother tongue was not English should be chosen for the responsible place of leading in a movement for the Revision of the English Scriptures." Probably no one else in America could boast a more widespread and diverse assemblage of friends and colleagues, and few were held in such high esteem by people from virtually every denomination in America.[37] All involved agreed that as many denominations as possible should be represented in the process and that such representation was of "almost paramount importance." Schaff exulted that "there never was a more faithful and harmonious body of competent scholars engaged in a more important work on the American Continent."[38]

Efforts to get the American point of view accepted, however, strained relations between the American and British committees and thoroughly tested Schaff's mediatory abilities. After he finally established the denominational representation of the American committee to the satisfaction of the British leadership — there had been problems in the attempt to secure adequate Episcopalian representation — he faced problems related to the ambiguity of the role of the American committee. Initially, the Americans understood their role as that of joint revisers whose decisions would be taken into full consideration by the British committee. Problems arose, however, as a consequence of the copyright agreement between the British committee and the university presses of Oxford and Cambridge. The Americans, who unlike the British had received no monetary support from the publishers, balked when the presses demanded of them a payment of five thousand pounds as a purchase price for the copyright. The refusal of the American committee to consider such a payment led to the probability of separation of the two committees' work and, at best, continued efforts by the Americans toward an independent version. Schaff expended his full powers of conciliation and urged the Americans to continue dialogue

37. Ibid., 377-78. Schaff also had abilities as a fund-raiser, and through his efforts some $50,000 were secured for the project. See *Philip Schaff Memorial Committee Pamphlet* (n.p., n.d.), 15. The Philip Schaff Manuscript Collection, The Burke Library, Union Theological Seminary, New York archives.

38. Schaff, *Companion,* 395. Schaff even went so far as to claim that the members "never raised a sectarian issue."

with the British. In the face of "a strong sentiment . . . in favor of independent action," the mediator favored a stance which emphasized "delay and further conference." He did not fear American inability to produce a completely reliable translation. On the contrary, he had full confidence in the American committees. But to separate before every possible avenue of conciliation had been exhausted was foreign to his character.

Evidence to support Schaff's claim that these efforts were the "greatest contest of my life" is readily available.[39] He met with the British committee in London during the summers of 1871, 1872, 1873, and 1875, and again stopped in England on his way to the Middle East in January 1877. Accounts of those meetings reveal both situations that tested the full scope of Schaff's diplomatic abilities and his remarkable determination — even stubbornness — in the face of opposition.[40] Time and again when cessation of relations seemed inevitable to everyone else, Schaff contrived to relieve tensions and provide a workable solution to the difficulty.

Finally, the committees and the presses reached acceptable compromises and carried the work to completion. The Americans completed their versions (which included an appendix of suggestions by the American committee that the British had refused to adopt), and presented them to the public, the New Testament in May 1881 and the Old Testament in May 1885.[41] Schaff was extremely gratified with the reception of the Revised Version. Various authorized and unauthorized publishers immediately sold two hundred thousand copies in New York alone, and Schaff could trumpet this "greatest literary sensation. It is a republication of the Gospel to the English-speaking world."[42] The enthusiastic acceptance of the version further revealed the depth of religious feeling in Great Britain and America. "Who will doubt," he queried, "that the New Testament has a stronger hold upon mankind

39. D. Schaff, *Life*, 370-72.

40. Schaff spoke of a "full and manly exchange of views" in the 1875 meeting. Schaff, *Companion*, 399.

41. For accounts of the negotiations, see D. Schaff, *Life*, 354-89; Schaff, *Companion*, 380-403; and S. L. Greenslade, ed., *The Cambridge History of the Bible: The West from the Reformation to the Present Day* (Cambridge: Cambridge University Press, 1963), 371-74.

42. D. Schaff, *Life*, 383.

now than ever before and is, beyond all comparison, the most popular book among the two most civilized nations of the earth?" Schaff estimated that as many as three million copies were "bought and more or less read" during the first year of publication in Great Britain and the United States. Exposure was also greatly increased through publication of extensive portions of the text in major newspapers like the *New York Times* and the *Chicago Tribune.* Schaff spoke triumphantly of the official adoption of the new version by the American Baptist denomination in 1883. "The Baptists," he exulted, "have broken the ice and showed the way to other denominations."[43]

The enthusiasm of the initial reaction was soon tempered by various criticisms of the work. Popular attitudes were slow to abandon the beloved King James Version; this was not unexpected. But criticisms from knowledgeable scholars, and particularly the stinging attack by Schaff's sometime close friend and colleague at Union Theological Seminary, Charles A. Briggs, wounded him deeply.[44] With characteristic imprudence, Briggs blasted the American Old Testament committee for their "extreme reactionary position" and "inconsistency and perversity" in refusing to accept the findings of recent textual criticism. Instead of seeking the best possible texts, the committee, Briggs charged, had "followed rather any ordinary texts they might have at hand." Even more damaging, however, was Briggs's assertion that "in the whole department of Biblical Theology the Revision has failed to adequately represent the original text."[45]

Briggs later apologized for the "fervor and fierceness" of his article on the Revised Version, explaining that it had been written under severe

43. Schaff, *Companion,* 404-6. Editions sold varied in price from 15 cents to 16 dollars. Peddlers on Wall Street prompted this reaction from one gentleman: "Well, the millennium must be at hand, sure enough! I never expected to live to see the Bible sold in Wall Street. They need it here badly enough, Lord knows! Here, young man, I'll take two copies, just to set a good example." *Companion,* 408.

44. For more on the relationship between Schaff and Briggs, see George H. Shriver, *Philip Schaff: Christian Scholar and Ecumenical Prophet* (Macon, Ga.: Mercer University Press, 1987), 88-93. Another criticism that Schaff took seriously was that of Frederick Field, a member of the American Old Testament company who thought the New Testament version sacrificed "poetic beauty and archaic flavor to pedantic fidelity." See Schaff, *Companion,* ix.

45. Charles A. Briggs, "The Revised English Version of the Old Testament," *The Presbyterian Review* 6 (July 1885): 493, 495, 513, 532.

time limitations and "at great personal inconvenience" due to the refusal of Dr. William H. Green, president of the Old Testament company, to write the article. Briggs also related his "painful surprise" that the American committee's work had "placed the Old Testament scholarship of America in a humiliating position before the world." While he regretted the tone of his article, especially the offense taken by "some of my very dear friends," Briggs insisted that his criticisms of the work of the committee remained valid.[46]

Despite Briggs's scathing criticisms and those of other, more diplomatic scholars, Schaff was confident that time would prove the value of the Revised Version, and that it would gain a breadth of acceptance that would make it a means of greater unity among Christians of all denominations. He concluded that, "whether the Revised Version may or may not replace King James' Version, it will remain a noble monument of Christian scholarship and coöperation, which in its single devotion to Christ and to truth rises above the dividing-lines of schools and sects."[47] The work fit well into Schaff's vision of Christian union and victory over evil in America. Regardless of criticisms by a few, the enthusiasm with which many received the new version gave a definitive answer to the "attacks and sneers of modern infidelity, which would fain make the world believe that the Bible is antiquated." The revision, in sum, was "the noblest monument of Christian union and co-operation in this nineteenth century."[48]

In a published account of the work done by the American committees, the authors paid tribute to Schaff's efforts:

> The committee desire to record, in this review of their labors, their acknowledgement of the great service rendered by their president, Dr. Philip Schaff. His untiring energy and constant devotion to the interests of the work, from its inception to its close, deserve the thanks of all who have coöperated in any way in the preparation of the Revised Version, and also of all who shall find in it help and light in their reading of the Word of God. It was owing to him, more than

46. C. A. Briggs, "The Discussion of the Revised Version of the Old Testament," *The Presbyterian Review* 7 (April 1886): 369-78, esp. 369.

47. D. Schaff, *Life*, 387.

48. Schaff, *Companion*, 406, 494.

> to any other, that the work was undertaken in this country, and to him likewise is largely due the success with which the means for carrying it forward have been secured.[49]

Upon his emigration to America, Schaff almost immediately recognized the active character of Americans, sensed the pervasiveness of the revivalist style, and became involved himself in various voluntary associations for the promotion of Christian goals. While he maintained critical distance from revivalism, his concern that people should hear the gospel of Jesus Christ led him to appreciate the pious motives and accomplishments of some revivalists, especially D. L. Moody. His work in the Sabbath observance and temperance movements revealed his concerns for American social and religious problems, and also disclosed the continuing "Americanization" of Schaff the immigrant. His efforts in biblical revision also show his acceptance of American ideals and his concern to provide American Christians with a version of the Bible which reflected accommodation to their distinctive situation.

As early as 1858 Schaff had spoken of the value of voluntary societies as "an auxiliary and handmaid to the Church and the ministry, in doing the work of the Church and ministry." Yet he insisted that they must never be confused with the church itself. Despite their addition to American religious diversity and despite the fact that some Christians could confuse the societies with the church, Schaff incorporated them into his vision of united evangelical-catholic Christianity. American Christianity was in a "peculiar transition state" in which the Spirit of God employed unexpected methods to bring about the reunion of the church. Therefore, rather than reject voluntary associations out of hand because of their obvious faults, Schaff was able to recognize their contributions to American Christianity through their formation of Christian character, as outlets for Christian zeal, as avenues for Christian service, and ironically, as agents for Christian union. Those who became involved in the societies usually found themselves yoked in common work with Christians of different denominations. Schaff was

49. *Historical Account of the Work of the American Committee of Revision of the Authorized English Version of the Bible, Prepared from the Documents and Correspondence of the Committee* (New York: Scribner's, 1885), 56, quoted in D. Schaff, *Life*, 389.

confident that such cooperation among individual Christians could only contribute to broader harmony within the church.[50]

Underlying all of these efforts was Schaff's conviction that although Americans were a unique people and American Christianity was a novel version of the ancient faith, they too could make an essential contribution to evangelical-catholic Christianity. God had in fact designed a unique role for these people and for this nation in the development of his kingdom.

50. Philip Schaff, "Speech of Dr. Schaff before the Pennsylvania Branch of the American Tract Society," *German Reformed Messenger* 24 (September 1, 1858): 1-2.

CHAPTER 6

The American Nation

A "Specifically American" National Character

During Philip Schaff's career in America, the larger international picture of the theoretical relationship between religious and civil authorities, institutions, and persons continued to concern him deeply. Exactly how should he interpret the place of America in the history of the world, and the place of American Christianity in the history of the church? Schaff frequently expressed his belief that the United States had a unique role on the stage of world history. The American nation, in his opinion, would be the scene of something new and marvelous in the sweep of national histories. Likewise, American Christianity would produce something "wholly new" in the history of the church, and both nation and church would incorporate the best from all past cultures and expressions of Christianity to produce something higher and better in both. Schaff's conception of the place of the American nation in the sweep of the history of the world was distinctive in a number of ways when compared to both other religiously minded thinkers and their more secularly or nationally minded counterparts.

Schaff was able to discern order in the seemingly chaotic mix of nationalities and ethnic groups in the United States by perceiving a unique American national character being shaped within the ferment. Schaff's views stood in sharp contrast to that of figures such as his colleague in the Evangelical Alliance, Josiah Strong, who equated "Protestant" with "Christian," and "Anglo-Saxon" with "American." In the face of massive immigration of non-Anglo-Saxon peoples, many of those who called themselves "native" Americans — that is, those of Anglo-Saxon descent — reacted with great energy against the dilution of their ideal of a pure America. Nativist sentiments fed on both religious and ethnic prejudices. According to Sydney Ahlstrom, following the Civil War, "there was widespread agreement that immigrant 'hordes' were threatening the American dream."[1] Strong could warn of "*the final competition of races, for which the Anglo-Saxon is being schooled.*" The result of the conflict would be the "survival of the fittest."[2]

As a non-Anglo-Saxon immigrant himself, Philip Schaff had a very different view of the possibilities of American ethnic pluralism. From his early view in his ordination sermon that most of even the German immigrants were a worthless lot, Schaff began to appreciate what could result from the blending of many peoples and cultures. Schaff used a model to answer the question "What is an American?" similar to that which he would use to answer "What is a Christian?" In both cases the union of numerous diverse parts would result in something "wholly new," something far better than any of the parts by itself. His own life may be seen as an embodiment of this cosmopolitan vision. During one of his many trips to Europe he described himself thus: "for England and Scotland I am too much of a German, for Germany and Switzerland too English, and for all too much of an American."[3]

Schaff constructed his ideal of American nationality on a foundational concept of particular national characteristics. This concept, drawn from his German Romanticist philosophical training, led him to discern the characteristics of every nation's people and measure their positive contribution to the development of the new American character. He defined "nationality" as "the peculiar genius of a people which animates its institutions, prompts its actions and begets a feeling of common interest and sympathy." It did not result from mere constitutional agreement, he insisted, but was due to "an instinct of human

1. Sydney E. Ahlstrom, *A Religious History of the American People* (Garden City, N.Y.: Doubleday, 1975), 2:326.

2. Josiah Strong, *The New Era: or The Coming Kingdom* (New York: Baker and Taylor, 1893), 79.

3. David S. Schaff, *The Life of Philip Schaff: In Part Autobiographical* (New York: Scribner's, 1897), 176.

nature in its social capacity, and expansion of the inborn love of self and kindred."[4] Yet in using this theory, Schaff was able to overcome the racism that clouded the thinking of some others who drew on the Romanticist heritage. A combination of characteristics of nearly all peoples would result from the commingling of races in America.[5]

All peoples, however, would not play equal roles in their contributions to America. Schaff also operated under the assumption that civilization through the centuries had moved from East to West, and naturally those nations in Western Europe where civilization had reached its highest development would contribute most to the new Western empire of the United States. Schaff was not without ethnocentrism in the major role he assigned to German thought and culture. The Germans, he said, are highly adaptable and excel in thought and theory. Their primary contribution to the American character would be their depth of thought and surpassing rationality. Both the Anglo-Saxons and the Germans were blessed with "mental energy and solidity," yet the Germans turned this mental energy inward and focused their attention on thought and theory. The Anglo-Saxons, in contrast, put their mental energies to work in practical ways "with will and action." The Germans were highly adaptable and often blended into foreign situations, but the unyielding Anglo-Saxons made everything serve themselves and their purposes. The Germans were "the most cordial and good-natured" people in the world. The Anglo-Saxons, Schaff admitted, have hearts also, but they "beat under a marble cover" allowing them to have perfect self-command and the proper demeanor to rule others. The British had in fact built an empire due to these characteristics and their "moral and intellectual energy."[6]

4. Philip Schaff, *American Nationality* (Chambersburg, Penn.: M. Kieffer, 1856), 3.

5. See Reginald Horsman, *Race and Manifest Destiny: The Origins of American Racial Anglo-Saxonism* (Cambridge: Harvard University Press, 1981), 25-27.

6. Quoted in D. Schaff, *Life*, 237. An example of German theoretical genius but total lack of practical understanding cited by Schaff was the Germans' missionary work in America with its "suicidal course" of fighting against use of the English language. It was more likely that "the course of the Mississippi be directed to Bavaria, and the Chinese converted by German preaching" than that the Germans would be successful in their attempts to avoid accommodation to American ways. The Germans had built up a theoretical world and assumed that "it must develope [sic] itself on the other side of the ocean just as it exists in

Schaff mentioned the contrast in a letter to his wife written during his first return to Europe in 1854. "The social life in Germany is certainly far more affectionate and hearty," he noted, "than in any other country, and forms a striking contrast to the stiff and dignified formality of England and the mere outward politeness of France." A rather whimsical example Schaff noted concerned the French and English who showed only enough interest in his personal life occasionally to ask him if he were married, while the Germans demanded to see pictures of his whole family![7] Schaff recorded his thoughts about the differences between the English and the Germans during his stay in England while journeying to Mercersburg, and in doing so revealed much about his own character. In England,

> I have received most cordial treatment, and have felt myself at home. The Englishman is not what we call genial [*gemüthlich*]. To his idea of character and manliness, there belongs a certain reserve of the emotions, and an intellectual composure bordering on coldness. A steel cuirass is strapped over his heart. He who in German fashion gives vent to his feelings, exposes himself, in the eyes of the deliberate and sober Englishman, to the charge of weakly emotionalism or lack of self-poise.

While Schaff coped with these differences of personality, more troubling was the English attitude toward the intellectual life.

> As for our *ideas*, we had better leave them at home unless they are thoroughly practical and easily intelligible to a sound common sense. Here they are for the most part looked upon as useless speculations, fancies and intellectual balloonings.[8]

---

their brain." Schaff's hopes for the Western hemisphere are voiced in *America: A Sketch of Its Political, Social and Religious Character*, ed. Perry Miller (Cambridge: Harvard University Press, 1961), 15ff. His views of German and Anglo-American dominance were very similar to those of the earlier American historians George Bancroft and John Lothrop Motley. See Horsman, *Race and Manifest Destiny*, 182-84.

7. Letter from Philip Schaff to Mary from Elberfeld, Prussia, 21 February 1854, Philip Schaff Correspondence Box, Philip Schaff Papers, Evangelical and Reformed Historical Society, Philip Schaff Library, Lancaster Theological Seminary, Lancaster, Pennsylvania. Hereafter referred to as ERHS.

8. Quoted in D. Schaff, *Life*, 87.

Despite English emotional reserve and their woeful lack of appreciation of German intellectual abilities, it was their positive characteristics that most interested Schaff. The combination of the best of both peoples would be a higher and greater people still, whose destiny would surely be global in scope.

> The German is the profounder thinker, the Englishman the sturdier character. The first rules the world by thought, conceiving it in all its varied relations. The second rules it by politics, making the world subservient to his wants. German life unfolds itself in various systems and schools of opinion, English life in various sects and political parties. But Germany and England dwell in the same ethical sphere. They complement one another. Idealism without the solid basis of realism turns to airy spiritualism; realism without idealism to bald materialism.[9]

While the Germans exerted a strong shaping influence, Schaff could maintain that "the basis of the American nationality is undoubtedly English," though, of course, modified by the unique American situation. The specific modification he had in mind was a greater capacity of Anglo-America for "receiving and working up foreign material." Whereas the Anglo-Saxons remained aloof and ruled, the Anglo-Americans were able to assimilate and combine the best of all peoples into a new nationality.[10]

Through the interaction of these two major contributors, along with the infusion of numerous other characters, the "American nationality" would arise. Already the distinctively "American" national character was beginning to appear. From the Anglo-Saxons Americans inherited their "organizing talent," their "self-control, . . . practical energy," and facility in business. Americans have "less solidity" than the English, however, and their spirit of enterprise often "degenerates even into fool-hardiness. Their reckless pursuit of novelty leads to wanton waste of human life" through

9. Ibid.

10. Schaff, *America,* 47. A significant part of the Americanization process was learning the ability to rule oneself. Philip Schaff, "Christianity in America," *Mercersburg Review* 9 (October 1857): 528. Reprinted in Charles Yrigoyen, Jr., and George M. Bricker, *Reformed and Catholic: Selected Historical and Theological Writings of Philip Schaff* (Pittsburgh: The Pickwick Press, 1979), 380.

"countless conflagrations in the cities, and disasters on steamboats and railroads." In Schaff's eyes, the distinctively "American" person — for good and evil — was taking shape.

> The main features of the American national character may be already quite plainly discerned, and reveal themselves as predominantly Anglo-Saxon; yet it is only in its formation state; and the more it develops, the more sensibility do the un-English elements, favored by the increasing emigration from the continental countries of Europe, modify the whole.[11]

The remarkable thing about Schaff's insights was that over all the "confused diversity" he saw in America, he was convinced that a higher unity ruled. In the "chaos of peoples" there were evident traces of a "specifically American national character," characterized by a freshness and energy never seen before. Though Germany and England predominated, all European nations had a part to play in this "ethnographic panorama."

> Here is the general congress of the noblest nations of Christendom, the sterling, energetic Briton; the strong-willed, enterprising Scotch; the hard-working, generous Irish; the industrious, deep-thinking German; the honest, liberty-loving Swiss; the hardy, thrifty Scandinavian; the even-tempered, tenacious Dutch; the easy, elegant Frenchman; the earnest, dignified Spaniard; the ingenious, imaginative Italian; the patriotic, high-minded Magyar and Pole.[12]

With a remarkable determination to see the good that stands in sharp contrast to his views only a decade earlier, Schaff lauded the contributions of immigrants. To counter the fears of "native" Americans — that is, Anglo-Saxons and other northern Europeans who had immigrated a few decades earlier — that immigration defiled the purity of

11. Schaff, *America,* 49. For German immigration statistics, see Ahlstrom, *Religious History,* 1:627. Schaff cites statistics in *America,* 28n. Schaff had been encouraged to help develop the "American nationality" by his former teacher, Dr. J. A. Dorner. See a letter from Dorner to Schaff quoted in D. Schaff, *Life,* 75.

12. Schaff, *America,* 45-46; Schaff, *American Nationality,* 16.

American blood and morality, Schaff insisted that America was truly "*favored* by the most extensive emigration from all other countries." The resulting chaos from "all the elements of the old world's good and evil, which will there wildly ferment together" would produce out of this "most fertile soil . . . fruit for the weal or woe of generations to come."[13]

13. Schaff, *America,* 71. Emphasis mine. Schaff reprinted the following in an article on the "Progress of Christianity in the United States of America," *The Princeton Review* 55 (September 1879): 250. He found these humorously nativist letters in the *New York Tribune,* 25 February 1879.

To the Honorable House of Representatives:

The undersigned, legal voters and citizens of the United States, respectfully ask that you prevent the immigration of any more Germans to this country, because they will drink lager, go on Sunday excursions, save their money, and are buying up all the land in the country.

ROBERT MACGREGOR
HUGH MACDOUGAL
SANDY MACPHERSON
and 1000 others.

To Yer Honers the Mimbers of congress:

We the unthersigned citizens of the United States of Amerikie respectfully petition you to tack into the "Haythen Chinee" bill the white nagers or Ratalians that are coming over here in dhroves and working ten or twilve hours a day for nothin' at all, and boarding themselves at that. Now what can an honest man do to airn a dacent livin' if you don't put a stop to it?

PATRICK O'REILLY
MICHAEL MCDERMOTT
WM. JAMES O'SULLIVAN
and 1000 others.

CONGRISHMAN: Vot for you no schtop dem Irishman shust de same mit Schineman? He drinks up all de viskey like nothings, votes every time all day long, and makes drubles mit us. And it is shust so easy mit de needle in de camels' eye ash to have de behind vordt mit the Irishman.

JACOB ROERHAUSEN
HANS BUMGARTEN
PETER VON STEINBURGER
and many others.

To Ze Grand Congress.

SHENTLEMEN: If you vill keeps out of ze countarie, all ze Germans, all ze Irish,

While the pessimism of many restricted their vision to just the problems of open immigration, Schaff's confidence in America's providential mission allowed him to focus on the good. Schaff called this "tide of emigration" one of the most "remarkable and important facts of modern times." It constituted a "migration of nations" that was even more amazing because it was peaceful and was accomplished "without sword or bloodshed." All of these ethnic groups must be assimilated into the one American character. "It is far better," he insisted, "for the Germans themselves to become amalgamated with the Anglo-Saxon race, and to coalesce with them into one American nation, than to be isolated and form a state in the state and an ecclesiola in ecclesia."[14] Such ideas did not bode well for Schaff's relations with his German countrypersons who desired to maintain completely their Teutonic heritage and language.

Go Forth, Noble Saxon Tongue

A fundamental part of Schaff's model of assimilation was the adoption of the English language. From the time of his marriage to "an American girl" in 1845, he used English in his home, and, despite considerable opposition among his German-American peers, encouraged the use of English in the German Reformed Church. Initially among the most strident advocates of keeping the German immigrants fully "German," Schaff's adoption of English is a prime example of his "Americanization." His inaugural address, given in 1844 and later enlarged and

---

all ze Anglasie, wis all ze, ze — vat you calls him — Shine — mans and evra boda but ze Frenchmans, you vill have one magnifishant Republic.

LOUIS DU BOISE
PAUL COGNAC.

14. Schaff, *America*, 27, 230. Ray Allen Billington, *The Protestant Crusade, 1800-1860* (New York: Macmillan, 1938), 193-211, points out that pessimists had a number of good reasons for their concerns. Many immigrants were extremely poor and relied on public assistance to survive. Crime statistics were markedly worse in immigrant areas; riots were common. Many "native" Americans were offended by immigrant drinking and lack of appreciation for Sabbath observance. Finally, natives feared for their jobs, since immigrants were usually prepared to work for lower wages.

published as *Das Princip des Protestantismus,* concluded with a section on the German language that was not included in John Williamson Nevin's English translation. It was deemed appropriate, though, for publication in the *Weekly Messenger* of the German Reformed Church. In that article, Schaff emphasized as nowhere else the necessity of maintaining the "pure German language" of the immigrants. He lamented the attitude by some of the most prominent among them that "the language of a LUTHER, LESSING, GOETHE, KRUMMACHER, cannot be too soon reduced to silence in our midst, and their children are ashamed to speak it or learn it." Their attitude was tantamount to an "inexcusable treason to the language of their fathers." In fact, Schaff noted that "according to common human calculation, the German for at least a hundred years to come must be preached along with the English; if indeed we may suppose it will ever go out of use entirely, something that strikes me always as very improbable."[15]

Some had suggested that Schaff use English in his seminary lectures, but he refused in the strongest terms.

> I cannot possibly accede to the suggestion of some of my friends, however much respected, that I should as soon as possible exchange the German in my lecture room for the English. I would consider this dishonorable treason to my fatherland, to my native tongue, and to the expectations of my countrymen still using the German in our Church itself.

Here was a champion for the cause of German identity who would not be denied.

> At the risk of offending English ears, in this sacred place and at this solemn hour I make the vow, with good conscience and mature deliberation, that in case of my remaining here, as much as in me lies and so long as a drop of blood rolls in my veins, I will with the interest of German theology and literature maintain the interest also of the German language, and teach, preach, act, suffer and die, true to my calling, as a missionary of the German Church in the German

15. Philip Schaff, "Conclusion of Dr. Schaf's Address," *Weekly Messenger* 10 (April 23, 1845): 2. Emphasis his.

> daughter Church of America. So help me God and his most holy gospel![16]

If one mark of strength of character is the willingness to admit error and change strongly held opinions in the face of compelling evidence, Schaff was a young man of exceptional fortitude. As the wisdom of changing to English became apparent, Schaff made such an about-face. As early as 1845 he used English in some addresses and correspondence, and in 1851 he preached an English sermon before the German Reformed synod. After 1854 he wrote his personal journals in English, and only four years after his declaration of unconditional loyalty to the German language, he lectured exclusively in English in his seminary classes. He had become convinced that it was only through adoption of English that the Germans could fit into American society and make their contribution to the emerging American nationality and evangelical-catholic Christianity. With the zeal of a convert he declared that

> the German has a great mission in America, although he can hardly be said as yet to have realized it. He will not fulfil it in any adequate manner by rigidly and stiffly secluding himself from the Anglo-Americans and making it his purpose to build up a state. Rather should he, in a cosmopolitan spirit, energetically appropriate the Anglo-American nature and its excellences and, as far as possible, penetrate it with the wealth of his own German temper and life.[17]

By 1887 Schaff had become convinced that the progress of humanity and the spread of Christianity depended on the preponderance of one language, and English, with its "heterogeneous" origin and its compatibility with American destiny, was ideally that language. Language, he believed, reflects the genius of a nation and serves the nation's special mission. Unity in language, Schaff asserted, served to "unite and consolidate our nationality and to increase our power and influence." He now looked beyond the German community in America with a vision that encompassed the entire nation. English, he insisted, "is emphatically the language of the modern age and of the coming age, of progressive intel-

16. Ibid.
17. D. Schaff, *Life,* 133, 156.

ligence and civilization. It is the prevailing language of Christian missions in heathen lands." Never had any language been entrusted with a nobler mission. America was the nation and English the language which would ultimately spread civilization and Christianity throughout the world.[18]

The thoroughly Americanized Schaff concluded that "as no other language can possibly compete with this powerful rival on the soil of North America, the Dutchmen, Frenchmen, and Germans should rejoice that the English rather than any other language . . . is destined ultimately to take the place of their beloved mother tongue." He concluded his address with a poetic flourish.

> Go forth, then, noble Saxon tongue,
> And speed the happy time
> When truth and righteousness shall reign
> In every zone and clime;
> When earth's oppressed and savage tribes
> Shall cease to pine and roam,
> All taught to prize the English words:
> Faith, Freedom, Heaven, and Home.[19]

Digesting the Nations

Schaff saw the American as Crèvecoeur did, as "a new man." In contrast, however, to Crèvecoeur's emphasis on the influence of the forces of the physical environment, Schaff maintained that it was the confluence of spiritual qualities that brought about the new creation. America was, in his eyes, "an ethnographic panorama," and America's first distinctive feature was the "commingling of nationalities." The nation, he said, "is truly '*e pluribus unum.*'"[20] Yet in it all, he discerned an order, a strong thread of unity that would bind the many together as one. As the Christian church was made up of the various denominations with

18. Philip Schaff, *The English Language: Heterogeneous in Formation, Homogeneous in Character, Universal in Destination for the Spread of Christian Civilization* (Nashville, Tenn.: Cumberland Presbyterian Publishing House, 1887), 55-56.

19. Ibid., 57-61. No reference is given for the source of the poem.

20. Schaff, *America,* 45; Schaff, "Progress of Christianity," 220.

their distinctive characteristics, held together by a consensus of common devotion to Christ, so the American national character was made up of various ethnic groups, none losing their distinctive character, but all joined in this "new" consensus, that of the American nationality.

In the "chaotic fermentation" of American Christianity and the developing character of Americans as a people, it was not the disorder that was important, because the chaos was that "which precedes the act of creation." In America, Schaff noted, "the cosmos lies in the chaos," and out of the turmoil arose "a thoroughly fresh and energetic national life, which instantly takes up and assimilates all foreign elements." He saw the nation in organic terms and creatively utilized the metaphor of digestion to illustrate American assimilation.

> The Americans have stronger digestive organs than any nation under the sun. They can eat English roast beef, German sauerkraut, Dutch kohl-slaw, Italian maccaroni, Scotch porridge, and Irish potatoes; and by way of keeping digestion, they drink a cup of French coffee, and smoke a Spanish cigar! If you don't grow fat on that process, it will not be for want of supply. No wonder that you suffer and complain so often of dyspepsia.

Others had used the digestion metaphor, but Schaff added a distinctive twist. All nationalities would be combined in the new American character, but Americans, Schaff insisted, "have a way of eating and assimilating without annihilating the foreign substance."[21] Schaff's American would be part of a great unity, but a unity always characterized by striking diversity. The principle of organic development demanded that the movement of history would preserve the essence of the historical past, even while it destroyed some of the nonessential aspects. The forces of development would raise the essential to a higher level, yet it would always bear the fundamental characteristics of its past.

21. Philip Schaff, "Speech of Dr. Schaff before the Pennsylvania Branch of the American Tract Society," *German Reformed Messenger* 24 (September 1, 1858): 1. Elsewhere he noted that "the American's digestive power is really astonishing. How many thousands and millions of Europeans has his stomach already received! and yet he has only grown firmer and healthier thereby." Schaff, *America,* 46. That Schaff spoke of French coffee rather than the more obvious wine was probably due to his sensitivity to the feelings of his friends involved in the American temperance movement.

The ferment of these fundamental elements produced a peculiar people with massive strengths and equally apparent weaknesses. Americans are full of "ambition and national pride," said Schaff. They are also "people of the boldest enterprise and untiring progress." They are so restless, he exclaimed, that "even when seated, they push themselves to and fro on their rockingchairs." Schaff became a little breathless himself when he described their "state of perpetual excitement in their business, their politics, and their religion," which "remind one of the storm-lashed sea." The expressions "help yourself" and "go ahead" are never out of their mouths. For all their frenetic activity, Americans are an average lot, he said, with "average intelligence, average morality, and average piety," but though there are fewer people of exceptional genius or virtue, there are also fewer of exceptional ignorance or wickedness. Schaff believed that these "average" people would play an extraordinary role in God's plan for his kingdom.[22]

Schaff's contemporary, Josiah Strong, also expressed passionate feelings about American destiny, but his hopes for the country were tempered by anxieties about what he saw as unfavorable trends. In 1885, Strong's *Our Country* warned of the perils of immigration, Romanism, Mormonism, intemperance, socialism, wealth, and the city. While Schaff was able to focus on positive aspects of some of those, Strong could not see beyond their detrimental effects on public morality and the political system. Both men used a common metaphor, but Strong came to a very different conclusion.

> Foreigners are not coming to the United States in answer to any appetite of ours, controlled by an unfailing moral or political instinct. They naturally consult their own interests in coming, not ours. The lion, without being consulted as to time, quantity or quality, is having the food thrust down his throat, and his only alternative is, digest or die.[23]

Quite to the contrary, Schaff had no doubts that America could "not only endure without harm such an uninterrupted stream of the

22. Schaff, *America,* 210, 54.

23. Josiah Strong, *Our Country: Its Possible Future and Its Present Crisis* (New York: The American Home Missionary Society, 1885), 46.

immigration of nations from the East," but the country could also "without difficulty and with incredible rapidity, denationalize it and assimilate it to itself." Schaff showed uncommon insight in his understanding that America could assimilate a diverse cross-section of peoples, and that they could learn to live together as Americans with surprisingly little conflict.[24]

Surmounting the "Unsurmountable Difference of Race"

There were groups that Schaff did not include, however, in his conception of the cosmopolitan American national character. As a man of his time, he segregated traditionally excluded groups like Native Americans, blacks, and the Chinese. In contrast to the Enlightenment emphasis on human equality, Americans had gradually come to accept a theory that maintained innate qualitative racial differences. During the late 1840s, the racial question was at the heart of scholarly discussion in the United States, and by the early 1850s, according to Reginald Horsman, the "inherent inequality of races was simply accepted as a scientific fact in America."[25] A corollary to the conception of different inborn capabilities among the races was the rejection of hopes to assimilate nonwhite peoples into American culture. Many of those who thus degraded nonwhite races also encouraged the belief of Anglo-Saxon superiority.

Initially, Philip Schaff seemed to share such views. While calling in 1856 for open immigration "by hundreds of thousands from the continent of Europe," Schaff believed that there was an "unsurmountable difference of race," between the "civilized nations of Europe" and the "red man, the negro and the Chinese."[26] Schaff at first paternalistically viewed these non-Caucasian races as "wards" of the churches and government. In his later writings, however, Schaff never repeated

24. Philip Schaff, *Der Bürgerkrieg und das christliche Leben in Nord-Amerika* (Berlin: Berlag von Wiegandt und Grieben, 1866), 7. An English translation by C. C. Starbuck was published in the *Christian Intelligencer* 37 (March 1-May 17, 1866). Both references will be given, and the *Christian Intelligencer* will be noted as *CI*. See *CI* 37 (March 1, 1866): 2.

25. Horsman, *Race and Manifest Destiny*, 133-34.

26. Schaff, *American Nationality*, 6, 8.

the idea of "unsurmountable difference" between races, and by 1879, he had taken an unpopular stance that, implicitly at least, assumed some sort of assimilation. The nature of the assimilation was that the Indians, for example, would be transformed into civilized Americans. He had come to hope in efforts to convert the "wild warrior to the obedient citizen." Schaff was appalled by unfair treatment of the tribes and spoke of "national guilt" for the government's policy of "expensive mismanagement and injustice" against the Indians. "The story of the aborigines, the original lords of the soil, now reduced to beggary and apparently doomed to extinction," he lamented, "is a sad tragedy that must fill every American Christian with mingled indignation, humiliation, and shame."[27]

Schaff agreed with Tocqueville, who, over forty years earlier, had seen through the empty promises of the federal government that it knew full well that it was unable to fulfill. "It is impossible," he said, "to destroy men with more respect to the laws of humanity."[28] Schaff's lament was similar. "The Indian problem," he moaned, "is as dark as midnight." Perhaps the only solution to the problem was continued work of dedicated Christians in schools and missions which would help the Indians take their place in American civilization. In expressing the view that the Indians could be transformed and take their place in American civilization, Schaff voiced a position that had become quite uncommon. There were few people after mid-century who believed that Indians, no matter how "civilized," could assume a permanent, equal place within American society.[29]

Schaff's development in this area may be traced to his exposure to meetings and discussions concerning the Native Americans following his move to New York. He attended various events, but one meeting in particular — at the Cooper Institute with the revealing but characteristic title of "Declining Indian Barbarism and Advancing American Civilization" — led him to reflect on injustices to the Indians. In his diary he recounted the deeply moving statements by the Indians.

27. Schaff, "Progress of Christianity," 244-47.

28. Alexis de Tocqueville, *Democracy in America,* trans. George Lawrence, ed. J. P. Mayer (Garden City, N.Y.: Doubleday, 1969), 339.

29. Schaff, "Progress of Christianity," 245-48; Horsman, *Race and Manifest Destiny,* 207.

> The Great Spirit made us both, he made you rich, us poor, he gave us land and gave you land. We gave you much of our land, and now you want to take the little that is left from us. We are all poor, because we are honest. I was once lean and meagre, now I am fat from the lies of your agents. The great father sent men to us whom he could not keep at home. We want land to hunt, we will live in peace, and only claim to be let alone.[30]

While the "Indian problem" vexed the government and made living on the western frontier dangerous, the racial problem that created the most apprehension among Americans was that of the blacks, both slave and free. New theories of racial inequality had merely affirmed what many Americans, both North and South, already believed. Few, even among those who abhorred slavery, believed in the equality of white and black races. Though he never repeated his statement of 1854 that assimilation was impossible for the blacks, neither did Schaff express much confidence that they could be assimilated. The solution that most appealed to him was that of colonization. Schaff viewed "the sore evil of negro slavery" as, in God's providence, a "striking instance of God's wisdom and mercy for over-ruling the wrath of man for his own glory."[31] God could use this evil, he believed, to bring about the good of Christianizing and civilizing Negroes, both in America and Africa. Schaff was not blinded by his concept of Providence, however, to the complete injustice of the system of slavery and its "contradiction of the first principle of that [American] government, that all men are born free and equal." He lamented the long survival of a system that "turned the Declaration of Independence into a lie," and maintained that the tragic civil war which finally ended slavery in America was "worth the cost." Schaff was deeply concerned for the welfare of blacks, but as a young man he failed to transcend the common conception of blacks as inferior. He spoke in 1854, for example, of the "black sons of Africa, rejoicing in the childlike cheerfulness of their nature, and even in freedom bowing instinctively before the superiority of the whites."[32]

30. Schaff diary, 16 June 1870, Box IV, The Philip Schaff Manuscript Collection, The Burke Library, Union Theological Seminary, New York. Hereafter UTS.

31. Schaff, "Christianity in America," 389; Schaff, "Progress of Christianity," 244.

32. Schaff, "Progress of Christianity," 212; Schaff, *America*, 42, 45.

By 1876, however, when he reported in the *New York Evangel* on "A Visit to Virginia," during which he spoke at the commencement exercises for twenty-four black graduates of Hampton Normal and Agricultural Institute, Schaff had become deeply impressed by the abilities of African Americans.

> The education of the negro is no more an experiment; it is an accomplished fact, and an encouraging success. The examinations of the three classes, the orations and recitations of the graduates, were highly creditable, and equal to the commencement exercises of many a white college of old standing.

Schaff also noted the students' singing was "worth a journey to Virginia," and spoke of his hope that Virginia, the "mother of Presidents," might also give birth to "many such institutions as Hampton."[33]

With the expansion of the United States to the Pacific coast, Schaff witnessed an immigration that moved counter to his idea of the flow of civilization from East to West. During the California Gold Rush of the late 1840s the Chinese had appeared, and in subsequent years their numbers had grown to the point that from 1860 to 1880 they comprised about nine percent of the state's population.[34] This was one immigrant group whom Schaff believed posed a threat to American civilization and religion. The "wholesale immigration of heathen Mongolians for permanent residence," he admitted, "might indeed endanger the Christian civilization of America." Many Chinese were infected with the "vices and filth of heathenism" and were generally "destitute of the ennobling influences of family life." Their significant numbers of immigrants had brought a reaction in the form of an "anti-Mongolian crusade" in the 1870s and 1880s, but Schaff did not share in the hysteria. Nothing on the massive scale that would cause difficulty had yet happened, nor could be expected to happen, and he could speak of the presidential veto of the Chinese

33. *The New York Evangel* article (25 May 1876) is found in Philip Schaff, "Autobiographical Scrapbook of Articles from Periodicals, 1870-1889," Box VI, UTS. His hopes for colleges like Hampton are expressed in his diary, 18 May 1876, Box IV, UTS.

34. John Higham, *Send These to Me: Immigrants in Urban America,* rev. ed. (Baltimore: The Johns Hopkins University Press, 1984), 34.

exclusion bill of 1879 in terms of American "national honor saved from disgrace."[35]

In fact, Schaff believed that most of the Chinese, like other immigrants, were beneficial for America. They were "intelligent, industrious, frugal, and peaceful." Few of them found their way to American hospitals or jails, and their work on the railroads had been of great benefit to the entire nation. The temporary immigration of Chinese workers created a wonderful opportunity for Christian missions, both to those Chinese who would remain, and to those who, having been converted, would return to China bearing the gospel as "the entering wedge for the conversion of that immense empire."[36]

In his attitude toward these excluded peoples, Schaff was an example of a not uncommon type; the benevolent, paternalistic, white male Christian who failed to recognize the true social equality of all human beings. While not excusing this blindness, it is instructive to note that Schaff spent a proportionally significant amount of time discussing these groups in comparison to other religious historians of his day, and that in all of his discussions of these groups Schaff was motivated by what he sincerely believed to be their best interests.[37] He condemned the conduct of many Americans toward these races, which he said too often manifested "the overbearing pride and oppression of a superior race." The only glimmers of hope in the entire situation were the scores of examples of true Christian devotion and a growing sense of our "national guilt" for past sins and our duty to address abuses. Schaff naively concluded in 1879 that "the negro problem is at last happily solved, and it is to be hoped that the justice done to the Africans will ultimately be granted to the Indians and Chinese."[38] Unfortunately it was.

35. Schaff, "Progress of Christianity," 249-52. Anti-Chinese agitation eventually led to exclusion legislation passed in 1882.

36. Ibid.

37. For example, in Schaff's *America* (1854), he spends only a handful of pages on these minority groups, but in "The Progress of Christianity in the United States of America" (1879), 9 of the 43 pages (21%) deal with these excluded groups and prospects for their futures. By way of comparison, Robert Baird's *Religion in America,* rev. ed. (New York: Harper and Brothers, 1856), spends only 22 out of 688 pages on Indians, and 11 on blacks (4.8% total), and Daniel Dorchester's *Christianity in the United States from the First Settlement Down to the Present Time* (New York, 1888) deals with these groups in about 20 out of 800 pages (2.5%).

38. Schaff, "Progress of Christianity," 244.

America's *Tendo-Achilles*

Possibly the views of American destiny most comparable to Schaff's did not belong to a clergyman or professional theologian, but a president, Abraham Lincoln. While both Schaff and Lincoln saw America's role in cosmic terms, both also refused to portray that role in uncritical ways, or to confine the participants to a narrow segment of race or ideology. Both identified the war between the states as a conflagration that threatened the progress of American destiny.

Without question the most troubling social issue in mid-nineteenth century America was the "peculiar institution" of chattel slavery. During his first few years in the land of his adoption, however, Schaff said very little about the problem. Through the first decade of his residence in America he had many other problems and issues to occupy his energies without opening the Pandora's box of slavery. In the *Principle of Protestantism,* for example, Schaff mentioned slavery only in passing as an important issue confronting the American denominations. Given his sensitivity to Christian union, it is somewhat surprising that he did not say more about the problem, since it was a principal contributing factor to division in some of America's major denominations.[39]

Schaff's return to Europe in 1854 and increasing attention to the problem among Americans, however, forced him to address the issue of slavery in order to explain it to his European hearers and outline for them his views about the solution to the problem. "Slavery," he admitted, "is unquestionably the greatest political and social difficulty of the Union." The nation had narrowly avoided division in 1850 through compromise legislation, which Schaff feared did not solve the problem. The practice of slavery, he conceded, "is certainly in most palpable contradiction to the first principle of that government that all men are born free and equal." His European audiences who prided themselves on their civilization and attainments in social justice could nod in agreement when he exclaimed, "What an anomaly, that the freest country in the world should maintain and defend a relic of barbarism

39. Schaff, *Principle of Protestantism,* 212. For example, the Methodists split into northern and southern denominations on 1 May 1845 over the issue of slavery, and the Baptists divided along sectional lines only a week later.

and heathenism, which humanity and Christianity, reason and revelation, and all the civilized nations of Europe condemn with one voice!" Lest his hearers become too comfortable in their conceit, however, Schaff was compelled also to point out that slavery did not have its origin under the American government itself, but had developed during the colonial period when the nations of Europe controlled the situation and the people of Europe came first to settle the new land. Slavery was a crime of both "European and American christendom (for it was under Spanish, French, Danish, and English rule that slavery came into the New world)."[40]

Nonetheless, Americans must now deal with this most threatening social evil in America, "the political and social canker, the *tendo-Achilles*, in the otherwise vigorous system of the United States." The "curse of slavery" might still cause the dissolution of the Union and possibly civil war, but there remained hope that America could avoid such a tragedy. Schaff was outspoken concerning the false picture of the American system given by radical abolitionists such as Theodore Parker and William Lloyd Garrison, who were "unsound, fanatical, and extremely radical in all political and social questions," and worst of all, "infidel in religion." While their indictments of slavery were warranted, this disease did not justify total condemnation of the American system. Not unaware of the evils of the slave system, Schaff could still maintain that "monsters, like Mrs. Stowe's Legree, are rare exceptions" and that the evil of slavery could be eliminated through orderly gradual emancipation.[41]

In addition to the need to discuss slavery in his formal lectures, various individuals confronted Schaff with the issue in private discussions, to the point that he found the topic tiresome. In a letter home he discussed his visits in Scotland where "enthusiasm for the author of *Uncle Tom's Cabin*" was "universally shared." "I am tired of talking on the subject," he complained, "for I can neither defend slavery nor on the other hand permit the unjust charges against America because of it." He was able both to blunt criticisms and vent his frustration, however, by reminding his British friends that "all the obnoxious and inhuman laws in the slave states were made under English rule."[42]

40. Schaff, *America,* 41-42, 44.
41. Ibid., 6-7.
42. D. Schaff, *Life,* 173.

As attitudes throughout the country hardened in response to the events of the 1850s, events drove Schaff to more exclusive support of the Northern cause. In a report on "Christianity in America" to the Evangelical Alliance meeting in Berlin in 1857, Schaff waxed eloquent in describing both the evils and eventual demise of the institution of slavery, and his optimism about the American situation, despite the disastrous measures that might be taken to eliminate the problem. The solution did not involve

> any undue foreign interference, which a nation as sensitive and high minded as the American will either indignantly repulse, or ignore; nor by political agitation, which so far at least has rather thrown back the process of emancipation and called forth a fanatical pro-slavery reaction in the southern States; nor by a dissolution of the Union and the terrors of a civil war, which may God in mercy prevent.

Deeply ingrained social problems like slavery could never be solved by violent force. As another illustration of the dominance of organic development over conflict in Schaff's thought, he insisted that the natural course of development and progress would alleviate the nation's distress and God in his providence would create something good out of the evil. The solution, Schaff thought,

> will be brought about partly by the silent influence of physical and material causes, such as climate, agriculture, industry, railroads; partly by the irresistible progress of Christianity, humanity and freedom; and especially by the adorable wisdom of the almighty ruler of events, who makes even the wrath of men to praise him, who delivered Israel from the bondage of Egypt, and of Babylon, and who will in his own good time gloriously solve this dark mystery by the elevation and salvation of the entire African race.[43]

Schaff desired emancipation but was essentially a social conservative who believed that massive social change required extensive time. "It must be remembered," he warned, "that it takes time to cure any evil of society, and that a gradual and silent cure is always the most safe

43. Schaff, "Christianity in America," 389-90.

and radical in the end."[44] Christ and his apostles did not demand immediate abolition of slavery within the Roman empire, because the "outward violence" and "sudden revolution" that would have been necessary to accomplish such a goal "would have only made the evil worse." Instead, they taught Christian principles which "exerted a silent influence" and created an "unconscious atmospheric influence," through which Christianity affected the surrounding world. Schaff completed his argument with examples of the significant numbers of Roman slaves who became Christians and the instances of manumission of slaves by Christian owners.[45]

Schaff's prayers that civil war might be avoided were not to be answered, and in the deteriorating situation of 1859 he wrote to his friend Henry Boynton Smith that a failure of leadership was partly to blame for the present predicament. "A propos politics I am sorry to confess that I am done with my friend James Buchanan as President of the U.S. and have given up the long cherished hope that he would yet recover himself in some way. He is gone, and every body looks towards the rising sun."[46] That Schaff could look to the "rising sun" reveals his steadfast optimism even during this period in which most Americans feared the sun was rapidly setting.

When war broke out, Schaff was quick to express his opinions about violations of biblical principles by those on both sides of the conflict. He had become convinced that abolition of slavery was based on biblical principles, but the example of New Testament teachings about slavery still pointed toward gradual emancipation as the ideal. In a work entitled *Slavery and the Bible: A Tract for the Times*, published in 1861, he contrasted the position of St. Paul with that of

44. Philip Schaff, "The Influence of the Early Church on the Institution of Slavery," *Mercersburg Review* 10 (October 1858): 616.

45. Ibid., 615-16. Eventually, according to Schaff, the procedure of manumission became a "solemn act" performed in the presence of the clergy and the whole Christian congregation.

46. Philip Schaff letter to H. B. Smith, Mercersburg, Pennsylvania, 8 February 1859. Philip Schaff Correspondence, ERHS. Schaff had not lost his sense of humor during the crisis period. In the letter he mentions "present theological writers" and names along with Mayer, Rauch, and Nevin, "Dr. *Schaff* author of many immortal works, too well known to be mentioned in this connection!!"

> our modern Abolitionists of the infidel type who secularize the holy philanthropy of the Gospel, subordinate the spiritual relations to the temporal, magnify the slavery question above every other moral question, denounce slavery under every form, in fierce, bitter, fanatical language, as the greatest sin and crime of our age and country, and our federal constitution, owing to its connection with it, as a 'covenant with death and an agreement with hell!'[47]

Schaff revealed his social conservatism most clearly in his discussion of the New Testament teaching concerning the relationship between masters and slaves. Abolitionists could take no comfort from this moderate's assertions that despite the spiritual freedom guaranteed by the Bible, servants should obey their masters in all things that did not violate the commands of God and "in the prospect of everlasting glory in heaven they might well forgo the comparatively small advantage of civil freedom in this present transient life." Further, "masters are nowhere required or even advised to emancipate their slaves" in the New Testament. Those who held slaves, however, should follow the instructions of Paul to Philemon and treat their slaves as brothers and sisters in Christ. Schaff preferred the term "servants" over "slaves" as being truer to the Greek usage in passages that refer to human bondage in the New Testament, and denoting a governmental relationship rather than a more degrading relationship of property ownership. The New Testament recognized governmental relationships between ruler and ruled and did not condemn them. It did, however, unconditionally reject buying and selling of human beings.[48]

Schaff was guided by the certainty that slavery had no place in Christian relationships and that emancipation on Christian principles, though a process involving centuries of time, was nonetheless inevitable. Christianity, said Schaff, "cures the root of the evil" and raises those in bondage to an "intellectual and moral condition" that allows them to participate in and contribute meaningfully to society. American slavery

47. Philip Schaff, *Slavery and the Bible: A Tract for the Times* (Chambersburg, Penn.: M. Kieffer and Co., 1861), 26. This paragraph is omitted from a reprint of this article in *Christ and Christianity.* The slave trade rightly received such censure, however, since "the very idea is utterly repugnant to the spirit of the gospel" (p. 24).

48. Ibid., 20-24.

had lingered for so long because it was an example of the most difficult type of the slavery problem in world history. Not only was American slavery a problem as a domestic institution and divisive political issue, but a deeper gulf separated slaves and masters: that of race. Thus, Schaff insightfully noted, "*the negro question lies far deeper than the slavery question,*" and therefore immediate emancipation provided no lasting solution.[49] Schaff continued to counsel moderation and non-interference between people of the North in affairs that were the "whole responsibility" of the States of the South.

The usually perceptive Schaff lagged far behind developments and seemed incredibly naive in his counsel to parties in the midst of civil war. He urged them to be responsible and calmly to alleviate the conditions that were the root causes of the outbreak of hostilities in the first place. Schaff seemed out of touch with the seriousness of the rift between the sections as he told those of the North to "take the vexing and perplexing question [of slavery] out of the turmoil of federal politics, and leave it to the several slave States, in the hands of Christian philanthropy, and of an all-wise Providence." At the same time he instructed the slaveholding states to "diminish as much as possible the evils and to prevent the abuses of slavery in their own midst, to provide for the proper moral and religious training of the negroes committed to their care, and thus to make the institution beneficial to both races while it lasts, and to prepare the way for its ultimate extinction without injury to either." It was up to the people of the North to offer their Southern neighbors "hearty sympathy . . . friendly counsel and . . . liberal cooperation" in this endeavor.[50]

Obviously neither side heeded Schaff's advice and he resigned himself to the tragedy of civil war, which eventually encompassed Mercersburg. From the beginning, Schaff was an ardent Unionist, but he was also able to view the conflict with enough dispassion to see the judgment of God against both sides. In a letter of 29 November 1861,

49. Ibid., 31.

50. Ibid, 32. Though these views in hindsight appear to be completely out of touch with the situation in 1861, they represented the feelings of a significant segment of the Northern population. In fact, this tract was a version of a sermon by Schaff to a union meeting of the Lutheran Church on 3 February 1861, which was published on request of those who heard it and who believed that "the extensive dissemination of such views, at this time, will produce great good."

Schaff lamented the blunders of Northern commanders but surmised that such setbacks served "to expose and humble our national vanity and pride." The only positive factor on the side of the North was the Port Royal affair, in which the North had captured "Mason — the fool of quality — and Slidell — the villain of quality."[51] Schaff distinguished, as surprisingly few could do at the time, between the purposes of God and the folly of human pretensions. All of the "national idols, mammon, cotton, slavery" were "shaken to the very foundation," heroes were made in one day and cast down the next. "All human wisdom is turned into folly, and human strength into weakness," but "in the mean time, 'God moves in a mysterious way his wonders to perform,'" and "the game is in the hands of Providence."[52]

On other occasions, Schaff could sound the patriotic call with the most ardent. He did not desire war, being opposed to it in principle, but it had come and in order to make the best of a bad situation, he became, in his words, "a war man for the sake of peace." In a war speech delivered in Lancaster, Pennsylvania, on 2 August 1862, Schaff insisted that the only honorable way to end the war was to fight it out to the finish. With the enthusiasm of a crusader he urged the able-bodied men in the crowd to

> enlist, enlist, enlist, under the star spangled banner, surmounted by the higher and holier banner which bears the inscription: By this thou shalt conquer! I appeal to you in the name of nationality against disintegration, of Union against disunion, of loyalty against treason, of liberty against despotism and slavery, of all that is dear to an American patriot. Enlist under the watchword: 'The Union and the Constitution — One and inseparable; Authority and Freedom now and forever.'

51. Philip Schaff, Letter "A," Mercersburg, Pennsylvania, 29 November 1861, Philip Schaff Correspondence, ERHS. William A. Clebsch, "Christian Interpretations of the Civil War," *Church History* 30 (June 1961): 212-22, lists Schaff with a mere handful of theologians, churchmen, and statesmen who refused to place full blame for the war on either North or South, but saw the conflict as judgment on the sins of the entire nation. See also Ernest Lee Tuveson, *Redeemer Nation: The Idea of America's Millennial Role* (Chicago: The University of Chicago Press, 1968; reprint ed. 1980), 187-214.

52. Schaff, Letter "A."

In language that echoed both the determination and the compassion of President Lincoln, Schaff continued,

> and having enlisted fight, fight, fight, that your children and children's children need never fight again. Fight with the sword in one hand, and the olive branch in the other. Fight till every star which has wandered away from its constellation shall be restored to its position and shine in its original lustre. Fight till the time honored banner of our nationality shall float over the cliffs of Vicksburg, the capitol of Richmond, and the Palms of Charleston as it now waves over this stand, an emblem of freedom and progress for all who from every quarter of the globe choose to make our magnificent country their home.[53]

As to the outcome of the war, Schaff sounded more like many of his fellow churchmen than he did Lincoln. While in his second inaugural address Lincoln pondered the inscrutable ways of Providence, in this unguarded and enthusiastic moment Schaff was characteristically optimistic, but he waxed overconfident about the righteousness of the Union cause.

> I have no misgiving as to the ultimate result. For we have *might* on our side, and what is better we have *right* on our side, and what is best of all, we have *God* on our side. Where God is there is victory. He rules supreme over all nations, and will overrule even the wrath of this causeless and wicked rebellion for his own glory and the good of our beloved country.[54]

Schaff kept a journal during the war, and after his death *Scribner's Magazine* published selections from June and July 1863. An editor's note by David Schaff revealed that Schaff himself narrowly escaped being taken prisoner by the Confederates because of his strongly Unionist public speeches since the beginning of the war. For the third time since the outbreak of hostilities, Schaff said, Rebel forces were either in or

53. Philip Schaff, "Conclusion to a War-Speech," 1. Given at the mass meeting at Lancaster, Pennsylvania, 5 August 1862. Philip Schaff Papers, ERHS.

54. Ibid., 2. Emphasis his.

near Mercersburg. With the troops of Lee once again invading the North, it appeared to Schaff that "the darkest hour of the American Republic and of the cause of the Union seems to be approaching." By June 16, the professors decided to suspend classes in the seminary because of the excitement and anxiety caused by the invasion, and in order to allow the students to enlist in the Union army. The professors encouraged their students to enlist. After all, Schaff sighed, "what are seminaries, colleges, and churches if we have no country and home?"[55]

On June 19 the Rebel cavalry arrived in Mercersburg, looking for horses and cattle for their army. Schaff had a "long conversation" with a Colonel Ferguson of the Confederate Army and was impressed by his courtesy as well as his determination. The Rebel soldiers were "very poorly and miscellaneously dressed," some with noble faces, but some looking "stupid and semi-savage." Schaff spoke bitterly of the abandonment of southern Pennsylvania by the Union forces. "The government," he lamented, "seems paralyzed for the moment." Confederate infantry arrived in Mercersburg on June 24 and Schaff again had conversations with officers and privates, including a major who was a distant relative to his wife. Schaff noted wryly that these Rebels were better equipped than those who had invaded the previous fall, since their victories had created a situation in which "Uncle Sam has to supply both armies."[56]

But the worst was yet to come. On the 25th, a guerrilla band of Confederate cavalry entered the town and threatened to burn it to the ground if citizens offered any resistance. The next day they engaged in what Schaff called "a regular slave-hunt . . . the worst spectacle I ever saw in this war." Some of those captured were escaped slaves, but Schaff insisted that two or three of those taken had been born free in that very neighborhood. Events brought out the worst in many people. There were some in the community, Schaff moaned, "who will betray their own neighbors." The situation was not one of theoretical detachment for Schaff and his family. On the contrary, they risked their own safety on behalf of their African American housekeeper and her son, who hid in the fields during the day and returned to Schaff's home under cover of darkness for food. The servant's daughter and her two children had already been captured and taken to Virginia.

55. Philip Schaff, "The Gettysburg Week," *Scribners Magazine* (July 1894): 21-22.
56. Ibid., 22-23.

Schaff was convinced that he had been in great danger. Years later, while visiting Libby Prison in Richmond, he reflected,

> What tales of horror [are] attached to this gloomy forbidding building! Here I might have found a miserable death like my friend and pupil Rice, in 1863, had I been in Mercersburg when Stuart's raid took 12 prisoners and carried them to Libby.[57]

Despite his outspoken Union sympathies and disgust with the behavior of the Rebels — particularly the guerrillas — stories of Union atrocities in southern territories convinced Schaff that "we deserve punishment in the North." The war and its accompanying events made Schaff hard pressed to maintain his optimistic view of American Christianity and civilization. "Such acts I should have thought impossible in America," he anguished, "after our boast of superior civilization and Christianity in this nineteenth century." Had there really been the progress in civilization that so many had believed? "This reminds one of the worst times of the Dark Ages, where might was right, and right had no might." Yet in his despair, Schaff affirmed, "God rules, and rules justly."[58]

Little did Schaff know that even as he wrote those words, one of the climactic battles of the war had begun. Just a few miles to the east, Union and Confederate armies clashed near the village of Gettysburg. On July 3 and 4 the citizens of Mercersburg held prayer meetings, and on the 5th the Union army brought hundreds of wounded Southern prisoners there, along with news of the decisive Union victory. Seminary staff and students cared for some six hundred wounded in the seminary building. Compelled by his gregarious nature, Schaff made the most of the opportunity to converse with the officers, men, and chaplains of the Confederate Army. On a few occasions, the chaplains led worship and prayer services attended by soldiers of both armies. By July 21, things began to return to normal and Schaff watched sadly as Union guards escorted away friends he had made among the Confederate officers.

The disturbances of the war helped Schaff make a decision that he had been considering for some years. The isolation of Mercersburg

57. Schaff, diary entry for 24 May 1873, Box IV, UTS.

58. Schaff, "The Gettysburg Week," 24-26.

had long been a hindrance to his scholarly pursuits, and the disruption of the Civil War was deeply frustrating for one who was accustomed to a life of constant production. Schaff obtained a two-year leave of absence from the seminary, during which he traveled in Europe and began his work with the New York Sabbath Committee. In 1865 he officially resigned his position at Mercersburg and took up residence in New York City, where he would spend the final twenty-eight years of his life.

Despite Schaff's hope that the battle of Gettysburg and the important Union victory at Vicksburg had sounded the death knell of the conflict, the war dragged on through 1864. In September of that year Schaff addressed an anniversary meeting of the United States Christian Commission, expressed his appreciation for their work, and reflected on the meaning of the war itself. The Commission had labored to "consecrate the war to holy purposes and turn its horrors into blessings for thousands of our soldiers and sailors who by the instrumentality of this institution [found] the Saviour whom they had lost or never known at home."[59]

In addition to the examples of individual salvation brought about by the war, a broader purpose was fulfilled in the providence of the God of nations. The Union cause could not fail because God had determined an important role for America in God's direction of world history.[60] The Union cause was righteous, Schaff insisted. This was a "war of self-defense of our country against domestic foes," else, Schaff insisted, "I would not defend it for a moment." In addition, God would honor the prayers and labors of hundreds of godly people who sought his aid on the Union side. Though Schaff failed to mention the prayers of equally godly people in the South, he obviously assumed that it was the righteousness of the cause of the Northern people — described in his war speech — that would make their prayers more effectual.

The most important assurance of success, however, was the purpose of God in allowing the establishment of the Union. "God does not permit a nation to perish," Schaff insisted, "before it has accomplished that mission for which he called it into existence." "If this country has no future," he added, "I do not know where to look for a future of

59. Philip Schaff, "Anniversary of the Christian Commission, Baltimore, Maryland," *German Reformed Messenger* 29 (October 19, 1864): 1.

60. See Clebsch, "Christian Interpretations of the Civil War," 212-22.

secular and ecclesiastical history on the face of the globe."[61] Division, in short, would violate the plans of the God of nature who had designed the geography of the North American continent to contain one nation free from the "border wars and endless discord" that had so plagued the new republics of Central and South America. The unique combination of religious fervor and seemingly unlimited space would allow the development of a Christian nation that would carry forth God's plan in the world.

Mysteries of Providence

In the heady atmosphere of optimism, Schaff could even express such ideas to European audiences. During the late spring and summer of 1865 Schaff was once more in Europe and was again asked to lecture on his adopted homeland. The lectures, later published as *Der Bürgerkrieg und das christliche Leben in Nord-Amerika,* offered Schaff's most developed understanding of the war. Schaff could speak of the war as "a righteous judgment of God upon a guilt of South and of North" alike; it was the "humiliation of an arrogant and boastful nation."[62] All of America's "moral maladies" had been laid bare before the world and immorality and injustice had increased, especially in the cities. Nonetheless, Schaff remained confident that the "hand of a special Providence which watches over them" would help Americans to regain their sense of divine mission.

More importantly, however, the war raised the question of whether the American nation could indeed fulfill the destiny for which God had prepared it. Looking back on the war, Schaff could answer that question in the affirmative, and could also argue that God had providentially used the horrors of the war to develop strength of character and maturity in America. Through the war, the nation had "learned more in four years than it would otherwise have learned in a hundred"; it had "borne fruits which are worth all the sacrifices of blood and treasure." The war had developed "the heroic element, the capability of sacrifice" in the American people. It had provided a "priceless wealth of historical tradi-

61. Schaff, "Christian Commission," 1.

62. Schaff, *Der Bürgerkrieg,* 8, 28; *CI* 37 (1 March 1866): 2; (22 March 1866): 1.

tions," and allowed the nation, for the first time, to enter its "age of manly vigor and independence." The process of assimilation of foreign peoples had been accelerated by the need for cooperation during the war. This redemptive "bloody baptism" had given the American people a renewed "hope for a glorious regeneration." As "'the blood of the martyrs is the seed of the Church' . . . the blood of the patriots [is] the seed of the state." Through it all, "the all-directing hand of God was visible."[63]

According to Schaff, Abraham Lincoln embodied and symbolized the deepest meanings of the war and had become "the second father of the North American Republic."[64] Schaff immediately recognized the profundity of Lincoln's understanding of the war. He argued that Lincoln's Second Inaugural Address had no peer in "genuine Christian wisdom and generosity."[65] Schaff's view of the conflict sounded like Lincoln's address as he insisted that "Providence . . . gradually unfolded its own programme before the astonished view of the world, and educated the nation, with its worthy President at its head, step by step, to the understanding of its appointed work and to the measures adapted for the discharge of this." The historian saw the assassination of Lincoln as another "mystery of Providence," which God turned from a catastrophe to a blessing through which the rebellion and slavery received their final death blows. Ever the optimist, Schaff put the war into his cosmic scheme of interpretation and was able to see the cosmos even in the chaos of war and reconstruction.

> A country in which so many streams of noble blood have flowed, in which so many sacrifices have been offered by Government and people, and in which the hand of God has so visibly and wonderfully

63. Ibid., 8-10; *CI* 37 (March 1, 1866): 2.

64. Ibid., 16; *CI* 37 (March 1, 1866): 3.

65. This section was not published in the Berlin, 1866 edition of *Der Bürgerkrieg.* It is found in *CI* 37 (March 15, 1866): 1. A passage that reveals something of the character of American Christianity in the 1860s, as well as Schaff's impatience with some interpreters, is his account of Lincoln's visit to Ford's theater. Some German Christians were offended that Lincoln had attended the theater on Good Friday. Schaff himself admitted "regret, in a religious point of view, that Lincoln went to the theater at all," but insisted that the president would never have done so on the Sabbath as was "the universal habit among Christian kings and princes in Europe."

> guided events to a happy issue, must, according to all human forecast, have a great future before it. It has endured the fiery trial, and has now first entered upon the age of manly vigor and independence.[66]

America as a nation had been chosen by God, according to Schaff. The chaos within the nation could never overcome the cosmos that Providence nurtured. Very early in his career Schaff came to believe that America was uniquely destined and qualified to support the work of God in the world. Americans were not individually superior to those who had lived before; on the contrary, they were characteristically average. Yet they and their nation had been chosen by God to bring about the unity of Christianity and ultimately the evangelization of the world. Americans had been given the responsibility to spread the Bible, civilization, and liberty throughout the world. In the United States all the forces of Europe, good and bad, fermented together and the situation appeared chaotic. Yet a transition was underway, and the spirit of God worked to fashion a beautiful creation out of the chaos. Specifically in America this new and beautiful creation was taking shape.

Schaff could not emphasize his point strongly enough. Despite the skeptics who could see nothing but the ferment and chaos, Schaff insisted in no uncertain terms that "the future lies with this country." God was using the American nation to develop a new people and to facilitate the reunion of his church. The choices were clear and the stakes were high.

> The only alternative therefore is either to believe in the speedy destruction of the world, or to look hopefully to the western hemisphere as the land of promise, to which in fact the massive emigrations from all parts of Europe seem to point.

Schaff had little doubt about what the outcome of the process would be. God would accomplish his purpose to "make this magnificent country — the richest inheritance ever given to man — Immanuel's land for all time to come."[67]

66. Ibid., 12, 16-17; CI 37 (March 1, 1866): 3.

67. Philip Schaff, *The Theology for Our Age and Country* (New York: Rogers and Sherwood, 1872), 19.

CHAPTER 7

Evangelical-Catholic Christianity in America

Patriotism vs. Nationalism

Philip Schaff believed that America's place in the history of the world was distinctive. The new nation would be the home of a new people who would combine the best characteristics of all the civilized peoples of the world. Most Americans felt the same way, but for Schaff, the nation was only a means to an end. In the providence of God America was emerging as a world leader, and in the cosmic scope of history the reason was clear: America had become so powerful in order to fulfill its divinely ordained mission. Schaff captured the excitement and energy, the chaos and ferment of the new land in his lectures to European audiences in 1854.

> Providence, who creates nothing in vain, has there made physical preparations on the grandest scale, and formed an immeasurable territory, containing the most fruitful soil, the most valuable mineral treasures and the most favorable means of commercial intercourse, as a tempting asylum for all European nations, churches and sects, who, there freed from the fetters of antiquated institutions, amid circumstances and conditions altogether new, and with renovated energies, swarm, and jostle each other, and yet, in an incredibly short space of time, are moulded by the process into one powerful nationality.[1]

1. Philip Schaff, *America: A Sketch of Its Political, Social and Religious Character,*

Schaff's exaltation of the nation was not crass nationalism, however. Instead, he provided an important corrective to the general drift of the times. While he shared the optimism of politicians, business leaders, and theologians about the future of America, something more profound than national power or wealth shaped his vision. America was indeed wealthy and powerful, and was becoming more so every day, but Schaff believed that America was great because she would be the scene for the final development of Christian history.

H. Richard Niebuhr noted a change in the attitudes of American Christians during the nineteenth century. "The old idea of American Christians as a chosen people who had been called to a special task," Niebuhr observed,

> was turned into the notion of a chosen nation especially favored. . . . As the nineteenth century went on the note of divine favoritism was increasingly sounded. Christianity, democracy, Americanism, the English language and culture, the growth of industry and science, American institutions — these are all confounded and confused.

The kingdom of God, noted Niebuhr, had become "a human possession."[2]

Americans rejoiced in their role as God's "new Israel," but their understanding of that role was in danger of degenerating into the kind of ethnocentrism that plagued the ancient Hebrew people. According to Albert K. Weinberg, in the opinions of many Americans this new "'kingdom of priests and a holy nation' was ordained to preserve not the law of man's duty to God, but the law of man's duty to man — democracy." This American version of an "anthropocentric theology" came perilously close "to changing the traditional dogma, that man exists *ad majorem gloriam Dei,* into the heresy that God exists *ad majorem gloriam hominis.*"[3]

---

ed. Perry Miller (Cambridge: Harvard University Press, 1961), 210. This passage is included in a section of the lectures entitled "The significance of North America for the future development of the kingdom of God," pp. 209-218.

2. H. Richard Niebuhr, *The Kingdom of God in America* (New York: Harper & Row, 1959), 179.

3. Albert K. Weinberg, *Manifest Destiny: A Study of Nationalist Expansionism in American History* (Gloucester, Mass.: Peter Smith, 1958), 128.

Schaff's major contribution to the concept of American destiny was his demand that American Christians must maintain the original notion that their chosenness was first and foremost an indication of duty. He never denied that American democracy and civilization were valuable contributions, but America's greatest gift to the world was her religion. The nation was significant primarily as the locus of developing Christianity, and in America the Christian church would reach its highest and perhaps final form. World history, in Schaff's opinion, played the part of "one crying in the wilderness, preparing the way for Him, who shall come." The modern world had been ushered in by the Protestant Reformation, according to Schaff, and it was in North America that "the fate of the Reformation is to be decided." All of the tendencies unleashed by the Reformation were present in their most fully developed form in the American land of freedom. The ultimate question, however, was a religious one. Would Protestantism

> at last break up into atoms [or] . . . come together, consolidate, concentrate itself, and out of the phoenix-ashes of all Christian denominations and sects, rise glorified, as the truly universal, evangelical Catholic Bride of the Lord, adorned with the fairest flowers of the church-history of all centuries?[4]

Like his colleague John Williamson Nevin, Schaff was highly optimistic about America's future but rejected uncritical nationalism and imperialism in the name of America's "manifest destiny." He blasted the "piratical schemes of our manifest-destinarians who would swallow, in one meal, Cuba, all Central America, Mexico, and Canada." He noted a clear difference between patriotism, "one of the noblest of natural virtues," and nationalism, which implied hatred or contempt of foreigners and disregarded the rights and welfare of other nations.[5]

The issue that had most engaged Schaff's thought and efforts throughout his career was the "church question," and he insisted that America would serve as "the theatre in which the question ultimately

4. Schaff, *America*, 212, 214-15.

5. Philip Schaff, *American Nationality* (Chambersburg, Penn.: M. Kieffer and Co., 1856), 22, 3-4. See also Richard E. Wentz, "John Williamson Nevin and American Nationalism," *Journal of the American Academy of Religion* 58 (Winter 1990): 617-32.

and practically must be solved."[6] In the 1850s, he characterized the story of the American churches as the "storm-and pressure period." Yet Schaff boldly insisted that the turmoil was "the chaotic fermentation that precedes the act of creation."[7] From the chaos of ferment would emerge the cosmos of a new creation. Out of unprecedented diversity would emerge the reunion of Christendom. Concerning the form the church would take in the land of opportunity, the words "evangelical catholic" are significant. Schaff's commanding vision focused on the realization of the evangelical-catholic church as the outcome toward which all the agitation of American freedom pointed.

Evangelical-Catholic Christianity

While the spiritual and physical unity of the church was his ultimate ideal, Schaff came to believe that denominational (as opposed to "sectarian") division in the American church, rather than being detrimental, was in fact beneficial. Each legitimate branch of the church had its contribution to make to the development and fullness of the presentation of the gospel, and to destroy any of them would hinder the progress of the church. Again Schaff utilized Hegel's conception of development derived from the German term *aufheben.* As the old forms are destroyed, the essence of the old is preserved and raised to a higher level. This model which could illuminate the relationships between denominations was the same as the one Schaff utilized to show the interaction of various ethnic groups that resulted in the "new" people called "Americans." As the best characteristics of every people would be retained and elevated in the new American character even while some old forms would disappear, so the process of development would retain the best of each branch of the Christian church and raise it to a higher level in the emerging evangelical-catholic Christianity, while correcting their individual weaknesses. A further parallel between the political and ecclesiastical spheres was Schaff's belief that as certain nations would dominate in forming aspects of the American character,

6. David S. Schaff, *The Life of Philip Schaff: In Part Autobiographical* (New York: Scribner's, 1897), 201.

7. Schaff, *America,* 213.

certain denominations would dominate aspects of evangelical-catholic Christianity.

Surprisingly, by the end of his life, Schaff was ready to accord the honor of the "centre of unification" to either the Greek Orthodox or the Roman Catholic "denominations."[8] Schaff's initial strongly negative attitude about Roman Catholicism and the development of his ideas toward greater tolerance and incorporation were discussed at length in chapter 2. Let it suffice to reemphasize here the novelty of Schaff's views about the Roman Catholic Church in America and the important role that he conceived for that church as it was changed by the American situation and by contact with the various Protestant groups. His opinions about Eastern Orthodoxy changed similarly. In fact, his original opinion of the Greek Church was even lower than his early ideas about Roman Catholicism. The Catholics, in their extreme conservatism, he said, had only been saved from stagnation by the prodding of Protestantism. Had the Protestants not goaded the Catholics, they "like the Greek Church (at least in great part), must have passed over into a state of putrefaction, so as to present at best only the spectacle of a praying corpse."[9] The Greeks had denied proper historical movement and found themselves in deepest stagnation and "dead formalism." As late as 1855, Schaff could speak of the Greek Church as "a mummy of Christianity in a praying posture."[10]

In his changing attitude about Greek Orthodoxy, Schaff provides a graphic example of his own lifelong belief that greater knowledge about other forms of Christianity brings with it greater appreciation for the things of value in those forms. His move from the hills of southern Pennsylvania to the metropolis of New York City probably

8. Philip Schaff, *The Reunion of Christendom: A Paper Prepared for the Parliament of Religions and the National Conference of the Evangelical Alliance Held in Chicago, September and October, 1893* (New York: Evangelical Alliance Office, 1893), 25.

9. Philip Schaff, *The Principle of Protestantism,* trans. John W. Nevin (Chambersburg, Penn.: Publication Office of the German Reformed Church, 1845; reprint ed., Philadelphia: United Church Press, 1964), 128.

10. Philip Schaff, *What is Church History? A Vindication of the Idea of Historical Development* (Philadelphia: J. B. Lippincott, 1846); reprinted in *Reformed and Catholic: Selected Historical and Theological Writings of Philip Schaff,* ed. Charles Yrigoyen, Jr. and George M. Bricker (Pittsburgh: The Pickwick Press, 1979), 123 [107] (references to page numbers in the original edition will be noted in brackets); D. Schaff, *Life,* 199. Schaff used "Greek Orthodoxy" as a generic term to describe all of Eastern Orthodoxy.

gave him his first opportunity for firsthand exposure to Orthodoxy in America, and a trip to Russia on behalf of the Evangelical Alliance — to plead with Czar Alexander II for religious liberty in his domains — let him personally witness Russian Orthodox worship. At that time he could still lament the mechanical character of Orthodox devotion, but he later spoke favorably of his experience of "spiritual communion of an American Presbyterian with an orthodox and pious Russian priest."[11] By 1893, Schaff recognized the special sphere of ministry for which the Greek Church was particularly adapted and called it a "glorious church" in whose language the New Testament and Septuagint had been passed on to all of Christendom. Her confessors and martyrs, her great writers and apologists, and her great creeds were a substantial legacy for all of Christian history. Only the Greek and Roman Churches could trace their origins back to the apostolic age, and that history provided the essential center for the emerging evangelical-catholic church.

Yet Schaff was far from accepting the Catholic or Greek views that if there was to be reunion of Christians, it would come when all Christians joined their particular communion. Neither Orthodox nor Catholics would recognize Schaff's evangelical-catholic church as their own. The Protestant principle would dominate the Catholic substance in Schaff's ideal, though Schaff's concessions to Orthodoxy and Catholicism made most Protestants very uncomfortable. Only as the church had developed through the centuries had it remained the legitimate bearer of the gospel to people from age to age, and development was a particularly Protestant characteristic. When the Catholic Church had refused to continue its development, it had become necessary for Protestantism to emerge. Included in the Protestant contribution to the emerging church were all the major denominations, and even smaller ones that had a legitimate contribution to make to developing Christianity. Schaff's guiding principle for inclusion was that "no labor in the

11. Philip Schaff, "Discord and Concord of Christendom, or Denominational Variety and Christian Unity," in *Christ and Christianity: Studies on Christology, Creeds and Confessions, Protestantism and Romanism, Reformation Principles, Sunday Observance, Religious Freedom, and Christian Union* (New York: Scribner's, 1885), 307. See also D. Schaff, *Life*, 344-45. Schaff reported on the deputation to Russia in his *Report of the Deputation of the American Branch of the Evangelical Alliance, Appointed to Memorialize the Emperor of Russia in Behalf of Religious Liberty* (New York: Office of the Evangelical Alliance, 1871).

Lord can ever be lost."[12] In fact, he claimed, the "cause of Christ would be marred and weakened if any one of the historic churches should be extinguished, or be absorbed into another."[13]

From his early views expressed in *The Principle of Protestantism* which only grudgingly, if at all, recognized value in the various denominations, Schaff had moved throughout his life toward an appreciation of the contributions the various groups could make to a full comprehension of Christian truth and life. Even in the 1850s, when he had learned to tolerate American denominational diversity, he found much that he regretted in the situation. For example, the Presbyterian and Congregational denominations which had emerged from the Puritanism of New England were to be admired for their "deep moral earnestness" and "stern self-discipline." Yet such emphases had led to "stripping the spirit of all covering whatever, as though the body were a work of the devil." Such lack of balance had led on the one hand to "stagnation" in theology, and on the other to the growth of Unitarianism. Likewise, while the Methodist founders Whitefield and the Wesleys showed great "wisdom, prudence, and moderation," their followers went to the "unnatural and wrong" extreme of separation from the Church of England and the excesses of revivalism.[14]

The Lutherans had come to America and had split into numerous bodies with ideologies, "representing almost all those of the mother church, besides specifically American tendencies." The three major divisions were the New Lutherans, Old Lutherans, and the Moderate or "Melanchthonian" Lutherans. The most Americanized were the New Lutherans, led by Samuel S. Schmucker, who had incorporated "American Puritanic and Methodistic elements," as well as almost exclusive use of the English language. For instance, the New Lutherans placed more emphasis on oratorical talent than theological education, and were very "active, practical, and progressive" in true American fashion. In contrast, the Old Lutherans were, "except in cases of happy inconsistency, very exclusive, and narrow-minded, and unable or unwilling to appreciate properly other churches and nationalities than their own." The Moderates followed a course much more congenial to Schaff, that

12. Philip Schaff, *Theological Propædeutic: A General Introduction to the Study of Theology* (New York: Scribner's, 1894), 241.

13. Schaff, "Discord and Concord of Christendom," 300.

14. Schaff, *Principle of Protestantism,* 145-46, 200-201.

of seeking a middle way between the extremes. Regrettably, some were indifferent in theology, but many were serious about their beliefs and their distinctive mission to "mediate . . . between European-German, and American interests."[15]

Thus, all three branches faced serious dangers as they tried to adapt to (or isolate themselves from) the American situation. The Old Lutherans, due to their extreme conservatism, risked falling out of step with the progress of the modern world and church. The New Lutherans were so concerned about fitting into American life that they had too easily accepted inferior American ways, in particular in their adoption of a conception of the Lord's Supper that was more rationalistic than even that of Zwingli. The moderates correctly sought a middle ground and harmony, yet they were perhaps ready to pay too dear a price for harmony.

Despite the difficulties, however, the Lutherans had a major contribution to make to evangelical-catholic Christianity. Lutherans must occupy a mediating position that would do justice both to their heritage and to their situation in the new world. In fact, Schaff's understanding of the Lutherans provides a paradigm for the development of a denomination in evangelical-catholic America. The Lutherans must find a way to be faithful to their "genius and history" and to communicate that to a "new country and people," yet without offending non-Lutherans. This process could purify the Lutheran gospel by removing outdated forms and also raise its essence to greater heights to allow a universal contribution. Of particular value from the Lutheran tradition was their deep respect for history, which could provide a corrective for the Reformed antihistorical tendency.[16]

The character of American Christianity was predominantly Reformed, Schaff believed, primarily due to Puritan sources but also through influence from German and Dutch Reformed bodies. The Dutch Reformed held the honor of being in America earlier than any Protestants except the Anglicans, and therefore contributed to America's Christian foundation. The Dutch had rather quickly assimilated into American life, for example in the use of the English language, but in Schaff's opinion they had gone too far and sacrificed some of their theological genius on the altar of accommodation. In their views of the

15. Schaff, *America,* 150, 152.
16. Ibid., 159.

sacraments and "kindred subjects," for example, they had "fallen in entirely with the reigning spirit of modern American Puritanism and Presbyterianism" with their "low Zwinglian theory." In other areas, however, they suffered from "theological stagnation" and seemed to assume that "the venerable Synod of Dort settled all theological questions in 1618, and left us nothing to do but to renew from time to time a sweeping commonplace protest against Arminianism, and more especially against Popery, as the veritable Antichrist and enemy of all civil and religious freedom." The Dutch Reformed denomination must "justify its separate denominational existence" by engaging in theological creativity on a level worthy of "its historical origin, its own resources, and its social standing in American Christendom." In other words, stop fighting out-of-date theological battles and get in step with the issues of the modern world — the church question, the issue of unbelief, and the reunion of Christians.[17]

The oldest Protestant church in the United States, the Protestant Episcopal, was "less numerous, popular, and energetic" than the other major denominations, yet had access to the "higher circles of society" and had very good prospects for growth. In fact, in one of his more glaring errors of prediction, Schaff thought that it had perhaps "the best prospects of ultimate success in the United States" of any Protestant denomination.[18] Such could happen, however, only if the church were more thoroughly Americanized. Less rigidity of liturgy and more liberal and friendly relations with other evangelical churches were two things Schaff suggested that might give the church greater appeal among all classes of people. Already there had been modifications in the American church, as opposed to the mother Anglican church, in favor of lay involvement and full separation from civil government. Modifications of the Thirty-Nine Articles had made the church fit the American situation better. This ability to modify nonessentials while maintaining a generally traditional core showed that the Episcopal Church in America had significant features to contribute to evangelical-catholicism.

One group whose significance Schaff initially failed to grasp was the Baptists. Admittedly they were numerous, if one counted all who opposed infant baptism, but they split too frequently over other issues

17. Schaff, *America,* 121, 124.
18. Ibid., 126, 135.

to present a unified front. Among those classified by Schaff as "baptists" in the 1850s were Mennonites and Disciples of Christ. Those we think of as Baptists proper also existed in numerous branches, and Schaff focused his attention on the "Regular or Calvinistic Baptists" as opposed to Free-Will Baptists. While he disagreed with their insistence on believers' baptism, he was more disturbed with their rejection of Christians who defended infant baptism. In their rigid logic, they were, "if possible, still more unchurchly and anti-catholic, than . . . the Puritans."[19] At this early stage of his career and with his top-down view of Christian development, Schaff did not envision the powerful influence of Baptists on American society, but he did admire their insistence on separation of church and state, and saw value in their critique of abuses of infant baptism.

Unlike many Christians, Schaff accorded the Quakers a place and contribution to developing evangelical-catholic Christianity. He lamented what he believed to be serious theological defects in their rejection of the sacraments and elevation of the Spirit above the written Word, but he had great admiration for their humanitarian work. "They will undoubtedly still long maintain themselves, and fill their place in the great family of Christendom," he maintained, "but they will always be limited to a very small sphere." Their position was precarious, Schaff thought, because if piety disappeared, "Quakerism sinks into the lowest rationalism and skepticism, or wanders into the wildest excesses of ultra democracy; the overstrained spiritualism ends in the flesh."[20]

By the end of his life, Schaff was prepared to praise the virtues of nearly all Christian groups across the theological spectrum and grant them a place in the kingdom of God. In the conclusion to his address, "The Reunion of Christendom," delivered to the Evangelical Alliance meeting held in conjunction with the World's Parliament of Religions at the Columbian Exposition of 1893, Schaff listed the participants in the developing evangelical-catholic Christianity. In his description of the major players in the drama, he described as "glorious churches" the following: Greek, Latin (Roman Catholic), Evangelical Lutheran, Evangelical Reformed, Episcopal, Presbyterian, Congregational, Baptist, and Methodist. In addition, the Society of Friends he saw as a "glorious society," and the Brotherhood of the Moravians "a glorious Brother-

19. Ibid., 172.
20. Ibid., 177-78.

hood." Schaff also praised the Waldenses, Anabaptists, and Socinians for their steadfastness under persecution and untiring demands for religious liberty. He chastised Unitarians and Universalists for their serious departures from orthodoxy, yet praised them for their criticisms which led to more balanced views among orthodox Christians. Finally, he lauded the Salvation Army "in spite of its strange and abnormal methods, as the most effective revival agency since the days of Wesley and Whitefield."[21]

Certainly Schaff tried to remain true to his assertion that "no labor in the Lord is lost." He insisted that "there is room for all these and many other Churches and societies in the kingdom of God, whose height and depth and length and breadth, variety and beauty, surpass human comprehension."[22] Schaff had certainly come a long way from his early belief that Christian union could only be real if based on institutional union.

Publications as a Means to Reunion

Though Schaff's ideas about the form of Christian union changed with time, the goal of the "reunion of Christendom" remained uppermost in his mind. To that end he founded the American Society of Church History, and joined various voluntary societies that facilitated cooperation among Christians of various denominations. That basic vision also provided the impulse for Schaff's editorial work with three scholarly journals: *The Mercersburg Review* (coedited by Schaff, with E. V. Gerhart, 1857-1861), *Der deutsche Kirchenfreund* (founded by Schaff in 1848 and edited by him until 1854), and the *Evangelische Zeugnisse aus den deutschen Kirchen in Amerika* (founded by Schaff in 1863 and edited by him until 1865 when it was discontinued). Through each of these, Schaff sought to build bridges between Germany and America in theology and practical church life, and to provide interdenominational forums for theological discussion.[23]

21. Schaff, *The Reunion of Christendom,* 40-45.

22. Ibid., 45.

23. For the *Kirchenfreund,* Schaff often had to labor as typesetter, printer, and binder as well as editor. See D. Schaff, *Life,* 161-63.

For example, the prospectus proposing the founding of the *Mercersburg Review* in 1849 stated that "the Mercersburg Review will bear no strictly denominational character." Five years later, Professor Theodore Appel of Marshall College reflected on whether or not publication of the *Review* should continue, and noted the difficulty of maintaining support for a periodical that "rises above denominational limits, and aims at a true catholicity."[24] Schaff's editorship supported that policy as he tried to make the voice of Mercersburg heard throughout the theological world. The *Kirchenfreund* aimed at a more limited German-speaking audience, but it also reflected the ecumenical ideals of its founder. David Schaff noted that "the effort to maintain its undenominational character was not without success, and it secured the cooperation of prominent adherents of the Lutheran, the Reformed and the Moravian churches."[25]

One of the ways to promote church union, according to Schaff, was to educate Christians about one another. To that end, Schaff organized and promoted a series of American denominational histories to be produced under the auspices of the American Society of Church History. Though Schaff did not live to see any of the volumes published, one of his longtime colleagues insisted that "the series is Dr. Schaff's work as much as if he had written it and followed it through the press."[26] The final result of the venture was a thirteen-volume set, published between 1893 and 1897, which Henry Warner Bowden has called "the most valuable literary achievement in an ecumenical vein" produced by the ASCH.[27] The initial volume, entitled *The Religious Forces of the United States*, was prepared by Henry K. Carroll and based upon statistics from the 1890 census. The final volume was a general history of American Christianity by Leonard W. Bacon which looked forward to Christian union in the future. In between were eleven volumes of denominational histories, written with a distinctively irenic tone.[28]

24. John Williamson Nevin, "Preliminary Statement," *Mercersburg Review* 1 (January 1849): 7-8; T. Appel, "The Review and the Quarterly," *Mercersburg Review* 5 (January 1853): 7-8.

25. D. Schaff, *Life*, 163.

26. Ibid., 465, quotes Methodist Bishop John F. Hurst.

27. Henry W. Bowden, *Church History in the Age of Science: Historiographical Patterns in the United States, 1876-1918* (Chapel Hill: The University of North Carolina Press, 1971), 64.

28. Authors and denominations of the histories were as follows: A. H. Newman,

Throughout the planning of the project, Schaff's ideal of denominational cooperation toward church union guided his efforts. The goals of the project, which were set forth in the *Papers* of the ASCH, indicated that the authors of the volumes must be ecumenically minded first-rate scholars. While they obviously would desire to portray their own denominations as positively as possible, they would also recognize the virtues of other communions. These would be volumes "decidedly irenical in spirit." Cooperation among the authors would set the pattern for the desired effect upon readers. The series would produce "large irenical results" since "a wide reading of histories of all the denominations . . . could not fail to be promotive, in a high degree, of truth and peace."[29]

Characteristically, the series included a history of the Roman Catholic "denomination" and to the author of that volume Schaff wrote, "I sincerely hope that the contemplated series of denominational histories prepared by competent scholars will not only be a valuable authentic contribution to our theological and historical literature, but also tend to remove ignorance and prejudice and to bring Christians nearer together." The same goal held true for the Protestant contributors. For example, Schaff wrote to Williston Walker, who was to write the volume on Congregationalism, "I confess to have a moral interest in the contemplated series as a means of bringing the different churches into closer union and ultimate coöperation."[30]

Baptist; Williston Walker, Congregationalist; H. E. Jacobs, Lutheran; J. M. Buckley, Methodist; R. E. Thompson, Presbyterian; C. C. Tiffany, Protestant Episcopal; E. T. Corwin, Dutch Reformed; J. H. Dubbs, German Reformed; J. T. Hamilton, Moravian; T. O'Gorman, Roman Catholic; J. H. Allen, Unitarian; R. Eddy, Universalist; G. Alexander, Methodist Church, South; J. B. Scouller, United Presbyterian; R. V. Foster, Cumberland Presbyterian; T. C. Johnson, Presbyterian Church, South; B. B. Tyler, Disciples of Christ; A. C. Thomas, Society of Friends; R. H. Thomas, United Brethren in Christ; and S. P. Spreng, Evangelical Association.

29. *Papers of the American Society of Church History*, First Series 3 (1891): 210. Quoted in Shriver, *Philip Schaff*, 96.

30. Quoted in D. Schaff, *Life*, 465. See also Shriver, *Philip Schaff*, 95-97.

American Religious Consensus?

An important background issue to Philip Schaff's ecumenism and cosmopolitanism is that of the quest for consensus — the supposed existence of a broad agreement about values, of common assumptions, ideals, or beliefs that serve to unify any particular society. The question is this: Is there, or was there in the nineteenth century, an American consensus, and if so, what was it? A number of options have been presented. Most prominent in the period under discussion was the conception, especially among leaders of the dominant religion, that the American consensus was somehow bound to Protestant Christianity. To be a true American was to be Protestant, and, for many, to be an Anglo-Saxon Protestant. The popularity of books like Josiah Strong's *Our Country,* first published in 1885, reflected decades of mounting fears about immigrants among the Protestants of America. During its first twenty years the book sold some 175,000 copies, and boasted influence comparable to that of Harriet Beecher Stowe's best-selling *Uncle Tom's Cabin.* Strong warned of the dangers of the growing Roman Catholic Church and the flood of "foreign" people who congregated in cities and threatened to undermine the American system of separation of church and state and the Protestant morality of American institutions.[31]

A second model which downplays the importance of the connection of American character with traditional Christianity but still assumes consensus is that proposed by religious historian Sidney Mead. Mead attempted to "delineate the religion of the Republic" and to point out its differences from denominational religion on theological and practical levels.[32] This religion of the republic, or "civil religion" as it has come to be called, has taken a number of forms, but always emphasizes the institutions, documents, and leaders of the American nation as central to the nonecclesiastical religiousness and nonchurchly value system of the American people.

31. Strong is discussed in Robert Michaelsen, *Piety in the Public School* (New York: Macmillan, 1970), 119-21. Important discussions of the theme of "Protestant America" are Robert T. Handy, *A Christian America: Protestant Hopes and Historical Realities,* rev. ed. (New York: Oxford University Press, 1984), and Martin E. Marty, *Righteous Empire: The Protestant Experience in America* (New York: Dial, 1970).

32. Sidney E. Mead, *The Nation with the Soul of a Church* (New York: Harper & Row, 1975), 5.

A recent variation of the civil religion type is that of Phillip Hammond, who applies the integration thesis of the sociologist Emile Durkheim to the religiously pluralistic situation of modern America, and argues that the legal system of the nation has taken the place of the traditional religions in providing order and uniformly acceptable meaning in the society. For Hammond, it is the "nine high priests in their black robes," who by interpreting the sacred texts of the nation provide the religious meanings for society.[33]

In sharp contrast to these proposals, R. Laurence Moore rejects the validity of consensus as an interpretive theme in American religious history. Instead, according to Moore, Americanness is a direct result of "outsiderhood"; it is the creative outsider who is "typically American."[34] It is the differentness of "outsider" groups that is characteristically American rather than any supposed consensus, be it Protestant or civil. Moore criticizes the American religious historians of the nineteenth and early twentieth centuries for their alleged creation of the myth of a Protestant consensus, and sees the efforts of those who promote the idea of consensus based on a religion of the republic as only extending the life of the myth of homogeneity. In the last two decades, says Moore, scholars of American religion have replaced the "stable pluralism" of earlier accounts with a more workable "unstable pluralism." "Conflict," he continues, "has replaced consensus. Contention has replaced comity."[35]

One of the histories critiqued by Moore is Philip Schaff's *America.* Moore insists that Schaff (along with Robert Baird before him and historians to the time of Winthrop Hudson after him) failed to give proper due to non-"mainline" groups, and because of his *desire* for Christian unity, overemphasized order in American religious history. Moore is correct in his assertion that Schaff emphasized Christian union, but he fails to give Schaff proper credit for the progressive nature of many of his views. For example, Moore claims that Schaff, like Baird, "attached no long-range significance to the proliferation of sects in

33. Phillip E. Hammond, "Religious Pluralism and Durkheim's Integration Thesis," in *Changing Perspectives in the Scientific Study of Religion,* ed. Allan W. Eister (New York: John Wiley & Sons, 1974), 115-42.

34. R. Laurence Moore, *Religious Outsiders and the Making of Americans* (New York: Oxford University Press, 1986), see especially p. xi.

35. Ibid., 20.

antebellum America. For the most part they were sects that Europe had dumped on America, and Schaff anticipated for them a short life in the New World."[36] While this accurately reflects Schaff's opinion during the early part of his career, Moore's generalization fails to show the development in Schaff's thought which eventually found him expressing deep appreciation for the positive contributions each group had already made and would continue to make in the future of American Christianity.

Schaff certainly insisted that consensus ruled, and due to the novelty of the American situation, he misread the extent of the pluralism of his day. Yet given the prevailing attitudes about religious liberty and pluralism in both Europe and America, it is indeed remarkable how quickly and clearly Schaff recognized the values of diversity. Nearly everyone in the late nineteenth century believed that consensus was necessary for the smooth functioning of society, and that consensus implied uniformity. In contrast, Schaff came to see that consensus could exist in a situation that appeared hopelessly chaotic to most interpreters. His ecumenism was far in advance of prevailing attitudes (at least in America), and his cosmopolitanism allowed him to broaden the idea of American nationality to include more than the Anglo-Saxon character, which most nineteenth-century Protestants increasingly emphasized as they faced the massive immigration of their day. Thus, in both religious and civil realms, Schaff's thought provided important transitions away from the narrowness of nativism and ethnocentrism and toward more contemporary notions of religious and ethnic pluralism.

Exceptions to the consensus through unity in diversity theme were few, but of them, the Church of Jesus Christ of Latter-day Saints was noteworthy. Even this irenic, positive man felt compelled to say that "I fear I can say nothing at all satisfactory about this phenomenon." Mormonism, Schaff insisted, was even "more unpopular than Romanism . . . and has much more affinity with Mohammedanism than with Christianity."[37] Like Robert Baird before him, Schaff found Mormonism to

36. Ibid., 8. In addition, it seems that Moore fails to consider adequately Schaff's conception of the unity in diversity of American Christianity. Initially Schaff desired outward institutional unity, but later came to believe that outward diversity could be beneficial as long as an inner unity of devotion to Christ allowed for mutual appreciation and cooperation among the churches.

37. Ibid., 198; Philip Schaff, "Christianity in America," in *Reformed and Catholic,*

be virtually incomprehensible. Yet Schaff's reasons for rejecting the movement were significantly different from those of Baird. According to Baird, Joseph Smith and other Mormon leaders were nothing more than "atrocious impostors" who had led astray a "body of ignorant dupes." The *Book of Mormon* was no less than the "absurdest of all pretended revelations from heaven," and the movement was destined to vanish because Smith would find that "America is not another Arabia, nor he another Mahomet."[38]

Schaff agreed that Mormon converts in America would be few, but not primarily because of the sect's unorthodox history and doctrines. Mormonism would fail because it was at war with the "whole policy and civilization" of the nation. Schaff believed that the sect was unimportant in historical terms, not merely because of its lack of numbers, but because it had exerted not the "slightest influence on the general character and religious life of the American people." There was, he said, an "irreconcilable antagonism of the American nationality with the pseudo-Christian, polygamistic, deceitful, rapacious, and rebellious Mormonism."[39] This champion of tolerance could not endure the scandal of pseudo-Christianity combined with the Mormons' vigorously exclusive idea of chosenness and refusal to tolerate others. Only those groups who had a positive contribution to make to the developing church in America were valid expressions, according to Schaff. Mormons could never fit into America either socially or religiously because they repudiated both fundamental unities, evangelical-catholic Christianity and cosmopolitan American nationality. While almost all religious groups could gain acceptance on the basis of loyalty to at least one of these areas of consensus, the Mormons refused to conform to either.

---

ed. Yrigoyen and Bricker, 386. This essay was originally published in *The Mercersburg Review* (October 1857).

38. Robert Baird, *Religion in the United States of America* (Glasgow: Blackie and Son, 1844; reprint ed. New York: Arno Press, 1969), 647-49.

39. Schaff, "Christianity in America," 361-62; Schaff, *America*, 198.

One Flock, but Not One Fold

According to Schaff, then, there was consensus within nation and church; a consensus that was much broader than the strictly Protestant America, or denominational exclusiveness promoted by many of his peers. From beginning to end during his fifty years of teaching, Schaff's commanding vision was the reunion of Christendom. When he first came to America, he hoped for an institutional union which would unite all legitimate communions in one evangelical-catholic church under the headship of Christ. Christians should never be satisfied with some "vague spiritual unity," however. True unity, he insisted, must begin internally, but must always manifest itself in "an outward way." The soul must form for itself a body. "Visibility lies necessarily in the conception of the church, which is the Body of Christ; the mark of unity consequently must also clothe itself in an outward form."[40]

Yet even in the 1840s and 1850s, Schaff was able to conceive of diversity in unity. Outward unity did not require "*one* visible head" such as the Catholics demanded, nor was a "single organization absolutely necessary."[41] To insist on "*one* constitution and *one* worship as alone true and valid, in the case at least of the militant church, is to fall back again into fleshly Judaism."[42] On the other hand, at that point in his career, Schaff, like nearly all of his European colleagues and most of his American friends, was scandalized by the seemingly total fragmentation of American Christianity. When he said that there need not be only *one* organization or *one* worship, what he had in mind was perhaps two, or at most three, and those would probably look a lot alike. It soon became obvious that such a model was unworkable in chaotic America.

Yet Schaff's vision did not die. Just weeks before his death in 1893, he produced his most impassioned plea for Christian union on the basis of evangelical-catholic Christianity. While the goal remained the same, however, he modified the external form. A moderate dose of American realism had tempered Schaff's idealism. Institutional unity was still the ultimate goal, since it would reflect complete internal unity, but Schaff

40. Schaff, *Principle of Protestantism*, 210.
41. Ibid.
42. Ibid., 111.

admitted that it might not come about until the second advent of Christ. Circumstances in America had led him to revise his conception of *how* God would unite the churches. Rather than an orderly series of institutional mergers, Providence had destined a period of ferment and seeming chaos in America which, despite appearances, would ultimately lead to a unity that was beyond human comprehension. Final union might have to wait for the *parousia.* There would still be unity in the church militant, but that unity would be in a form of cooperation among a plurality of external organizations.

In 1885, Schaff had described modes of doctrinal union, both proper and improper. Among those that would not work, he listed absorptive union, negative union, and union produced through the formation of an eclectic creed. Absorptive union, which involved incorporation of all denominations and sects into one of them, was inappropriate since each had a contribution to make and "the leading denominations will last to the millennium." "Christians" and "Disciples of Christ," among others, desired "negative" union based on allegiance to the Bible alone. According to Schaff, however, such a union would be disastrous, since such primitivism or restorationism in its disdain for tradition "would undo the whole history of Christianity." Finally, an eclectic creed, a "mechanical compound of heterogeneous elements," would satisfy no one, and the patchwork result would violate the organic, living nature of proper creeds which were inspired by the spirit of truth.[43]

The type of union that Schaff favored he called "conservative." Conservative union, based on a "broad and comprehensive evangelical catholic platform," recognized all denominations and their creeds as having legitimate contributions to make to the organic unfolding of full Christian truth. Significantly, this type of union would not attempt "an amalgamation or organic union of denominations."[44] In 1871, in his inaugural address as professor at Union Theological Seminary, Schaff reaffirmed what he had always believed: "True union is essentially inward and spiritual." He revealed the difference in his thought from his early years at Mercersburg in the next lines where diversity had also become a dominant motif.

43. Schaff, "Creeds and Confessions," 146-47.
44. Ibid., 146-48.

> It does not require an external amalgamation of existing organizations into one, but [they] may exist with their perfect independence in their own spheres of labor. It is as far removed from indifference to denominational distinctions, as from sectarian bigotry and exclusiveness. It is quite consistent with loyalty to that particular branch of Christ's kingdom with which we are severally connected by birth, regeneration, or providential call. Every one must labor in that part of the vineyard where Providence puts him, and where he can do [the] most good. The Church of God on earth is a vast spiritual temple with many stories, and each story has many apartments; to be in this house at all, we must occupy a particular room, which we are bound to keep in order and adorn with the flowers of Christian graces.

The key to reunion is that those involved in the work of their particular denomination

> live on the best terms of courtesy and friendship with our neighbors and brethren who occupy different apartments in the same temple of God, who love and worship the same Christ, who pray and labor as earnestly as we for the glory of our common Master and the salvation of souls, and with whom we expect to spend an endless eternity in the many mansions of heaven.[45]

Another typology of union Schaff developed and proposed at the 1893 meeting of the Evangelical Alliance involved three kinds of union: voluntary association of individual Christians, federal union, and organic absorption. The first was the sort of union that the Evangelical Alliance promoted, as well as such groups as tract and Bible societies, YMCA and YWCA, and Sunday school societies. Schaff saw such unity as highly valuable, but looked beyond it to more universal kinds of union. Organic absorption is what he formerly called "absorptive" union, but here Schaff noted particular examples where such union had, in fact, worked. For example, the Protestant Union Church of Prussia in the early 1800s and the reunion of Old School and New School Presbyterians in 1869 had been absorptive, and both had served valuable purposes.

45. Schaff, *Theology for Our Age and Country*, 16-17.

Federal or confederate union is very much like what Schaff earlier called "conservative" union, with denominations remaining independent to do their own particular work, but

> all recognizing one another as sisters with equal rights, and coöperating in general enterprises, such as the spread of the gospel at home and abroad, the defense of the faith against infidelity, the elevation of the poor and neglected classes of society, works of philanthropy and charity, and moral reform.[46]

Schaff had come a long way from his initial insistence that internal union must be manifested in outward union. In 1884, he could come close to contradicting his earlier scoffing about "vague spiritual unity" and insist that "unity of outward organization is not absolutely necessary for the unity of the Church. *This is essentially spiritual.*"[47] The Savior had promised one *flock*, Schaff said, but never one *fold*. "There may be many folds, and yet one and the same flock under Christ, the great arch-shepherd of souls. Even in Heaven there will be 'many mansions.'"[48]

Union Despite Rugged Individualism

Evangelical-catholic Christianity was emerging in America, but there were significant problems still to be overcome. One of the key elements of evangelical-catholic Christianity was proper respect for the church, and a serious weakness of American Christianity, in Schaff's eyes, was its general lack of "church feeling." In their individualism, Americans both fragmented the church and lost the essential sense of community as the body of Christ. Nurtured on the ideals of the individual's importance and freedom, Americans transferred such ideas to the church, and frequently community suffered. The Christianity of too many Americans reflected the American ideal of "rugged individualism" rather than more biblical models of community. In addition, too many assumed that

46. Schaff, *The Reunion of Christendom*, 14-15.
47. Schaff, "Discord and Concord of Christendom," 301. Emphasis mine.
48. Ibid., 302.

since there were so many alternative Christian groups, attachment to any particular one of them could not be especially important.

Schaff believed that the attempt to foster individual piety apart from the larger Christian community was a serious error. Piety is not a life of isolation, but

> genuine obedience toward the church coincides with the highest degree of personal piety. The life of the single member in the body and for the body as a whole, constitutes also its own most healthy and vigorous state. Separated from the body, it is given over at once to a process of dissolution.[49]

To find Christ, the seeker must look to the church. The church is the "*continuation* of the life and work of Christ on earth."[50] Christ's individual person had been withdrawn from the world, but Schaff insisted that "his generic existence is still present really and substantially."[51] American Christians needed to realize their place as organically united with historical tradition and all other persons who were followers of Christ. Such ideas could only have sounded strangely alien to American ears, or worse still, smacked of Puseyism or Romanism. As we have seen, Schaff's battle to foster proper "church feeling" in America was fraught with dangers.

A corollary to the lack of church feeling among American Christians was a failure to appreciate the sacraments of the church sufficiently. Schaff completely agreed with the ideas of his colleague John W. Nevin expressed in *The Mystical Presence*. Nevin argued that American churches, even those of Reformed heritage, had departed from the sacramental views of Calvin and adopted the more rationalistic Zwinglian position. The organicism of the Mercersburg men allowed them to take the mysteries of the sacraments more seriously. Using language similar to Calvin's to describe the presence of Christ in the church and sacraments, Schaff insisted that

> the Lord, therefore, through the Holy Ghost, is present in the church, in all its ordinances and means of grace, especially in the word and

49. Schaff, *Principle of Protestantism*, 169.
50. Schaff, *History of the Apostolic Church*, 8. Emphasis his.
51. Schaff, *What is Church History?*, 50 [34].

> the sacraments; present, indeed, in a mystical, invisible, incomprehensible way, but none the less, really, efficiently, and manifestly present, in his complete theanthropic person.[52]

According to Schaff, the danger was clear. The American lack of proper "church feeling" led to consequences far more serious than even sectarian division. In Germany, for example, "the undervaluation of the church and her symbols led gradually to the undervaluation of the apostles and their writings, and terminated finally in the denial of the divinity of Christ himself."[53] Schaff was no docetist and recognized the church's need of continual reform. He was not prepared to allow theoretical separation of visible, multiple, earthly, and corruptible churches from the one invisible, pure church. The two were distinguishable, but God had chosen to work on earth through the visible, corruptible church, and the effort of some to establish the pure church on earth was folly. According to Schaff, even the "true, pure, or invisible Church is made up of men, and bears throughout a true human character. It is not, however, for this reason the product of men, but, as indicated even by its name, stands before us as a purely supernatural organization."[54]

The church, then, is not just another voluntary human organization that may be rejected for reasons of convenience or taste. Instead, even in all its corruption, it stands as "bearer of all God's revelations, the channel of Christianity, the depository of all the life powers of the Redeemer, the habitation of the Holy Ghost."[55] Schaff could go so far as to insist that while

> there are thousands of church-members who are not vitally united to Christ, and who will therefore be finally lost . . . there are no real Christians any where who are not, at the same time, members of Christ's mystical body, and as such connected with some branch of his visible kingdom on earth. Church-membership is not the *principle* of salvation — which is Christ alone — but the necessary *condition* of

52. Schaff, *History of the Apostolic Church,* 8.
53. Schaff, *Principle of Protestantism,* 131.
54. Schaff, *What is Church History?,* 48 [32].
55. Ibid.

it; because it is the divinely-appointed means of bringing men into contact with Christ and all his benefits.[56]

It would be hard to exaggerate the foreignness of such ideas to the thinking of many nineteenth-century American Christians. Their Christianity depended on individual response to the preaching of the gospel and particularly on individual understanding of the Bible. Going to church was necessary, being a church member was commendable, but it was the individual, whose rights had been guaranteed by the American Constitution and Bill of Rights, who was also most important in religion. Nineteenth-century Americans worked with a distinctively "American" definition of the church. Whereas Schaff viewed the church in the more traditional way as God's primary agent of activity in human history, Americans had come to see it as a voluntary association which helped the individual Christian to reach practical goals such as spiritual growth and the gaining of converts. Small wonder, then, that opponents suspected Schaff of Anglo-Catholic, or even Roman Catholic sympathies.

Americans were correct to emphasize spiritual growth, though. Evangelical-catholic Christianity was clearly orthodox, but at the same time deeply pious. Schaff had himself experienced conversion and nurture among the pietists of Württemberg and believed that a life of piety was the basis for defense against doctrinal and moral error. In fact, pious devotion to Christ was one of the strongest bonds of unity between Christians of nearly every stripe. Theological differences often could be overcome by common devotion to Christ. For example, Schaff noted that in worship, Calvinists could sing Wesley's "Jesus Lover of My Soul" while Arminians joined in singing Toplady's "Rock of Ages," "forgetting the theological conflict of the two authors."[57] While Schaff insisted on orthodoxy in the area of essential doctrines, in the sphere of what he deemed nonessential matters he could say that "the piety of the heart often protests against the theology of the head, and love is better than logic."[58] For Schaff, in areas of dispute, the heart sought harmony and fellowship even when the head could not find agreement. A ruling principle in evangelical-catholic Christianity — and Schaff's entire life

56. Schaff, *History of the Apostolic Church,* 9.

57. Quoted in D. Schaff, *Life,* 426.

58. Schaff, "Discord and Concord of Christendom," 308.

— given in his address at opening ceremonies for the 1892 school year at Union Theological Seminary, was "HERESY IS AN ERROR; INTOLERANCE IS A SIN; PERSECUTION IS A CRIME."[59] Likewise, Schaff's four life-mottoes sum up well the general character of evangelical-catholic Christianity.

1. Christ is all things in all things.[60]
2. I am a Christian and nothing Christian is foreign to me.[61]
3. My given name is "Christian," my surname is "Reformed."[62]
4. In necessary things, unity; in doubtful things, liberty; in all things, charity.[63]

Schaff developed concepts of two areas of consensus, but how did he understand the relationship between them? If Schaff did not find consensus in the concept of "Anglo-Saxon" or "Protestant America" as did many of his peers, what role did Christianity play in Schaff's scheme in which American nationality provided the consensus for the nation as a whole? Continuing to employ the organism metaphor of which Schaff himself was so fond, it is possible to illustrate Schaff's conception of this relationship by envisioning Christianity as the vital soul of the national organism. His romantic philosophical heritage had provided him with a model which viewed society as an organism with religion serving as its "life-blood." Schaff used these metaphors to insist that religion was an essential part of a properly functioning society.[64]

From his coming to America in 1844 to his death in 1893, the guiding vision of Philip Schaff was the reunion of the Christian church. Soon after arriving in the new world, he became convinced that America played a distinctive role in providential history. American Christians

59. Quoted in D. Schaff, *Life,* 439. Emphasis his.

60. "Χριστος τα παντα εν πασιν."

61. "Christianus sum, nihil Christiani a me alienum puto."

62. "Christianus mihi nomen, Reformatus cognomen."

63. "In necessariis unitas, in dubiis libertas, in omnibus caritas." All from a stray sheet taken from "Dr. Schaff's notebook in his own handwriting." Philip Schaff Papers, ERHS.

64. See B. M. G. Reardon, *Religion in the Age of Romanticism: Studies in Early Nineteenth Century Thought* (Cambridge: Cambridge University Press, 1985), 12.

had a duty to nurture an evangelical-catholic Christianity which would combine the best of all denominations in a higher and fuller union than had yet been seen on earth. This vision was so clear for Schaff that it guided his developing understanding of how American Christian diversity, rather than being a hindrance to reunion, was actually the method God had chosen to use.

Rather than struggle vainly against the American system, Schaff availed himself of its opportunities, all the while maintaining his vision of reunion. His involvement in publications and organizations of various kinds uniformly reflected his commitment to Christian union. His models for Christian union changed significantly during his career as he came to terms with the realities of the American religious situation. Yet he never lost sight of his ideal of evangelical-catholic Christianity which would be unifying, historical, sacramental, and churchly.

Epilogue

Many of the issues that face today's interpreters of American religion were issues with which Philip Schaff also wrestled. Religious freedom, which led to the "threats" of sectarianism, Romanism, and rationalism; the American experiment of separation of church and state, the role of voluntary associations, American destiny, and the possibility and shape of united Christianity were and are issues of intense debate among Americans. Schaff's analyses, developed over a nearly half-century career as a scholar of religion in America, supply to these discussions valuable insights both for historical context and present understanding.

This volume has demonstrated that as an interpreter of both the amazing diversity and underlying unity of American Christianity during the latter half of the nineteenth century, Schaff had no peer. While others were befuddled and dismayed by the seeming confusion and chaos, Schaff maintained a constant vision of purpose and order. His early life and training had implanted within him a cosmic vision of the purpose of God in the world, and he refused to allow that vision to die. Put to the severest test in the American "wilderness of sects," Schaff could affirm that despite appearances, God was working out a plan of union and within the chaos God was creating the cosmos of a "wholly new" united Christianity.

Schaff's fundamental vision of the church's oneness faced the challenge of American religious freedom and the plethora of sects that had arisen there. He found himself continually revising his understanding of the role of division within the church, to the point that while he initially saw denominational divisions as antithetical to Christian union, finally he accepted such divisions as God's ultimate method of reunion. Throughout his life in the midst of religious freedom's ferment, Schaff consistently discerned an unbroken thread of unity, and he labored diligently to help others see it too.

At a time when most Protestant interpreters allowed no more than a subordinate role for Roman Catholicism, Schaff found a place for that church within his vision of united Christianity. Having at first identified Romanism as one of the three major threats to religion in America, Schaff modified his views of Roman Catholicism in the United States to the point that he could not only offer Catholics the hand of fellowship, but even suggest that they might play a central role in bringing about united evangelical-catholic Christianity. His guiding vision of Christian union and confidence in the progressive historical work of God overcame fears of Catholic dominance and allowed him to accept the providential inclusion of Catholic input toward united Christianity.

Schaff's views of intellectual life in America also followed this pattern. Initially, he feared the corrosive effects of rationalism and lamented the shallowness of American attempts to neutralize that threat. The more he came to know the American situation, however, the more he appreciated its virtues. The characteristic American emphasis on practicality, in contrast to the German focus on abstract theory, could indeed contribute to Christian life, and, finally, to Christian union. Rather than spend his time protesting against American weaknesses, Schaff set to work utilizing American strengths. In all of his endeavors, whether publishing, speaking, teaching, or organizing, Schaff was convinced that improving the life of the mind would lead inevitably to greater cooperation and union among Christians. The combination of German theory with American practicality could provide the intellectual foundation for united evangelical-catholic Christianity.

Schaff was one of the first interpreters of American religion to wrestle with the theological as well as practical implications of the separation of church and state. He immediately recognized the benefits of the American situation for both authorities, and sought to convince his European mentors of the value of the American system. The greater vitality of "free" Christians, the increased opportunity for service through voluntary associations, and the freedom from governmental interference in religious matters that American Christians enjoyed more than outweighed the problems of the system. Once again, despite appearances to the contrary, rather than a hindrance to Christian unity the separation of civil and religious authorities was one of the most favorable promoters of union.

As an American Christian, Schaff became involved in the characteristically American institutions called voluntary societies. These organizations, which on the surface appeared to increase American religious diversity, could also be powerful agents for unity, he realized. Perhaps the activity that most reveals Schaff's "Americanization," his involvement with and support of voluntary societies, reflects the modification of his initial ideas about how Christian union would come about. The central core of Schaff's vision remained the reunion of Christianity, yet he was able to incorporate into that vision various methods and institutions that seemed, on the surface at least, to postpone reunion. While voluntary associations initially complicated the Christian picture in America, Schaff came to believe that their work in fact helped bring about unity through the cooperation of people from various denominations in Christian service. Such cooperation could only lead to deeper mutual understanding and greater unity.

Reflecting the common European opinion of America, when Schaff first immigrated he believed himself to be entering a wilderness of religious confusion and cultural barbarism. Very quickly, however, he realized that despite its cultural backwardness and religious problems, America was the land of destiny. While that idea was not uncommon — among Americans at least — Schaff's vision for America was distinctive because of the breadth of peoples included in the American "nation" and, most significantly, he placed religion at the center of American purpose. America's destiny was one of responsibility, to be the location of reuniting Christianity.

The reunited church would be the fulfillment of Schaff's lifelong vision, but he found it necessary to accept only limited reunion during his lifetime. The ultimate goal was evangelical-catholic Christianity, which would combine the best of all denominations and express the fullness of the Christian gospel in complete unity and harmony, but Schaff was forced to modify his timetable and be content with lesser forms of union. Yet the vision did not die. It endured with remarkable steadfastness, and Schaff worked diligently to bring it to fruition.

Final Wish

In August, 1893, Schaff went to view the Statue of Liberty with his son and grandson and stood looking out over New York Harbor and the Atlantic Ocean toward the land of his birth. He then turned and looked westward toward New York and the land of his adoption. Perhaps he spent a few moments reminiscing about his career of forty-nine years and the changes that had taken place in his own life and in the country he loved. Yet his vision of the future swept the clouds of memory aside and he exclaimed,

> How I should like to come back fifty or a hundred years from now and visit the great city and the country to which it is the gateway! No one can dream what its destiny is to be and what great chapters in the history of the church and state are yet to be enacted in its borders.[1]

Schaff died without seeing his unfailing desire for the reunion of the church fulfilled. Yet those who benefit from his legacy continue to feel his influence. His tombstone in New York's Woodlawn Cemetery aptly captures the guiding principles of his life:

VIVAT INTER SANCTOS

REV. PHILIP SCHAFF. JAN. 1, 1819–OCT. 20, 1893

A TEACHER OF THEOLOGY FOR FIFTY YEARS.

HISTORIAN OF THE CHURCH.

PRESIDENT OF THE AMERICAN COMMITTEE OF BIBLE REVISION.

HE ADVOCATED THE REUNION OF CHRISTENDOM.

1. David S. Schaff, *The Life of Philip Schaff: In Part Autobiographical* (New York: Scribner's, 1897), 91.

Selected Bibliography

Manuscript Collections

Farewell Address to the German Reformed Church, 1892. Philip Schaff Papers. Evangelical and Reformed Historical Society. Philip Schaff Library. Lancaster Theological Seminary. Lancaster, Pennsylvania. (Hereafter cited as ERHS.)

Heilman, U. H. "Lectures on Church History begun October 3, 1860 at Mercersburg by Philip Schaff." Philip Schaff Papers. ERHS.

Hoffheins, John A. "Lecture Notes on Modern Church History. September 17, 1863." Philip Schaff Papers. ERHS.

Lectures by Philip Schaff at Mercersburg, 1845-61. Philip Schaff Papers. ERHS. Includes: Philippians, Introduction to New Testament, Matthew, John, Epistles of John, Acts, Romans, Galatians, Dogmatics, Symbolics, Hebrews, and History of the Church in the United States.

Lectures by Philip Schaff on Modern Church History. September 17, 1863. Philip Schaff Papers. ERHS.

Lectures on Church History delivered by Philip Schaff at Mercersburg 1847. Unidentified Student Manuscript in Philip Schaff Papers. ERHS.

Letters of Contributors to *Lange's Commentary* to Philip Schaff (1858-1886). Philip Schaff Papers. ERHS.

Letters of Members of the American Committee on Bible Revision (1870-85). Philip Schaff Papers. ERHS.

Manuscript correspondence between W. J. Mann and Philip Schaff. Chicago, 1958. Joseph Regenstein Library. University of Chicago.

Russell, C. C. "Notes of Dr. Schaff's Lectures on Church History (311-590)." 1855-56. Philip Schaff Papers. ERHS.

Schaff, Philip. "Autobiographical Reminiscences of My Youth Till My Arrival in America for My Children." Begun December 31, 1871, concluded March 1890. Philip Schaff Papers. ERHS.

———. Autobiographical Scrapbook of Articles from Periodicals, 1870-1889. 2 vols. The Philip Schaff Manuscript Collection. The Burke Library. Union Theological Seminary, New York. (Hereafter cited as UTS.)

———. Correspondence. Box II. UTS.

———. Diaries. Box IV. UTS.

———. Lecture notes taken by Philip Schaff as a student at Tübingen, Halle, and Berlin. Philip Schaff Papers. ERHS.

Super, H. W. Lecture notes on Symbolic Theology, Delivered by Philip Schaff 1846-47. Philip Schaff Papers. ERHS.

Thompson, Joseph B. Lecture Notes taken in Encyclopedia of Theology/Symbolic Theology 1847-48. Philip Schaff Papers. ERHS.

Publications by Philip Schaff

America: A Sketch of the Political, Social, and Religious Character of the United States of North America. New York: Scribner's, 1855; reprint edited by Perry Miller. Cambridge: Harvard University Press, 1961.

Amerika: Die politischen, socialen und kirchlich-religiösen Zustände der Vereinigten Staaten von Nord-Amerika mit besonderer Rücksicht auf die Deutsche, aus eigener Anschauung dargestellt. Berlin, 1854. Second edition, enlarged, 1858.

"America, the General Character of the Political, Social, and Religious Circumstances of the United States." *Mercersburg Review* 6 (October 1854): 600-624 and 7 (January 1855): 45-67.

American Nationality. Chambersburg, Penn.: M. Kieffer and Co., 1856.

The Anglo-American Sabbath. New York: American Tract Society, 1863.

Anglo-Germanism or the Significance of the German Nationality in the United States. Chambersburg, Penn.: Publication Office of the German Reformed Church, 1846.

An Appeal to Germans In Behalf of the Sunday Clause in the Excise Law of 1866. New York: John A. Gray and Green, 1867.

"Anniversary of the Christian Commission, Baltimore, Maryland." *German Reformed Messenger* 29 (October 19, 1864): 1.

Bibliotheca Symbolico Ecclesiae Universalis, The Creeds of Christendom. 3 vols. 6th ed. Revised. New York: Harper and Brothers, 1931.

Der Bürgerkrieg und das christliche Leben in Nord-Amerika. Berlin: Berlag von Wiegandt und Griben, 1866. An English translation by C. C. Starbuck appeared in the *Christian Intelligencer* 37 (March 1-May 17, 1866).

"The Card of Dr. Schaff." *The Christian Messenger* 38 (February 21, 1872): 64-65.

Christ and Christianity: Studies on Christology, Creeds, and Confessions, Protestantism and Romanism. Reformation Principles, Sunday Observance, Religious Freedom, and Christian Union. New York: Scribner's, 1885.

"Christianity in America." *Mercersburg Review* 9 (October 1857): 493-539.

Christianity in the United States of America. Document XIV of Evangelical Alliance Documents. New York: Bible House, Astor Place. n.d. [A report prepared for the Seventh General Conference of the Evangelical Alliance held in Basel, Switzerland, September, 1879.]

Church and State in the United States or the American Idea of Religious Liberty and Its Practical Effects with Official Documents. New York: Scribner's, 1888.

A Companion to the Greek New Testament and the English Version. New York: Scribner's, 1883.

"Conclusion of Dr. Schaf's Address." *Weekly Messenger* 10 (April 23, 1845): 2.

Creed Revision in the Presbyterian Churches. New York: Scribner's, 1890.

"Development of the Idea of the Church." *Reformed Quarterly Review* 35 (July 1888): 287-96.

The English Language: Heterogeneous in Formation, Homogeneous in Character, Universal in Destination for the Spread of Christian Civilization. Nashville: Cumberland Presbyterian Publishing House, 1887.

"The Evangelical Church Diet of Germany." *Mercersburg Review* 9 (January 1857): 1-28.

"The Friendship of Calvin and Melanchthon." *Papers of the American Society of Church History*. First Series 4 (1892): 143-63.

"The German Evangelical Church of the United States in its Relation to the Mother Church in Germany." *Mercersburg Review* 7 (January 1855): 136-62.

Germany, Its Universities, Theology, and Religion. Philadelphia: Lindsay and Blakiston, 1857.

"The Gettysburg Week." *Scribners Magazine* (July 1894): 21-30.

The Harmony of the Reformed Confessions, as Related to the Present State of Evangelical Theology. New York: Dodd, Mead and Co., 1877.

History of the Apostolic Church with a General Introduction to Church History. Trans. Edward D. Yeomans. New York: Scribner's, 1854.

"Impressions of England." *Mercersburg Review* 9 (July 1857): 329-58.

"The Influence of Christianity on the Family." *Mercersburg Review* 5 (October 1853): 473-91.

"The Influence of the Early Church on the Institution of Slavery." *Mercersburg Review* 10 (October 1858): 614-20.

In Memoriam. Our Children in Heaven. Printed for private circulation. New York, 1876.

"The Intermediate State, from Dr. Schaf's Work, Sin Against the Holy Ghost." *The Christian Intelligencer* 16 (July 9, 1846): 206.

Introduction to the American Edition. New York: Harper and Brothers, 1881. [This was the introduction to B. F. Westcott and F. J. A. Hort, *The New Testament in the Original Greek.*]

"Introduction to the Church History of the United States." *Weekly Messenger* 14 (December 20, 27, 1848; January 10, 17, 24, February 7, 14, 21, 1849): 2754, 2760, 2768, 2772, 2776, 2784, 2788, 2792.

"Katholizismus und Romanizismus." *Literarische Zeitung* (Berlin), no. 40 (1843): 633ff; no. 61 (1843): 969ff.

"Letter for The Christian Intelligencer." *The Christian Intelligencer* 17 (July 23, 1846): 6.

"The Mission and Opportunity of American Christianity." *Reformed Church Review* 51 (April 1904): 161-83.

The Moral Character of Christ, or the Perfection of Christ's Humanity, a Proof of His Divinity. Chambersburg, Penn.: M. Kieffer and Co., 1861.

"Neander as Church Historian." *Mercersburg Review* 4 (November 1852): 564-77.

"Ordination of Professor Schaff." *Weekly Messenger* 9 (September 4, 1844): 1869-1870.

"Other Heresy Trials and the Briggs Case." *The Forum* 12 (January 1892): 621-33.

The Person of Christ: The Perfection of His Humanity Viewed as Proof of His Divinity. New York: American Tract Society, 1882.

"Princeton and Mercersburg." *Weekly Messenger* 13 (June 7, 1848): 2650.

Das Princip des Protestantismus. Chambersburg, Penn.: In der Druckerei der Hochdeutsch-Reformirten Kirche, 1845.

The Principle of Protestantism as Related to the Present State of the Church. Trans. John W. Nevin. Chambersburg, Penn.: Publishing Office of the German Reformed Church, 1845; reprint ed. Philadelphia: United Church Press, 1964.

"The Progress of Christianity in the United States." *Princeton Review* 55 (September 1879): 209-52.

The Progress of Religious Freedom as Shown in the History of Toleration Acts. New York: Scribner's, 1889.

"Protestantism and Romanism." *Reformed Church Messenger* 40 (March 11, 1874): 2-3.

"Recollections of Neander." *Mercersburg Review* 3 (January 1851): 73-90.

"Religion in the United States of America." In *The Religious Condition of Christendom: Described in a Series of Papers Presented to the Seventh General Conference of the Evangelical Alliance, Held in Basle, 1879,* edited by J. Murray Mitchell, 79-117. London: Hodder and Stoughton, 1880.

"Religious State of Germany." *German Reformed Messenger* 22 (March 5, 12, April 2, 1856): 4265, 4269-4270, 4281.

Report of the Deputation of the American Branch of the Evangelical Alliance, Appointed to Memorialize the Emperor of Russia in Behalf of Religious Liberty. New York: Office of the Evangelical Alliance, 1871.

The Report of the Rev. Dr. Philip Schaff of His Mission to Europe on Behalf of the Alliance. Document III of Evangelical Alliance Documents. New York: Baker and Godwin, 1870.

The Reunion of Christendom: A Paper Prepared for the Parliament of Religions and the National Conference of the Evangelical Alliance Held in Chicago, September and October, 1893. New York: Evangelical Alliance Office, 1893.

"Rome Fifty Years Ago." *The Homiletic Review* 29 (January 1895): 3-9 and (March 1895): 195-204.

Slavery and the Bible. Chambersburg, Penn.: M. Kieffer and Co., 1861.

"Speech of Dr. Schaff Before the Pennsylvania Branch of the American Tract Society." *German Reformed Messenger* 24 (September 1, 1858): 1-2.

"The State Church System in Europe." *Mercersburg Review* 9 (January 1857): 151-66.

Die Sunde wider den Heiligen Geist. Halle: Johann Friedrich Lippert, 1841.

Theological Propaedeutic: A General Introduction to the Study of Theology. New York: Scribner's, 1894.

The Theology for Our Age and Country. New York: Rogers and Sherwood, 1872. [Address delivered at his inauguration as Professor of Apologetics, Symbolics, and Polemics in the Union Theological Seminary, October 18, 1871.]

The Toleration Act of 1689: A Contribution to the History of Religious Liberty. London: James Nisbet and Co., 1878.

The University: Past, Present, and Future. New York: Published by the University of New York, 1889.

"A Vindication." *Weekly Messenger* 12 (April 14, 1847): 2410.

What is Church History? A Vindication of the Idea of Historical Development. Philadelphia: J. B. Lippincott and Co., 1846. Reprinted in *Reformed and Catholic: Selected Historical and Theological Writings of Philip Schaff,* edited by Charles Yrigoyen, Jr. and George M. Bricker. Pittsburgh: The Pickwick Press, 1979.

Schaff, Philip, ed. *A Commentary on the Holy Scriptures by John Peter Lange.* 25 vols. New York: Scribner's, 1864-1880.

———, ed. *Der Deutsche Kirchenfreund: Organ für die gemeinsamen Interessen der amerikanisch-deutschen kirchen.* 5 vols. Mercersburg, Penn., 1848-1853.

———, ed. *A Dictionary of the Bible Including Biography, Natural History, Geography, Topography, Archaeology, and Literature.* Philadelphia: American Sunday School Union, 1890.

———, ed. *The International Revision Commentary on the New Testament.* 6 vols. New York: Scribner's, 1881-84.

———, ed. *The Revision of the English Version of the Holy Scriptures by Cooperative Committees of British and American Scholars of Different Denominations.* New York: Harper and Brothers, 1877.

———, ed. *The Schaff-Herzog Encyclopedia of Religious Knowledge.* 3 vols. New York: Funk and Wagnalls, 1882-84.

Schaff, Philip, and S. Irenaeus Prime, eds. *History, Essays, Orations, and Other Documents of the Sixth General Conference of the Evangelical Alliance, Held in New York, October 2-12, 1873.* New York: Harper and Brothers, 1874.

Schaff, Philip, and David Schaff. *History of the Christian Church.* 8 vols. 5th ed. Revised. Grand Rapids, Mich.: Eerdmans, 1950.

Schaff, Philip, et al., eds. *The American Church History Series. Denominational Histories.* New York: The Christian Literature Company, 1896.

The Semi-Centennial of Philip Schaff. New York: privately printed, 1893.

Selected Primary and Secondary Sources

Ahlstrom, Sydney E. *A Religious History of the American People.* 2 vols. Garden City, N.Y.: Doubleday, 1975.

Anglo-American Bible Revision. By Members of the American Revision Committee. Philadelphia: American Sunday School Union, 1879.

Appel, Theodore. *The Life and Work of John Williamson Nevin.* Philadelphia: Reformed Church Publication House, 1889.

———. *The Mercersburg Theology.* Manheim, Penn.: Sentinel Printing House, 1953.

Baird, Robert. *Religion in America.* Rev. ed. New York: Harper and Brothers, 1856.

———. *Religion in the United States of America.* Glasgow: Blackie and Son, 1844. Reprint, New York: Arno Press and The New York Times, 1969.

Barrows, John Henry, ed. *The World's Parliament of Religions.* 2 vols. Chicago: Parliament Publishing Co., 1893.

Beker, J. Christiaan, *Paul the Apostle: The Triumph of God in Life and Thought.* Philadelphia: Fortress Press, 1980.

Billington, Ray Allen. *The Protestant Crusade, 1800-1860.* New York: Macmillan, 1938.

Binkley, Luther J. *The Mercersburg Theology.* Lancaster, Penn.: Franklin and Marshall College, 1953.

Boorstin, Daniel J. *The Americans: The National Experience.* New York: Vintage Books, 1965.

Bowden, Henry Warner. *Church History in the Age of Science: Historio-*

graphical Patterns in the United States 1876-1918. Chapel Hill: University of North Carolina Press, 1970.

———. Introduction to *Religion in America* by Robert Baird. New York: Harper & Row, 1970.

———. "Philip Schaff and Sectarianism: the Americanization of a European Viewpoint." *Journal of Church and State* 8 (Winter 1966): 97-106.

———. "Science and the Idea of Church History: An American Debate." *Church History* 36 (Summer 1967): 308-26.

———, ed. *A Century of Church History: The Legacy of Philip Schaff*. Carbondale, Ill.: Southern Illinois University Press, 1988.

Bricker, G., and C. Yrigoyen, eds. *Reformed and Catholic: Selected Historical and Theological Writings of Philip Schaff*. Pittsburgh: Pickwick Press, 1979.

Briggs, Charles A. "The Discussion of the Revised Version of the Old Testament." *The Presbyterian Review* 7 (April 1886): 369-78.

———. "The Revised English Version of the Old Testament." *The Presbyterian Review* 6 (July 1885): 493-532.

Bushnell, Horace. *Barbarism the First Danger: A Discourse for Home Missions*. New York: American Home Missionary Society, 1847.

Carroll, H. K. *The Religious Forces of the United States*. New York: The Christian Literature Company, 1893.

Cherry, Conrad, ed. *God's New Israel: Religious Interpretations of American Destiny*. Englewood Cliffs, N.J.: Prentice-Hall, 1971.

Clebsch, William A. "Christian Interpretations of the Civil War." *Church History* 30 (June 1961): 212-21.

Cole, Charles C. *The Social Ideas of the Northern Evangelists, 1826-1860*. New York: Columbia University Press, 1954.

Cremin, Lawrence A. *American Education: The National Experience, 1783-1876*. New York: Harper & Row, 1980.

De Crèvecoeur, J. Hector St. John. *Letters from an American Farmer*. 1782. Reprint, New York: E. P. Dutton, 1957.

De Tocqueville, Alexis. *Democracy in America*. Translated by George Lawrence. Edited by J. P. Mayer. Garden City, N.Y.: Anchor, 1969.

Dillenberger, John. *Protestant Thought and Natural Science*. Garden City, N.Y.: Doubleday, 1960.

Documentary History of the American Committee on Revison, Private and

Confidential. Prepared by order of the committee for the use of the members. New York: n.p., 1885.

Documents of the New York Sabbath Committee, 1857-1869. 2 vols. New York: Sabbath Committee Room, 1867, 1869.

Dolan, Jay P. *The American Catholic Experience: A History from Colonial Times to the Present.* New York: Image, 1987.

Dorchester, Daniel. *The Liquor Problem in All Ages.* New York: Phillips and Hunt, 1884.

"Dr. Schaff's Reception at Mercersburg." *Weekly Messenger* 9 (August 21, 1844): 1863.

"Dr. Schaff's Second Trial for Heresy." *Reformed Church Messenger* 66 (October 6, 1898): 2-3.

"Dr. Schaff's Work on the Sin Against the Holy Ghost." *Christian Intelligencer* 17 (July 23, 1846): 6.

Fisher, G. P. "Dr. Schaff as an Historian." *Papers of the American Society of Church History.* First Series 7 (1895): 3-11.

Flower, Elizabeth, and Murray G. Murphey. *A History of Philosophy in America.* 2 vols. New York: Capricorn Books, 1977.

Gaustad, Edwin Scott. *Historical Atlas of Religion in America.* New York: Harper & Row, 1962.

———, ed. *The Rise of Adventism: Religion and Society in Mid-Nineteenth-Century America.* New York: Harper & Row, 1974.

Goliber, Thomas J. "Philip Schaff: (1819-1893): A Study in Conservative Biblical Criticism." Ph.D. dissertation, Kent State University, 1976.

Greenslade, S. L., ed. *The Cambridge History of the Bible: The West from the Reformation to the Present Day.* Cambridge: Cambridge University Press, 1963.

Hales, E. E. Y. *The Catholic Church in the Modern World: A Survey from the French Revolution to the Present.* Garden City, N.Y.: Doubleday, 1960.

Hammond, Phillip E. "Religious Pluralism and Durkheim's Integration Thesis." In *Changing Perspectives in the Scientific Study of Religion,* edited by Allan W. Eister, 115-42. New York: John Wiley and Sons, 1974.

Handy, Robert T. "Freedom and Authority in Doctrinal Matters: Some Protestant Struggles." *Journal of Ecclesiastical Studies* 12 (Summer 1975): 335-47.

———. *A Christian America: Protestant Hopes and Historical Realities*. Rev. ed. New York: Oxford University Press, 1984.

———. *Undermined Establishment: Church-State Relations in America, 1880-1920*. Princeton, N.J.: Princeton University Press, 1991.

Hatch, Nathan O. *The Democratization of American Christianity*. New Haven: Yale University Press, 1989.

Hatch, Nathan O., and Mark A. Noll. *The Bible in America: Essays in Cultural History*. New York: Oxford University Press, 1979.

Helfenstein, Jacob. *A Perverted Gospel or the Romanizing Tendency of the Mercersburg Theology*. Philadelphia: William S. Young, 1853.

Hennesey, James. *American Catholics: A History of the Roman Catholic Community in the United States*. New York: Oxford University Press, 1981.

Higham, John. *Send These to Me: Immigrants in Urban America*. Rev. ed. Baltimore: Johns Hopkins University Press, 1984.

———. *Strangers in the Land: Patterns of American Nativism, 1860-1925*. New York: Atheneum, 1975.

Historical Account of the Work of the American Committee of Revision of the Authorized English Version of the Bible, Prepared from the Documents and Correspondence of the Committee. New York: Scribner's, 1885.

Hodge, Charles. "Is the Church of Rome a Part of the Visible Church?" *Biblical Repertory and Princeton Review* 18 (April 1846).

———. "Schaff's Protestantism." *Biblical Repertory and Princeton Review* 17 (October 1845): 626-36.

Hoffecker, W. Andrew. *Piety and the Princeton Theologians: Archibald Alexander, Charles Hodge, Benjamin Warfield*. Grand Rapids, Mich.: Baker Book House, 1981.

Hofstadter, Richard. *Anti-Intellectualism in American Life*. New York: Vintage, 1963.

"Honors to Dr. Schaff." *Weekly Messenger* 19 (July 19, 1854): 4126.

Horsman, Reginald. *Race and Manifest Destiny: The Origins of American Racial Anglo-Saxonism*. Cambridge: Harvard University Press, 1981.

Hovenkamp, Herbert. *Science and Religion in America, 1800-1860*. Philadelphia: University of Pennsylvania Press, 1978.

Hughes, Richard R., ed. *The American Quest for the Primitive Church*. Urbana: University of Illinois Press, 1988.

Hurst, J. F. "Dr. Schaff as Uniting Teutonic and Anglo-Saxon Scholarship." *Papers of the American Society of Church History.* First Series 6 (1894): 7-12.

Hutchison, William R. *The Modernist Impulse in American Protestantism.* New York: Oxford University Press, 1976.

"Inauguration of Dr. Schaff." *Weekly Messenger* 10 (November 6, 1844): 1907.

Jacobs, Henry E. "Dr. Schaff and the Lutheran Church." *Papers of the American Society of Church History.* First Series 6 (1894): 13-19.

Janeway, J. J. *Antidote to the Poison of Popery in the Publications of Professor Schaff.* New Brunswick: N.J.: J. Terhune and Sons, 1854.

———. *A Contrast Between the Erroneous Assertions of Professor Schaf and the Testimony of Credible Ecclesiastical Historians; in Regard to the State of the Christian Church in the Middle Ages.* New Brunswick, N.J.: Ternine and Son, 1852.

Johnson, Kathryn L. "The Mustard Seed and the Leaven: Philip Schaff's Confident View of Christian History." *Historical Magazine of the Protestant Episcopal Church* 50 (June 1981): 117-70.

Jordan, Philip D. "Cooperation without Incorporation: America and the Presbyterian Alliance 1870-1880." *Journal of Presbyterian History* 55 (Spring 1977): 13-35.

———. *The Evangelical Alliance for the United States of America, 1847-1900: Ecumenism, Identity and the Religion of the Republic.* New York: Edwin Mellen Press, 1982.

Kaul, A. N. *The American Vision: Actual and Ideal Society in Nineteenth-Century Fiction.* New Haven: Yale University Press, 1963.

Kennedy, William Bean. *The Shaping of Protestant Education: An Interpretation of the Sunday School and the Development of Protestant Educational Strategy in the United States, 1789-1860.* New York: Association Press, 1966.

Kieffer, Moses. "Theological Seminary at Mercersburg: Earlier Reminiscences, 1838-1851." *Weekly Messenger* 36 (July 6, 1870): 2.

Kliebard, Herbert M., ed. *Religion and Education in America: A Documentary History.* Scranton, Penn.: International Textbook Co., 1969.

Kremer, A. R. "Memories of Dr. Philip Schaff at Mercersburg." *Reformed Church Messenger* 85 (November 16, 1916): 8-9.

Kuklick, Bruce. *Churchmen and Philosophers: From Jonathan Edwards to John Dewey.* New Haven: Yale University Press, 1985.

Lange, John Peter. *The Gospel According to Matthew.* Edited by Philip Schaff. New York: Charles Scribner, 1865.

Levin, David. *History as Romantic Art: Bancroft, Prescott, Motley, and Parkman.* Stanford, Calif.: Stanford University Press, 1959.

Lewis, Tayler. "The Church Question." *Weekly Messenger* 11 (January 21, 28, February 5, 1846): 2153, 2161. [Review of Schaff's *The Principle of Protestantism.*]

Lindberg, David D., and Ronald L. Numbers, eds. *God and Nature: Historical Essays on the Encounter Between Christianity and Science.* Berkeley: University of California Press, 1986.

Mackenzie, Ross. "Reformed Tradition and the Papacy." *Journal of Ecclesiastical Studies* 13 (Summer 1976): 359-67.

Mandelbaum, Maurice. *History, Man, and Reason: A Study in Nineteenth-Century Thought.* Baltimore: The Johns Hopkins Press, 1971.

Maritain, Jacques. *Reflections on America.* 1958. Reprint, New York: Gordian Press, 1975.

Marty, Martin E. *Religion and Republic: The American Circumstance.* Boston: Beacon Press, 1987.

———. *Righteous Empire: The Protestant Experience in America.* New York: Dial Press, 1970.

McGiffert, A. C., Jr. "Making of an American Scholar: Biography in Letters." [A. C. McGiffert and Philip Schaff] *Union Seminary Quarterly Review* 24 (Fall 1968): 31-46.

McKee, Elsie Anne, and Brian G. Armstrong, eds. *Probing the Reformed Tradition: Historical Studies in Honor of Edward A. Dowey, Jr.* Louisville, Ky.: Westminster/John Knox Press, 1989.

Mead, Sidney. *The Lively Experiment: The Shaping of Christianity in America.* New York: Harper & Row, 1976.

———. *The Nation with the Soul of a Church.* New York: Harper & Row, 1975.

Merk, Frederick. *Manifest Destiny and Mission in American History.* New York: Vintage, 1963.

Meyer, John Charles. "Philip Schaff's Concept of Organic Historiography as Related to the Development of Doctrine." Ph.D. dissertation, The Catholic University of America, 1968.

Michaelsen, Robert. *Piety in the Public School.* New York: Macmillan, 1970.

Miller, Rufus W. "Philip Schaff, Prophet and Pioneer in Christian Unity." *Reformed Church Messenger* 81 (December 19, 1912): 11.

———. "Philip Schaff, Prophet and Pioneer in Christian Unity and the Manifestation of Unity." *Reformed Church Review* 61 (April 1914): 234-62.

Minear, Paul S. "Who Seeks Church Unity?" *The Christian Century* 73 (February 15, 1956): 202-4.

Moore, James R. *The Post-Darwinian Controversies: A Study of the Protestant Struggle to Come to Terms with Darwin in Great Britain and America, 1870-1900.* Cambridge: Cambridge University Press, 1979.

Moore, R. Laurence. *Religious Outsiders and the Making of Americans.* New York: Oxford University Press, 1986.

Nevin, John Williamson, *Catholic and Reformed: Selected Theological Writings of John Williamson Nevin.* Edited by Charles Yrigoyen, Jr. and George H. Bricker. Pittsburgh: The Pickwick Press, 1978.

Nevin, John Williamson. "True and False Protestantism." [Review of Schaff's *The Principle of Protestantism.*] *Mercersburg Review* 1 (January 1849): 83-105.

Nichols, James Hastings, ed. *The Mercersburg Theology.* New York: Oxford University Press, 1966.

———. *Romanticism in American Theology: Nevin and Schaff at Mercersburg.* Chicago: The University of Chicago Press, 1961.

Niebuhr, H. Richard. *The Kingdom of God in America.* New York: Harper and Brothers, 1935.

———. *The Social Sources of Denominationalism.* 1929. Reprint, New York: Meridian, 1975.

Noll, Mark A. *Between Faith and Criticism: Evangelicals, Scholarship, and the Bible in America.* San Francisco: Harper & Row, 1986.

———, ed. *Charles Hodge: The Way of Life.* New York: Paulist Press, 1987.

———, ed. *The Princeton Theology, 1812-1921.* Grand Rapids, Mich.: Baker Book House, 1983.

Papers of the American Society of Church History. First Series. 7 vols. 1889-95.

Payne, John B. "Schaff and Nevin, Colleagues at Mercersburg: The Church Question." *Church History* 61 (June 1992): 169-90.

Penzel, Klaus. "Church History and the Ecumenical Quest: A Study of the German Background and Thought of Philip Schaff." Th.D. dissertation, Union Theological Seminary, New York, 1962.

———. "Church History in Context: The Case of Philip Schaff." In *Our Common History as Christians: Essays in Honor of Albert C. Outler,* ed. John Deschner et al., 217-60. New York: Oxford University Press, 1975.

———. "Philip Schaff: A Centennial Reappraisal." *Church History* 59 (June 1990): 207-21.

———. "The Reformation Goes West: The Notion of Historical Development in the Thought of Philip Schaff." *Journal of Religion* 62 (July 1982): 219-41.

———, ed., *Philip Schaff: Historian and Ambassador of the Universal Church, Selected Writings.* Macon, Ga.: Mercer University Press, 1991.

Powell, Milton, ed. *The Voluntary Church: American Religious Life (1740-1865) Seen Through the Eyes of European Visitors.* New York: Macmillan, 1967.

Pranger, Gary. "Philip Schaff (1819-1893): Portrait of an Immigrant Theologian." Ph.D. dissertation, The University of Illinois at Chicago, 1987.

Proudfit, J. W. "Dr. Schaff as Church Historian." *The New Brunswick Review* 1 (August 1854): 278-325.

———. "Dr. Schaff's Works on Church History." *The New Brunswick Review* 1 (May 1854): 1-63.

Prugh, P. C. "A Reminiscence or Two of Dr. Philip Schaff." *Reformed Church Messenger* 86 (February 22, 1917): 8-9.

Reardon, Bernard M. G. *Religion in the Age of Romanticism: Studies in Early Nineteenth Century Thought.* Cambridge: Cambridge University Press, 1985.

"Reminiscences of Dr. Schaff." *Reformed Church Messenger* 61 (November 16, 1893): 3.

"Reply to Dr. Schaff's Letter." *The Christian Intelligencer* 17 (July 30, 1846): 10.

"Report of the Committee on the Resolutions of the Philadelphia Classis in Reference to Dr. Schaf's 'Principle of Protestantism.'" *Weekly Messenger* 11 (November 6, 1845): 2110.

Richards, George W. "The Life and Work of Philip Schaff." *Bulletin of the Theological Seminary of the Evangelical and Reformed Church in the United States* 15 (October 1944): 155-72.

———. "The Mercersburg Theology Historically Considered." *Papers of the American Society of Church History*. Second Series 3 (1912): 117-49.

———. "The Mercersburg Theology: Its Purpose and Principles." *Church History* 20 (Summer 1951): 42-55.

———. "Philip Schaff — Prophet of Christian Union." *Christendom* 10 (Autumn 1945): 463-71.

Richey, Russell E., ed. *Denominationalism*. Nashville: Abingdon, 1977.

Rorabaugh, W. J. *The Alcoholic Republic: An American Tradition*. New York: Oxford University Press, 1979.

Rossiter, Clinton. *The American Quest, 1790-1860: An Emerging Nation in Search of Identity, Unity, and Modernity*. New York: Harcourt Brace Jovanovich, 1971.

Rupp, I. Daniel. *He Pasa Ekklesia, An Original History of the Religious Denominations at Present Existing in the United States, Containing Authentic Accounts of Their Rise, Progress, Statistics, and Doctrines*. Philadelphia, 1844.

Sanders, Thomas G. *Protestant Concepts of Church and State*. New York: Holt, Rinehart and Winston, 1964.

Schaff, David. *The Life of Philip Schaff: In Part Autobiographical*. New York: Scribner's, 1897.

———. "Philip Schaff, the Advocate of the Reunion of Christendom." *Reformed Church Review* 64 (January 1917): 1-13.

Schaff, Philip. *Saint Augustine, Melanchthon, Neander*. New York: Funk and Wagnalls, 1885.

Schlesinger, Arthur M., Jr. *The Age of Jackson*. Boston: Little, Brown, 1945.

Schlesinger, Arthur M., Sr. *A Critical Period in American Religion, 1875-1900*. Philadelphia: Fortress Press, 1967.

Schneck, B. S. *Mercersburg Theology Inconsistent with Protestant and Reformed Doctrine*. Philadelphia: J. B. Lippincott and Company, 1874.

Shahan, Thomas J. "Dr. Schaff and the Roman Catholic Church." *Papers of the American Society of Church History*. First Series 6 (1894).

Shriver, George H. "Philip Schaff as a Teacher of Church History." *Journal of Presbyterian History* 47 (March 1969): 74-92.

———. *Philip Schaff: Christian Scholar and Ecumenical Prophet*. Macon, Ga.: Mercer University Press, 1987.

———. "Philip Schaff's Concept of Organic Historiography Interpreted in Relation to the Realization of an 'Evangelical Catholicism'

Within the Christian Community." Ph.D. dissertation, Duke University, 1960.

———, ed. *American Religious Heretics: Formal and Informal Trials in American Protestantism.* Nashville: Abingdon, 1966.

Smylie, J. H. "Philip Schaff: Ecumenist; the Reunion of Protestantism and Roman Catholicism." *Encounter* 28 (Winter 1967): 3-16.

SR, "Protestantism of Mercersburg Contrasted." *German Reformed Messenger* 11 (October 15, 1845): 2096.

Stokes, Anson Phelps. *Church and State in the United States.* 3 vols. New York: Harper and Brothers, 1950.

——— and Leo Pfeffer. *Church and State in the United States.* Rev. Ed. New York: Harper & Row, 1964.

Strong, Josiah. *Our Country: Its Possible Future and Its Present Crisis.* New York: American Home Missionary Society, 1885.

———. *The New Era, Or the Coming Kingdom.* New York: Baker and Taylor, 1893.

Tiffany, C. C. "Dr. Schaff and the Episcopal Church." *Papers of the American Society of Church History.* First Series 6 (1894).

Trost, Theodore L. "Philip Schaff's Concept of the Church with Special Reference to His Role in the Mercersburg Movement, 1844-1864." Ph.D. dissertation, New College, Edinburgh University, 1958.

Tucker, Gene M., and Douglas A. Knight, eds. *Humanizing America's Iconic Book: Society of Biblical Literature Centennial Addresses, 1980.* Chico, Calif.: Scholars Press, 1982.

Tuveson, Ernest Lee. *Redeemer Nation: The Idea of America's Millennial Role.* Chicago: The University of Chicago Press, 1968. Reprint, 1980.

Tyler, Alice Felt. *Freedom's Ferment: Phases of American Social History from the Colonial Period to the Outbreak of the Civil War.* 1944. New York: Harper & Row, 1962.

Tyrrell, Ian R. *Sobering Up: From Temperance to Prohibition in Antebellum America, 1800-1860.* Westport, Conn.: Greenwood Press, 1979.

Weinberg, Albert K. *Manifest Destiny: A Study of Nationalist Expansionism in American History.* Gloucester, Mass.: Peter Smith, 1958.

"Welcome to Dr. Philip Schaff." *Weekly Messenger* 9 (August 28, 1844): 1867.

Wentz, Richard E. "John Williamson Nevin and American Nationalism." *Journal of the American Academy of Religion* 58 (Winter 1990): 617-32.

White, Andrew D. A *History of the Warfare of Science with Theology in Christendom.* New York: George Braziller, 1955.

Winebrenner, John. *History of All the Religious Denominations in the United States.* Harrisburg, Penn.: John Winebrenner, 1849.

Woodbridge, John D.; Mark A. Noll; and Nathan O. Hatch. *The Gospel in America: Themes in the Story of America's Evangelicals.* Grand Rapids, Mich.: Zondervan, 1979.

Yrigoyen, Charles. "Mercersburg's Quarrel with Methodism." *Methodist History* 22 (October 1983): 3-19.

Index